JOHN MILTON AND THE ENGLISH REVOLUTION

JOHN MILTON AND THE ENGLISH REVOLUTION

A Study in the Sociology of
Literature

Andrew Milner

Barnes & Noble Books
Totowa, New Jersey

For my parents
Dorothy and John Milner

First published 1981 by
THE MACMILLAN PRESS LTD
London and Basingstoke
Companies and representatives
throughout the world

First published in the USA 1981 by
BARNES & NOBLE BOOKS
81, Adams Drive
Totowa, New Jersey, 07512

MACMILLAN ISBN 0 333 27134 3
BARNES & NOBLE ISBN 0 389 201235

Printed in Hong Kong

Contents

Acknowledgements

I would like to acknowledge the aid and assistance which I have received from Colin Barker, Ian Birchall, Verity Burgmann, Michael and Paul Crook, Geraldine Gillespie, Andrew Keogh, Professor David Martin, Richard Milner, Chris Sill, Colin Sparks, Kaye Stearman, Dr Alan Swingewood, Robert Tickner, Pam Townshend, Kathryn Wench, the staffs of the British Library of Political & Economic Science and the University of London Library, and T. M. Farmiloe of the Macmillan Press.

1 Literature and Society: The Problem of Method

When Lucien Goldmann began his first major work, the early study of the tragic philosophy of Immanuel Kant, he found it necessary to apologise to his readers for the apparent 'rashness' of his initial decision to commence the analysis with an account of a set of problems which were empirical and sociological, rather than, in the conventional sense of the term, philosophical.[1] In France itself, Goldmann's own later study of Jansenism, *The Hidden God*,[2] established, almost single-handedly, the right to exist of a sociology of literature and of philosophy. But in England events have proceeded rather less rapidly. The predominant empiricism of English literary-critical ideology has proved stubbornly and tenaciously resistant to all attempts at theorisation. Leavis's refusal *as a matter of principle* to indulge in generalisation, a refusal made explicit in his famous reply to Rene Wellek,[3] is thus indicative of a wider, more general, and specifically English disdain for theoretical analysis. Against the background of such an intellectual climate, it appears necessary to attempt a brief justification, at least, for beginning a study of the prose and poetical works of John Milton with a 'theoretical' chapter which takes as its prime focus the general problem of the relationship between 'literature' and 'society'. Such a lengthy discussion of methodology is, in fact, necessitated by the existence of an intellectual orthodoxy which is not only anti-theoretical in general, but which is also specifically committed to a view of the sociology of literature as an impossible or, at best, an undesirable project. The anonymous authors of a recent, collectively composed account of various approaches to the study of literature, define this orthodoxy—that is, the literary-critical orthodoxy of the English-speaking world—in the following manner:

> The core assumption which gives coherence to traditional literary-criticism as a practice is that *literary works are communications of a*

radically distinctive kind. They are autonomous productions of the activity of literary expression. It is in the name of this claim that studies of the author's life, his times and his society, his stated purposes, his working drafts, etc. are *subordinated* to the reading and interpretation of *the text itself.*[4]

This particular form of literary-critical ideology has been especially influential in the United States where, since the late 1930s, literary criticism has been premised, to a quite remarkable extent, on the more general propositions of the New Criticism of John Crowe Ransom.[5] In England, the position has been complicated somewhat by the 'sociological' aspirations of the Leavis school. But nonetheless, in so far as Leavisian literary criticism has attained a degree of general acceptance, it has done so by virtue of the peculiar combination of its insistence on the specificity of the literary text, and its elitist hostility to 'mass' culture, rather than of its more serious sociological intentions. Recent years have, of course, witnessed a number of major sociological incursions into literary-critical territory. But its essential contours remain much the same as ever. A reasonably prolonged discussion of method thus proves necessary in order to establish, as it were, the very ground upon which we stand. Let us turn now to an extended survey of the terrain which lies before us.

1   Marx's Sociology of the Forms of Consciousness

Our starting point, the most salient feature in the sociological 'landscape', is surely Marx's notion that literary production, as a form of intellectual production, is not completely autonomous, that it is, in some way, dependent upon extra-literary factors, and that, moreover, the economic factor in social life plays an especially privileged role in the complex process of determination of which social reality, including literary production, is the outcome. Marx's own initial interests were, in fact, essentially 'aesthetic' rather than properly 'sociological'. Along with the other Left Hegelians, he had accepted Hegel's notion of an opposition between the classical ideals of Greek art and the anti-aesthetic nature of modern bourgeois reality. But he had rejected both Hegel's own willingness to come to terms with that reality, at the price of art, as Hegel himself perceived it, and the romantic rejection of reality in the name of art, propounded by Marx's one-time collaborator, Bruno Bauer.[6] Rather, he sought to establish his own materialist sociology as an alternative to these two, equally 'speculative', aesthetic theories. And in the course of this break with Hegelianism, Marx moved from the earlier speculative aesthetic towards a new, materialist sociology of the forms of consciousness. Before we proceed to a precise analysis of the structure of that sociology, it is, however, necessary to emphasise the extent to which Marxist sociology remained a *Hegelian* sociology, the extent to which Marx's materialism remained a *dialectical* materialism. The central category of the Hegelian system is, of course, that of *totality*: for Hegel, the whole is always prior to the parts which it contains within itself. Now this central methodological principle is clearly taken over into Marx's sociology. It is indeed, as Goldmann suggests, a fundamental principle of dialectical materialism that 'the knowledge of empirical facts remains abstract and superficial so long as it is not made concrete by its integration into a whole; and that only this act of integration can enable us to go beyond the incomplete and abstract phenomenon in order to arrive at its concrete essence'.[7] This approach informs the whole of Marx's work, and not merely his earlier youthful writings. Indeed, the section on 'The Method of Political Economy' in the Introduction to the *Grundrisse* evidences a thoroughgoing Hegelianism. Here Marx notes that: 'It seems to be correct to begin with the real and the concrete, with the real precondition, thus to begin, in economics, with e.g. the population.'[8] But population thus conceived is a mere abstraction, argues Marx, since it can yet be analysed into classes, and these in turn can be analysed in terms of exchange relations. Thus population has to be understood, not as a concrete fact, but rather as 'a rich totality of many determinations and relations'.[9] 'The concrete is concrete', Marx writes, 'because it is the concentration of many determinations, hence unity of the diverse.'[10] A genuinely scientific sociology must, then, proceed not in terms of the analysis of abstract 'facts', but rather in terms of an understanding of the interrelationships between the different elements which make up any particular totality, and this totality must in turn be understood in terms of its interrelationships with other elements in a wider totality, and so on. It follows, then, that society itself (and by this we mean a real concrete society, and not the abstract 'society' of functionalist mythology) has to be seen as a concentration of many determinations. This conception of society as a totality of interrelated and contradictory elements does not, and indeed cannot, allow within itself the notion of art and literature as mechanical 'effects' of some other economic 'cause'. This does not imply any necessary rejection of the formulation of a determining base and a determined superstructure, a formulation which is, as we shall see, at the core of the Marxist sociology of consciousness. What it does imply, however, is a rejection of any notion of determination couched in the terms of mechanical causation. With this cautionary note in mind, we can turn now to a detailed analysis of the structure of Marx's sociology of the forms of consciousness.

How, then, does this sociology of consciousness develop? Marx begins, in *The Holy Family*, simply enough by asserting the primacy of material reality against the speculative metaphysics and speculative aesthetics of the idealist school. He characterises the Hegelian method as one in which, firstly, abstractions are constructed out of the diverse elements of reality, and secondly, these abstractions are then endowed with an active independence which is seen as generating the different concrete realities. In this way, the abstract is made concrete, and the concrete abstract.[11] But this critique of critical criticism is still not yet a sociology proper. The first workings out of the Marxist sociology of consciousness are, in fact, to be found in *The German Ideology*, written with Engels only a year later. There, Marx and Engels formulated the distinctively new, and distinctively sociological, proposition that: 'Life is not determined by consciousness, but consciousness by life.'[12] This statement is clearly the starting point for any Marxist sociology of consciousness, in that it directs our attention away from 'consciousness' as an isolated phenomenon, and towards the analysis of the structure of 'life' itself. And it is Marx's and Engels's concrete analyses of the real content of 'life', and in particular their understanding of the *class* nature of society, which add real analytical power to this initial formulation. On this basis they are able to offer sociological explanations of a whole range of phenomena. They are able, for example, to locate the material basis of the illusion of 'pure' consciousness in the existence of the division of material and mental labour; to analyse political struggles, such as the struggle for the franchise, as the forms in which class struggles are fought out; and to interpret the ruling ideas of any age as the ideas of its ruling class. This initial proposition that 'life' determines 'consciousness' receives a much more precise formulation in the later *A Contribution to the Critique of Political Economy*, where Marx writes that, 'The mode of production of material life conditions the general process of social, political and intellectual life. It is not the consciousness of men that determines their existence, but their social existence that determines their consciousness.'[13] It should be emphasised that this reformulation in no way represents a change in substantive content; it merely represents a move in the direction of greater precision. But Marx does go on, here, to suggest a more sophisticated analysis of the precise relationship which pertains between the economic 'base' and the ideological 'superstructures'. He adds that: 'It is always necessary to distinguish between the material transformation of the economic conditions of production, which can be determined with the precision of natural science, and the legal, political, religious, artistic or philosophic—in short, ideological forms in which men become conscious of this conflict and fight it out.'[14] Now this distinction between the economic conditions of production 'which can be determined with the precision of natural science', and the ideological forms, which cannot be determined with such precision, suggests something about the precise meaning of the term determination in the base/superstructure formulation. In much of the Marxist literary criticism of the Stalin period, whether produced in the Soviet Union itself or by westerners sympathetic to Moscow-affiliated Communist Parties, determination was normally understood in the sense of mechanical causation, such that any given mode of production of necessity causes to come into being the appropriate ideological superstructures. Thus, for example, Christopher Caudwell wrote that 'Modern poetry is capitalist poetry'.[15] Now, as we have already noted, this conception of determination as a causal process is incompatible with the wider precepts of Marx's sociological method. But it is equally incompatible with the version of the base/superstructure formula which Marx himself here employs. For if the relationship between base and superstructure is indeed one of mechanical causation, and if we can measure the transformation of the economic conditions of production with the precision of natural science, then it *must* follow that we can do likewise with the ideological forms. The fact that Marx specifically states that such precision is impossible, clearly suggests that the process of determination, in Marx's view at least, cannot be a simple causal one.

How, then, are we to understand Marx's concept of determination? What is the precise relationship between the mode of production and the other elements within the social totality? This relationship can perhaps best be understood if we consider the social system as, in Perry Anderson's words, 'a complex totality, *loaded* by the predominance in the long run of one level within it—the economy'.[16] This is, in fact, precisely the relationship between the different elements in the social totality which Engels pointed to when he argued that:

> Political, juridicial, philosophical, religious, literary, artistic etc. development is based upon economic development. But all react upon one another and also upon the economic base. It is not that the economic position is *the cause and alone active*, while everything else only has a passive effect. There is, rather, interaction on the basis of economic necessity, which ultimately always asserts itself.[17]

Such a conception of the social totality clearly implies a concept of determination which is very far removed from that of mechanical causation. Raymond Williams has argued for a revaluation of the concept of determination 'towards the setting of limits and the exertion of pressure, and away from a predicted, prefigured and controlled content'.[18] Now such a revaluation is indeed necessary: much of Marxist literary criticism, and especially that developed under the political auspices of Stalinism, has in fact used the notion of determination precisely in the sense of causation. But it needs to be emphasised that Williams's 'revaluation' is not so much a revaluation as a rediscovery of Marx's own Marxism. Marx's concept of determination is, then, concerned not with causation, but rather with *the setting of limits*. But if it is important to remember that the economic base does not mechanically 'cause' the appropriate ideological forms, it is equally important to remember that it does, nonetheless, set certain very definite objective limits on the possibilities for their development. Many Marxist sociologists, and in particular those influenced by the early work of Georg Lukács, have tended, in their concern with the 'totality', to abandon not only the concept of causation, but also the concept of determination itself, and in so doing they have tended to develop the notion that art can, in some way, transcend ideology. Let us consider, very briefly, one such example. Ian Birchall, in an essay on 'the total Marx', argues that Marx's references to *Timon of Athens* in *Capital* and in the *Economic and Philosophic Manuscripts* imply that Shakespeare was in some way able to transcend the limitations of Elizabethan society.[19] The first of Birchall's references can easily be discounted. In *Capital*, Marx merely inserts a quotation from Act IV of *Timon*,[20] on the levelling power of money, as an illustration of his general argument, and makes no direct reference whatsoever to Shakespeare's own ideological position. In the *Economic and Philosophic Manuscripts*, however, Marx does directly discuss Shakespeare's views, and in particular he emphasises the playwright's ability to recognise two of the main properties of money, its 'godlike' capacity to transform all human and natural qualities into their opposites, and its 'whoreish' role as the universal procurer of human beings.[21] But at no point does Marx suggest that these Shakespearian insights represent some miraculous transcendence of the limits of Elizabethan ideology. Now Birchall's interpretation of Marx's comments on Shakespeare rests on the implicit assumption that such insights are inexplicable in terms of the social structure of Elizabethan England. The only possible explanation of Birchall's adherence to such a view must be that he regards Shakespeare as a poet of the rising bourgeoisie who should, as such, be incapable of a truly critical stance *vis-à-vis* the developing bourgeois society. But such an analysis of Shakespeare's position in Elizabethan society is essentially superficial. Certainly, Shakespeare came from the bourgeois class; but, as an Elizabethan dramatist, he was also a servant of the court. Caudwell came much closer to a truly sociological analysis when he defined the dramatist as a bourgeois 'with a feudal *status*'.[22] But even Caudwell is insufficiently precise, since the status of court player is a product, not of feudalism in general, and certainly not of medieval feudalism, but rather of that specific moment in the development of feudal society which gives rise to the specific political form of absolutism. The Elizabethan dramatists were, then, not bourgeois with a feudal status, but rather, as Colin Sparks has argued, a *noblesse de robe*, that is, a section of the bourgeoisie tied inextricably to the institutions of the absolutist state.[23] And, as Goldmann demonstrated, the social position of such groups characteristically gives rise to a tragic world vision which is capable of perceiving the limitations of bourgeois society in just such a way as does Shakespeare. It is only in the light of such concretely sociological analyses, and not by reference to some metaphysical transcendence of the limitations of existing forms of consciousness, that *Timon of Athens*, or for that matter any other work of art, can be fully understood.

In Marx's and Engel's own scattered comments on the relationship between art and society, there is contained an insistence on the 'dialectical' nature of that relationship which precludes both the ahistorical idealism characteristic of literary-critical orthodoxy, and that economic determinism which became the single most distinctive feature of official Marxist writing on literature in the course of the

Stalin period. Since the death of Stalin, modern Marxism, and in particular, modern western Marxism, has been pre-eminently pre-occupied with the problem of developing a theory of the superstructures which avoids the pitfalls of the earlier economic determinism. The danger remains, however, that any attempted reconciliation between the theory of totality and the theory of a determining base and determined superstructure will remain merely formal. Elizabeth and Tom Burns have described the notion of the dialectic, somewhat uncharitably, as 'a life-raft on which it is possible to stand between the clear sky of scientific positivism and the deep waters of post-Kantian phenomenology, and await rescue'. [24] Whilst this would represent an extremely unfair comment on the founders of Marxism themselves, it does, perhaps, have a certain pertinence to more recent dialectical sociologies. [25] And it is certainly true that, all too often, the word 'dialectical' is invoked, not in order to solve a problem, but rather in order to wish it away. If the notion of the dialectic is to prove at all useful, we have an obligation to explain how a dialectical relationship functions, to specify the precise moments of the dialectic. And in respect of literary studies, at least, Marx and Engels can themselves be of little assistance, for neither of them ever worked out a fully developed theory of literature. For such an elaboration, we have to turn elsewhere and, in particular we have to turn to Lucien Goldmann's genetic structuralism.

2   *Goldmann's Genetic Structuralism* [26]

Perhaps the most important feature of Goldmann's sociological method is that resolution of Marxism with structuralism which enables him to render explicit the structuralist premises upon which Marx's work rests. [27] For Goldmann, as for Marx, sociological analysis is concerned with the way in which 'facts' are related, rather than with 'facts' in the raw. And Goldmann is insistent that any relationship which exists between literature and society has to be understood in terms of *structure* rather than in terms of *content*. As he himself puts it: 'The essential relationship between the life of society and literary creation is not concerned with the content of these two sectors of human reality, but only with the mental structures, with what might be called the categories which shape both the empirical consciousness of a certain social group and the imaginary universe created by the writer.' [28] In rendering explicit a notion of structure which is only implied in Marx's writings, Goldmann absolves the 'base determines superstructure' theory from the charge of economic determinism. For it is only when both the material base and the various superstructures are understood in terms of their direct empirical content that this theory leads of necessity to a vulgar economic determinism. It is, for example, Caudwell's attempt to reduce the *content* of literature to the *content* of social life which leads him to the notion that modern poetry is merely 'capitalist' poetry. But if we define both the economic base and the superstructures as sets of structural relationships, as Goldmann does, then we are able to understand literature, not as a reflection of reality, but rather as a distinct mode of practice, which stands in a relationship of *structural homology* to the various other modes of human practice. It can be seen, then, that despite the persistency of his attacks upon structuralist orthodoxy, Goldmann is, in fact, very much a structuralist. It remains true for Goldmann, as for any other structuralist writer, that 'comprehension is the bringing to light of a significant structure immanent in the object studied'.[29] His studies of Kant, Pascal and Racine are just as concerned to find 'the primal plan on which everything else depends',[30] as is Todorov's essay on Henry James. However, where Goldmann parts company with mainstream structuralism is in his insistence that 'structures are born from events and from the everyday behaviour of individuals and that, except for the most formal characteristics, there is no permanence in these structures'.[31] From Goldmann's standpoint, and from the standpoint of Marxism generally, most structuralist analysis is incomplete in that it contents itself with the description of a set of structural relations, the existence of which is taken as given, rather than attempting to explain the processes by which such structures are produced.[32] And this incompleteness leads to distortion in that the structure of a particular set of relations can only be fully understood in the context of an analysis of its origins, and of its relationship to other structures. In its insistence on the production of structures, rather than on the mere fact of their existence, Goldmann's structuralism becomes profoundly historical. The central task of the sociologist is defined thus: 'It is when he replaces the work in a historical evolution which he studies as a whole, and when he relates it to the social life of the time at which it was written—which he also looks upon as a whole—that the enquirer can bring out the works's objective meaning.'[33] Sociology should, then, focus itself, at one and the same time, on both the internal structures of given literary works and the wider social structures which give rise to these purely literary structures. As Goldmann himself admits,[34] this notion of structure derives from the earlier writings of Georg Lukács. But whilst a notion of structure certainly is present in Lukács's earlier writings, both pre-Marxist and Marxist, it is quite definitely absent from the later 'socialist realist' writings which constitute the main foundations of Lukács's reputation as a literary critic and sociologist of literature. In the writings of the Stalin period, Lukács's work was obsessively concerned with the notion of literature as a realistic reflector of the real content of life. In fact, Goldmann's work achieves a reconciliation between the theory of society as a totality and the theory of a determining base and a determined superstructure, a reconciliation which succeeds in building on the achievements of the young Lukács. By contrast, much of Lukács's own subsequent work represents an intellectual regression towards that deterministic Marxism which *History and Class Consciousness*[35] had set out to challenge.

Goldmann's structuralism does not in itself represent a substantial revision of the Marxist theory of literature. His conception of the base/superstructure relationship as *mediated* through the *world visions* of the different social classes does, however, entail such a revision. Goldmann argues, in his earlier writings at least, that there exists, not a direct structural homology between individual works of literature and the nature of social reality, but rather a set of structural homologies between, on the one hand, the individual work of literature and the world vision of the social class to which the writer belongs, and on the other, that world vision and the real social life of the times. The term 'world vision' here refers to 'the whole complex of ideas, aspirations and feelings which links together the members of a social group (a group which, in most cases, assumes the existence of a social class) and which opposes them to members of other social groups'.[36] Such world visions can exist on two different planes: 'that of the *real* consciousness of the group, . . . or that of their *coherent* exceptional expression in great works of philosophy or art'.[37] It is this latter plane which corresponds most clearly to what Goldmann terms the 'maximum possible consciousness' of the group. 'Any great literary or artistic work', he argues,

> is the expression of a world vision. This vision is the product of a collective group consciousness which reaches its highest expression in the mind of a poet or a thinker. The expression which his work provides is then studied by the historian who uses the idea of the

world vision as a tool which will help him to deduce two things from the text: the essential meaning of the work which he is studying and the meaning which the individual and partial elements take on when the work is looked at as a whole.[38]

Goldmann employs this notion of the world vision, with some considerable success, in his studies of Kant, Pascal and Racine. There he relates the structure of the 'tragic vision' as a world vision both to the structure of the philosophical writings of Pascal and Kant, and of the theatre of Racine, and to the social structure of seventeenth-century France and eighteenth-century Germany. The efficacy with which Goldmann is able to elucidate the internal structures of both Jansenism and Kantianism clearly suggests the value of this concept of the world vision to the sociology of literature and of philosophy.

Nonetheless, Goldmann's theory of the world vision contains within itself certain problematic elements. In the first place, it is difficult to accept his rigorous distinction between *world visions* and *ideologies*. Goldmann maintains that such a distinction can, in fact, be made on the basis of the *partial*, and hence distorting, character of the latter, as opposed to the *total* character of the former. In his view, only world visions, that is, those mental constructs which do not distort the nature of reality, can give rise to great works of art, since only world visions can give a *coherent* account of reality. Furthermore, Goldmann argues that world visions can only be produced by rising social classes. Indeed, he firmly maintains that we can 'link *world-views* to *social classes* so long as they still possess an ideal bearing on the totality of the human community; and . . . ideologies to *all other social groups*, and to social classes *in decline* when they no longer act except to defend, without much faith or confidence, privileges and acquired positions'.[39] Marxists have, of course, always drawn the distinction between true and false consciousnesses. However, for Marx, only true proletarian consciousness can involve the elimination of all distorting elements. All other class consciousnesses are inherently distorting in that they are always an ideological expression of the particular interests of the class concerned. This does not, though, imply that all other class consciousnesses are necessarily incoherent. Indeed, it is difficult to understand Goldmann's insistence that distortion and incoherence are necessarily related. There would appear to be no *a priori* reason why a particular ideology should not give an account of reality which is, at one and the same time, both false and internally consistent. Most ideologies are precisely of this nature. Classical

Greek philosophy, medieval Catholicism, Azande witchcraft, bourgeois political economy, Stalinist Marxism—all give an account of
reality which is both distorted and coherent. Even the notion that
'rising' social classes necessarily offer a 'better' understanding of
reality than 'declining' social classes is extremely suspect. The passage
from *Timon of Athens*, which Marx quoted with such approval,
clearly suggests that the sixteenth and seventeenth-century *noblesse de
robe*, and presumably also the old feudal nobility, were able to achieve
a much clearer insight into the fetishism of capitalist society than
were the more revolutionary Puritan sections of the bourgeoisie.
Goldmann's distinction between world visions and ideologies rests, in
fact, on an extremely schematic theory of history as a process of linear
progress in which each successive rising class moves progressively
nearer to a correct, coherent account of reality. But the problem of
ideology cannot be dealt with in this *a priori* manner. Rather, we
require concrete analyses of the structures of different social class
world visions, analyses such as those which Goldmann himself carried
out in his studies of the tragic vision. The distinction between world
visions and ideologies can only be an obstacle to the development of
such a sociology of literature.

The second major weakness of Goldmann's theory of the world
vision consists in its essentially *formalist* character. For Goldmann
conceives of the world vision, in typically Weberian (and Lukácsian)
terms, as an *ideal type*. The very considerable extent to which
Goldmann's methodology derives, in this respect at least, from that of
the German sociologist, Max Weber, necessitates a somewhat lengthy
digression to consider the precise nature of the latter's sociological
method. Weber's sociological individualism was, in fact, conceived as
a response to both the Marxist theory of social class and the positivistic
notion of 'society' as a supra-individual entity. Now any individualistic social science, such as that which Weber proposes, is
immediately faced with one central problem, that of explaining the
structured, non-random nature of social behaviour. Once we allow
that social behaviour follows certain patterns, which it quite clearly
does, it becomes extremely difficult to maintain a strict adherence to
the notion that the motive forces behind such behaviour are purely
individual. Indeed, the only way in which such an adherence can be
maintained is by positing the notion of 'typical' behaviour. And it is
this notion of the typical which is, in Weber's sociology, the central
mediating agency between, on the one hand, the observed re-
gularities of social behaviour and, on the other, the notion that the

social world consists only of discrete individuals. This notion of the typical assumes a central importance, in particular, as the basis for Weber's development of a certain methodological tool which he termed the 'ideal type'. Weber defines the ideal type in the following manner:

An ideal type is formed by a one-sided *accentuation* of one or more points of view and by the synthesis of a great many diffuse, discrete, more or less present and occasionally absent *concrete individual* phenomena which are arranged according to those one-sidedly emphasized viewpoints into a unified *analytical* construct (*Gedankenbild*). In its conceptual purity, this mental construct (*Gedankenbild*) cannot be found empirically anywhere in reality.[40]

It is, then, essentially an abstraction, the purpose of which is to cast light on the nature of social reality. 'It has the significance', writes Weber, 'of a purely ideal *limiting* concept with which the real situation or action is *compared* and surveyed for the explication of certain of its significant components.'[41] These comparisons are effected, argues Weber, 'by the application of the category of objective possibility',[42] that is, by the consideration of what *would* happen given certain initial limiting assumptions. Thus, for example, in Weber's view, the significance of the battle of Marathon can only be understood on the basis of a comparison between the two *possible* outcomes of that battle.[43] Weber is particularly insistent on the value of ideal types in understanding the significance of ideological formations. He argues that

those 'ideas' which govern the behaviour of the population of a certain epoch, i.e., which are concretely influential in determining their conduct, can, if a somewhat complicated construct is involved, be formulated precisely only in the form of an ideal type, since empirically it exists in the minds of an indefinite and constantly changing mass of individuals and assumes in their minds the most multifarious nuances of form and content, clarity and meaning.[44]

Finally, we may note that these ideal types are of two different kinds: those which refer to certain concrete historical phenomena— for example, the ideal type of 'capitalism', and those which have a more general ahistorical applicability—for example, ideal types such as 'rationality', 'power', 'authority', etc.

These, then, are the central features of the Weberian 'ideal type' approach to sociological theory. In what ways does this approach differ from that of Marxist sociology? The central difference between the two methodologies consists in their differing conceptions of the role of abstraction in social theory. For Marx, the aim of sociological theory was the reconstitution of the social totality in theoretical form. Thus abstractions, such as for example 'surplus value', are only of value in that they constitute an instrument by which the social scientist moves from the totality of empirically-given reality to the totality of reality grasped theoretically. Weber, however, subscribed to an essentially tragic, neo-Kantian epistemology which conceived of reality as fundamentally unknowable. The goal of abstraction then becomes, not the reconstitution of the social totality, but rather the elucidation of *certain facets* of reality through the medium of a comparison between the abstraction and the concretely given reality. Whereas Weber was concerned with the analysis of 'objective possibilities', Marx was concerned with the understanding of 'objective realities'. This difference between their respective epistemologies explains their differing conceptions of the nature of ideological formations. Whereas Weber maintained that the essence of such formations could only be understood abstractly, Marx held that they could, indeed, be grasped in their concrete essence. Thus, for Marx, neither true nor false consciousness is seen as an abstraction. Rather, they are each concretely existing forms of consciousness. True proletarian consciousness, for example, is *not* an abstraction; it is, in fact, that consciousness concretely attained by the proletariat in the process of revolutionary struggle. It follows, then, that the very notion of an ideal type is alien to the Marxist methodology. But, in addition to this general rejection of ideal typology, we must add a specific objection to the notion of general ahistorical ideal types. Marx's sociology not only aims to reconstitute the social totality in theoretical form, but also conceives of that totality as subject to a process of constant historical *change*. It cannot allow the existence of universal categories, such as 'rationality' or 'power', since it recognises their substantive content as constantly transformed, made and remade, in the course of human history.

Now this Weberian ideal typology is, in fact, taken over into the work of the young Lukács. In *The Theory of the Novel*, for example, Lukács's typology of the novel form is precisely an ideal typology. In

Lukács's view, the central problem in the modern world is 'the in-commensurability of soul and work, of interiority and adventure — . . . . the absence of a transcendental "place" alloted to human endeavour'.[45] He identifies two broad types of such incommensurability, and argues that they each give rise to a particular type of novel. The first of these, that is the incommensurability which arises when the soul is too narrow with respect to the complexity of reality, gives rise to the novel of 'abstract idealism', of which Lukács cites Cervantes's *Don Quixote* as the classical example.[46] The second type of incommensurability is that in which the soul is broader than is allowed for within the conventional world of reality, an incommensurability which gives rise to the novel of the 'romanticism of disillusionment', and here Flaubert's *L'Education sentimentale* provides Lukács with his main example of such a novel.[47] Finally, Lukács identifies in Goethe's *Wilhelm Meister* a third type of novel which effectively constitutes an attempted synthesis of the other two types.[48] These three types of novel are not, in fact, concrete variants of the novel form; rather, they are abstractions with which concrete literary works are compared. Furthermore, they are constructed precisely on the basis of the formalistic category of objective possibility. Given that the central problem in the modern world is the incommensurability between the soul and the world, it follows *logically* that there can be only these three *possible* types of novel. It is, of course, barely remarkable that Lukács's pre-Marxist writings should bear the stamp of that intellectual climate which he shared in common with Max Weber. But the presence of a similar formalism in the avowedly Marxist *History and Class Consciousness*, a work which clearly exercised some considerable influence over Goldmann's own intellectual development, is rather more surprising. But the theory of class consciousness which Lukács outlines in *History and Class Consciousness* clearly derives from Weber as well as from Marx. Lukács takes from Marx the very notion that we can speak of class consciousness, as opposed to individual consciousnesses. But his analysis of the nature of those class consciousnesses is couched in entirely Weberian terms. He argues that: 'By relating consciousness to the whole of society it becomes possible to infer the thoughts and feelings which men would have in a particular situation if they were able to assess both it and the interests arising from it in their impact on immediate action and on the whole structure of society. That is to say, it would be possible to infer the thoughts and feelings appropriate to their objective situation.'[49] For Lukács, then, 'class consciousness consists in fact of the appropriate and rational reactions "imputed" (zugerechnet) to a particular typical position in the process of production'.[50] Thus Lukács distinguishes between 'imputed' class consciousness and psychological consciousness in terms of the Weberian category of objective possibility. Indeed, he actually argues that: '*The objective theory of class consciousness is the theory of its objective possibility.*'[51] Class consciousness, thus conceived, is in fact a Weberian ideal type. Lukács argues that, given firstly, the characteristically Weberian assumption of 'rationality' and, secondly, an analysis of the nature of objective reality, we can then proceed to *deduce* the appropriate form of class consciousness. In this way, class consciousness becomes an abstraction constructed by the scientific observer (presumably, the revolutionary) for his own purposes. Now, neither Marx, nor Lenin ever conceived of true consciousness in such a manner. Marx did not, for example, 'deduce' the nature of the dictatorship of the proletariat from any notion of objective possibility. On the contrary, he concluded that the Commune was the appropriate political form of such a dictatorship only on the basis of a concrete analysis of the civil war in France.[52] As Lenin quite rightly comments: 'Marx did not indulge in utopias; he expected the *experience* of the mass movement to provide the reply to the question as to what specific forms the organization of the proletariat as the ruling class will assume and as to the exact manner in which this organization will be combined with the most complete, most consistent, "winning of the battle of democracy".'[53] The Weberian formalism, which Lukács bequeathed to Goldmann, is entirely his own and not that of either Marx or Lenin.

To return from this somewhat prolonged digression, the precise extent to which Goldmann's theory of the world vision derives from both Weberian and Lukácsian formalisms should now be readily discernible. Goldmann's world vision is, quite clearly, an ideal type. 'It is not an immediate empirical fact,' he writes, 'but a conceptual working hypothesis indispensable to an understanding of the way in which individuals actually express their ideas.'[54] Indeed, Goldmann employs the specifically Weberian category of 'objective possibility', when he argues that: '*The maximum of potential consciousness of a social class always constitutes a psychologically coherent world-view which may be expressed on the plane of religion, philosophy, literature or art.*'[55] There is, of course, a certain contradiction in Goldmann's work here. On the one hand, he follows Lukács in developing a theory of class consciousness which is based on the notion of an opposition between *real* consciousness and an '*imputed*' maximum possible consciousness. On the other, however, he insists, unlike Lukács, on the concrete embodiment of these maximum possible consciousnesses in works of literature and philosophy. As long as we are able, in fact, to understand these maximum possible consciousnesses as actually realised in the real consciousnesses of certain individuals and *groups*, then it becomes possible to cleanse Goldmann's sociology of this formalistic residue. The tragic vision then becomes, not a maximum possible consciousness, but rather a maximum real consciousness, and much of the substantive content of Goldmann's analysis can remain unaltered. But Goldmann's formalism does not remain at this level. On the contrary, it leads him on into a realm of, at times, astonishing abstraction. Thus, behind Goldmann's analysis of the tragic vision, there rests a further, much more abstract notion, the notion of what one can only term the 'meta-world vision' of totality. For Goldmann strongly emphasises the continuity between Pascal, Kant, Hegel, Marx and Lukács.[56] Now a world vision which finds expression in Pascal and Lukács, Kant and Marx, cannot possibly represent any social group's collective consciousness. It can *only* be a Weberian ideal type, and furthermore, an ideal type of the most profoundly ahistorical nature. Goldmann's belief in this meta-world vision is, in fact, not only a consequence, but also a cause of his general formalism. It is precisely Goldmann's inability to understand the extent to which there exists a profound breach between Kantianism and Marxism which helps to explain the formalistic nature of his sociology. For Goldmann, like Lukács, defines his sociological method in essentially neo-Kantian terms. This is evident, of course, in his adherence to the ideal type method. But it is also evident in his 'theory of the wager'. In *The Hidden God*, Goldmann identifies the wager on the existence of a non-provable God as central to Jansenist philosophy.[57] Kantianism, too, contains a similar wager, a wager on the existence of the 'noumenon', the thing-in-itself. And Goldmann argues that Marx's sociology is also based on such a wager. Thus he writes of the Marxist 'faith' 'in the future that we must make for ourselves by what we do . . . this faith becomes a "wager" which we make that our actions will, in fact, be successful'.[58] Now, of course, there is a sense in which Marxism does rest on a sort of wager. Like all other belief systems, including natural science, Marxism makes the 'wager' that its own fundamental axioms, which are untestable precisely because they are axiomatic, are nonetheless correct. But such 'wagers', which are common to all belief systems, are quite different to those genuine wagers which we find only in tragic philosophy. Whereas tragic man conceives of his wager as a *wager*, all non-tragic belief systems conceive of their axioms as *certainties*. Furthermore, in the case of both Marxist sociology and natural science, the wager is merely an initial 'act' which permits other subsequent, and consequent, actions, which do not partake of the nature of a wager. In tragic philosophy, however, the wager is not only the beginning, but also the middle and the end of the theory. Goldmann's attempt to conflate the Jansenist wager on God with the Marxist and natural scientific 'wagers' on the certainty of their own axioms, thus results in an essentially Kantian conception of sociology as a wager in the face of an unknowable reality.

3   A Note on the Problem of Aesthetics

Thus far, our discussion of Goldmann's theory of literature has centred around an analysis of the specifically *sociological* aspects of that theory. But there is, in fact, a second element within that theory, that is an *aesthetic* which takes as its central criterion of value the notion of *coherence*. As we have seen, world visions can exist on two planes, that of the real consciousness of the group and that of their coherent expression in works of art. Goldmann argues that: 'Great philosophical and artistic works represent *coherent* and adequate expressions of . . . world views.'[59] This notion of coherence is here employed as both a sociological and an aesthetic concept. Goldmann maintains not only that all works of art do in fact coherently express a world vision, but also that 'it is precisely because their work has such a coherence that it possesses artistic, literary or philosophical worth'.[60] This definition of aesthetic value leads Goldmann almost of necessity into a rigidly deterministic account of the sociological preconditions for the creation of great works of art. Since artistic value is defined in terms of coherence, it follows that only those social groups which give rise to coherent world visions, as opposed to ideologies, can possibly produce great works of art. For Goldmann, then, 'any valid literary work or philosophical vision takes in the whole of human life. It thus follows that the only groups whose world view is likely to find expression in such works or systems are those whose ideas or activities tend towards the creation of a complete vision of man's social life',[61] — that is, of course, rising, as opposed to declining, social classes. One of the great merits of Goldmann's sociology is its insistence on the need for a direct analysis of the art-object as art-object, its insistence on the integrity of the literary text. In his sociology, 'all positive study must always begin with an effort to dissect the object studied, so that the object is seen as a complex of significant reactions, the structure of which can account for most of the partial empirical aspects they present to the research worker'.[62] From this it follows that 'the research worker must account for the whole of the text and must add nothing to it'.[63] In his sociological work, then, Goldmann is acutely aware of the dangers of that eclecticism which follows from any too-hasty concern to analyse the literary work in non-literary terms. And yet, paradoxically enough, Goldmann's *aesthetic* is defined precisely in *non-literary* terms. The notion of coherence is not, in fact, a specific literary concept, but rather a concept derived from the method of philosophy. Certainly, one can speak of philosophical systems as 'incoherent' in the sense that they lack internal consistency. But is a work of art similarly obliged to demonstrate internal consistency? Is it not often the case that the function of artistic form is precisely to integrate into itself inconsistent and often contradictory elements? As Barthes says, 'the work of art is what man wrests from chance'.[64] Goldmann's aesthetic seeks to subsume literary activity under the general category of philosophical activity. At the same time, of course, Goldmann also defines aesthetic value in crudely sociological terms. In his theory, the work of art is little more than the maximum possible consciousness of a particular social class. Any work of art which expresses an 'ideology' rather than a 'world vision' is automatically debarred from attaining lasting artistic value. We have already argued that this rigid distinction between ideologies and world visions is sociologically untenable. And we must accept, surely, that no ideological formation can be ruled aesthetically infertile in this *a priori* manner. But even this modification of the theory cannot save Goldmann's aesthetic. Literary worth can only be explained in literary terms, that is, in terms which seek to elucidate the specifically *literary* effect which a particular work of literature achieves, and not by reference to any *merely* external philosophical or sociological criterion.[65]

In practice, of course, Goldmann's aesthetic is rather more innocuous, and also rather less rigorous, than the above account might suggest. If Goldmann had rigorously followed through the logic of his own declared position, he would have been obliged to begin each of his analyses with an investigation into the progressive or regressive nature of the social class to which the writer belongs, and a corresponding enquiry designed to determine whether that class's belief system should be understood as an ideology or as a world vision. Such an aesthetic would have provided Goldmann with a critical method entirely independent of the declared preferences of both the reading public and the professional practitioners of literary criticism. But, in fact, he does no such thing. Rather, he tends to accept existing judgements as to the literary worth of particular works of art, and seeks merely to justify those judgements in terms of his own philosophical and sociological criteria. This approach renders Goldmann's aesthetic rather more flexible, and rather less dogmatic, than its formal characteristics might suggest. But it also renders it perilously close to the status of *tautology*. Given that all great works of art are coherent expressions of a world vision, as opposed to an ideology, and given that a particular work is indeed an example of great art, then that work of art must, in Goldmann's view, embody such an expression. The circularity of the argument derives, clearly, from Goldmann's reluctance actually to apply his own aesthetic criteria directly to the study of works of literature, and his corresponding willingness to accept, as given, the existing aesthetic status of such works. But if the argument is circular, it is at least inoffensive. It manages to avoid that dogmatism, characteristic of many aesthetic theories, which seeks to erect a particular notion of literary worth into a universally applicable ideal and to impose that ideal upon those, both writers and readers, who are unprepared to accept it. Goldmann succeeds in maintaining, against the weight of his own declared aesthetic principles, a healthy respect for the declared literary preferences of others, a respect which is markedly absent both from orthodox Eastern European Marxist theories of aesthetics and from western aesthetic theories such as those propounded by, for example, both Leavis and T. S. Eliot.

If Goldmann's own aesthetic is merely formally dogmatic and substantively tautologous, how, in fact, should an aesthetic proceed? This question is, of course, far more readily posed than it is answered, and perhaps the only answer that can, at present, be given is an answer in the negative—that is, one which seeks to demonstrate how an aesthetic should not proceed. We referred earlier to Marx's critique of critical criticism in *The Holy Family*. There, Marx identifies the 'speculative' nature of idealism in its tendency to construct abstract ideals out of the diverse elements of reality and to impose those ideals upon that reality. Thus, for example, Marx charged Szeliga that: 'After having constructed out of the real world the category of "mystery", he constructs out of this category the real world.'[66] Now the dogmatic nature of Goldmann's aesthetic derives from precisely such a procedure. Goldmann identifies a particular ideal, that of coherence, an ideal which is perhaps appropriate to certain particular cultural forms, and elevates that ideal to the level of a universally applicable criterion of literary merit. Goldmann's own aesthetic is, as we have suggested, saved from the full consequences of this procedure by its lapse into tautology. But in general, most aesthetic theories do indeed become fully 'speculative', and hence fully dogmatic. Thus, for example, both Lukács and Leavis, in their own very different ways, attempt to construct a universal aesthetic out of a particular set of criteria of worth derived, essentially, from the study of the modern realist novel. The problem with all such aesthetics is, clearly, their *indifference to the real*. They are obliged, of necessity, to deny the validity, the reality, of all aesthetic experiences which fall outside the compass of their own particular criteria. To take the example most obviously relevant to our own particular project, Leavis finds it necessary to effect a wholesale repudiation of the previously accepted definition of Milton's literary worth. Leavis argues, not only that he personally dislikes Milton's verse, but also that all those readers who have claimed, over the past three centuries, to have found something of value in *Paradise Lost*, are simply wrong. Lukács dismisses Kafka's modern readership in exactly similar terms. The problem here is really quite simple. Both Leavis and Lukács actually subscribe to a conception of aesthetics which is *legislative* rather than *scientific*. They each attempt, not to understand why certain people enjoy certain literary forms, but rather to demand of their readers that they change their literary tastes and conform to those of the all-knowing, all-perceiving literary critic. The speculative dogmatism of their respective aesthetic theories derives, surely, from their prior commitment to the notion that there can be only *one*, universally applicable, set of criteria of literary worth. For if this is the case, and if a particular critic is especially enamoured with a certain type of literature, then he is bound to represent the standards of worth appropriate to that literature as universally applicable ideals. Furthermore, the very notion itself of such an ideal is inherently dogmatic, rather than scientific. One only has to attempt to trace out the history of a particular writer's reputation over any considerable period of time in order to discover the remarkable changeability of empirical human taste. Thus, the twentieth-century disdain for Milton's epic poetry, pioneered by both Eliot and Leavis, can only aspire to universality on the basis of a corresponding disdain for the real aesthetic experiences of many thousands of individuals over a period of some three centuries. This notion of a mythical, universally applicable, aesthetic ideal is, then, perhaps the single most important obstacle to the development of a truly scientific aesthetic.

What, then, are the possible alternatives? At the opposite extreme, there is, of course, the notion that all aesthetic experience is merely subjective and that no objective criteria of value can possibly exist. Such a notion of aesthetics would run parallel to that of ethics outlined in Professor Ayer's *Language, Truth and Logic*, in which ethical terms are seen as essentially 'pseudo-concepts' which serve merely to express feeling and emotion.[67] But the central weakness of such individualistic relativisms as that outlined by Ayer is their inability to account for the *structured* nature of ethical, and hence also of aesthetic, responses. Aesthetic and moral preferences are not normally perceived as merely subjective, as mere expressions of personal emotion. Rather, they are experienced as possessing an objectivity which defines them as essentially inter-personal rather than personal constructs, and an external coerciveness reminiscent of the Durkheimian notion of a 'social fact'.[68] An emotive theory of aesthetics will not, in fact, work quite simply because aesthetic notions are essentially social rather than individual in their origins. What, then, of the possibility of some form of sociological relativism? Such a theory would represent standards of aesthetic value as objective and external with respect to the individual, but as subjective and internal with respect to the relevant community, be it the society, the class, or the group. This is clearly the notion of literary worth to which T. S. Eliot subscribes in his famous essay on 'Tradition and the Individual Talent'. There, Eliot defines the 'ideal order' of an existing literary tradition, in terms neither of an abstract ahistorical ideal nor of a merely personal subjectivity, but rather of an essentially social, and changing, response on the part of present communities to the literature of both the past and the present. Thus: 'The existing monuments form an ideal order among themselves, which is modified by the introduction of the new (the really new) work of art among them. The existing order is complete before the new work arrives; for order to persist after the supervention of novelty, the whole existing order must be, if ever so slightly, altered.'[69] The danger to which such sociological relativisms are always exposed is that of collapsing into a type of collective 'emotivism', which concedes the objectivity of aesthetic value with respect to the particular community, only in order to deny it in the face of history. If pushed to such extremes, sociological relativism finds itself incapable of any explanation of the problem of lasting value in art. Eliot himself does not, however, take this course. Rather, his 'Hegelianism' leads him to posit a notion of *history* in which artistic development is seen as a process of movement, in the direction of greater refinement and greater complexity, which operates in such a fashion as to abandon nothing *en route*.[70] A somewhat analogous Hegelianised Marxism led both Lukács and Lifshitz to very similar conclusions. And, indeed, this is the solution at which Marx himself hints, in his few brief comments on classical Greek art, in the Introduction to the *Grundrisse*.[71]

There is, however, an unfortunate paradox here. Whilst both Lukács and Eliot formally adhere to this Hegelian notion of aesthetic value as an essentially historical product, they both tend to repudiate that notion in the substantive practice of their literary criticism. In the case of Eliot this is, perhaps, excusable. Eliot's sustained polemic against Milton and Dryden, and in particular the former,[72] and his corresponding panegyric on the metaphysical poets,[73] were deliberately designed, as Frank Kermode quite rightly observes,[74] as an essentially propagandist intervention in order to justify the new Symbolist poetics. Eliot's subsequent retraction of much of his earlier hostility to Milton[75] clearly suggests the extent to which that hostility had been motivated, at least unconsciously, by such immediate, tactical considerations.[76] But Lukács's own stubborn commitment to a dogmatist aesthetic persisted right through until his death. In part, of course, this dogmatism derives from the simple 'social control' requirements of the Stalinist state bureaucracy, for which Lukács acted, in general at least, as a loyal and faithful servant. But Lukács's personal belief in the need for a legislative, rather than a scientific, aesthetic also has certain very clear origins in the theoretical nature itself of Stalinist Marxism. Marx's rejection of the *post festum* character of Hegelian philosophy, his insistence on the unity of theory and *praxis*, is one of the most obviously distinctive features of his system. And Lukács himself clearly viewed the legislative nature of his aesthetic as corresponding to the function of *praxis* in general Marxist theory. To put it rather crudely, Lukács conceived of literary theory as the theory of which censorship was the practice. It follows necessarily that such an aesthetic must be concerned with the problem of devising literary 'rules of conduct', rather than with that of understanding real patterns of behaviour. Doubtless, this is a plausible enough application of certain of Marx's very general categories to the specific problem of literary criticism, although it is belied somewhat by Marx's own youthful opposition to censorship. [77] But in so far as it makes the determination of literary worth the prerogative of certain particular individuals and groups, in practice the theoreticians of the Soviet Communist Party, rather than of the total historical process, it appears as distinctly un-Hegelian in its aspirations. If a scientific aesthetic is to be fully developed, one suspects that the practice of which it will be the theory is that of literary creation itself, rather than that of censorship. Our account of the potentialities of such an aesthetic has been necessarily tentative. We have insisted that it must be scientific, rather than legislative, in character, that it must be designed so as to enable us to comprehend real literary phenomena, rather than to persuade or coerce its 'victims' into the acceptance of standards of literary value which are imposed from without. And we have suggested that it must contain within itself a Hegelian appreciation of the nature of the historical process, an appreciation which can only be made concrete by reference to specific sociological analyses. Almost certainly it will require, too, an as yet undeveloped theory of the nature of the structural categories which inform individual aesthetic appreciation. For, whilst it is obviously true that realised literary tastes are a sociological, rather than a psychological, construct, these sociological processes presumably act upon other essentially psychological processes, of which they are, in part, both cause and consequence. But all of this is little more than speculation. At the present stage of our scientific knowledge, we possess a reasonably sophisticated theoretical apparatus for the development of a sociology of literature, an apparatus substantially bequeathed to us by Lucien Goldmann. But, unfortunately, we suffer from the corresponding lack of such an apparatus in the field of scientific, as opposed to speculative, aesthetics. In the absence of such an apparatus, a general injunction in favour of a healthy respect for declared literary preferences will provide us with a safe enough guide as to our future procedures.

4   Lukács and Socialist Realism

Despite the very considerable reservations which we have made with respect to the excessive formalism of Goldmann's sociological method, there can be little doubt that his theory of mediation represents a very considerable advance in the direction of greater methodological sophistication. In *The Hidden God* especially, Goldmann presents a set of concrete analyses, which clearly demonstrate the value of his theory of the world vision, and which are still, in many respects, a model of how a Marxist sociology of literature should proceed. Certainly, that theory is noticeable in its absence from the later, and markedly less satisfactory, *Towards A Sociology of the Novel*.[78] Goldmann's heritage is a problematic heritage, but nonetheless a fruitful one. And it appears as especially fruitful when we compare its achievements with those of the official 'socialist realist' school to which the older Lukács subscribed. Goldmann's sociology had, of course, derived substantially from the work of the young Lukács. But Lukács himself came to renounce the central principles around which his own earlier work had been constructed. It has been argued that this renunciation was forced on Lukács by his return to the Soviet Union in the 1930s, and that both it and his adoption of the theory of socialist realism were to some extent tactical manoeuvres dictated by the prevalent conditions in Stalin's Russia. But, whilst the form which this renunciation took was indeed determined by such tactical considerations, the sincerity of its content cannot really be doubted. Long after Stalin's death, in 1967, Lukács reaffirmed that 'I sincerely did believe that *History and Class Consciousness* was mistaken and I think that to this day.'[79] And Lukács, far from being a reluctant collaborator in the development of the theory of socialist realism, was, in fact, one of its prime authors. Helga Gallas has demonstrated the prominent role which Lukács played in the development of the theory of socialist realism *before* its adoption as official Stalinist dogma at the First Soviet Writers Congress in 1934.[80] Lukács's initial formulations of the theory of socialist realism were elaborated, quite independently of official Communist doctrine, in the journal *Linkskurve*, at a time when the Comintern was politically committed to the 'third period' line, a line which implied a literary theory much closer to that of the Proletcult[81] than that of socialist realism. Lukács did, of course, denounce the 'excesses' of socialist realism, but he did so only in terms which expressed his continuing commitment to the theory itself. In *The Meaning of Contemporary Realism*, he criticises official Soviet literature for its 'naturalism' and 'revolutionary romanticism', each of which he sees essentially as an aberration from genuine socialist realism.[82] But, these aberrations apart, Lukács was convinced of 'the superiority—historically speaking—of socialist realism'.[83] In fact,

Lukács's later writings represent the most thorough and systematic statement of the theory of socialist realism, that is, of the only theory of literature developed under the political auspices of official, post-Leninist, Communism.

We have already referred, in passing, to Lukács's socialist realist aesthetic, and we have suggested that it is essentially legislative, rather than scientific, in character. But let us now consider the nature of that aesthetic in a little more detail. Lukács's earlier pre-Marxist writings had contained both an aesthetic and a sociology, although obvious a non-Marxist one.[84] But in his later socialist realist writings, the sociological element becomes almost entirely subordinated to the claims of the aesthetic. As Colin Sparks has pointed out, here 'the vital mediation between . . . literary analysis and the sociology of the world vision remains absent. The disjuncture between the two aspects of the theory is papered over, simply by failing to develop the second with any rigour.'[85] Sparks, however, seeks to retain that aesthetic as an essential element within the Marxist theory of literature, and fails to perceive the full extent of its dogmatism, its concern not with understanding the processes of artistic production and appreciation, but rather with laying down certain categorical principles as to what constitutes 'acceptable' and 'unacceptable' literature. Bertolt Brecht, one of the many victims of Lukács's attacks, understood this rather more clearly when he described Lukács (and Gábor and Kurella) as 'enemies of production. Production makes them uncomfortable. You never know where you are with production; production is the unforeseeable. You never know what's going to come out. And they themselves don't want to produce. They want to play the *apparatchik* and exercise control over other people. Every one of their criticisms contains a threat.'[86] The aesthetic of Lukács's later writings functions very much as a set of general rules designed to help in the administration of a literary 'command economy'.[87]

How then, does this system of rules develop? In form, at least, it derives from Engels. We suggested earlier that neither Marx nor Engels ever elaborated a fully developed theory of literature. There are, however, certain scattered references to their own particular literary tastes contained in both those of their writings which were intended for publication and, more especially, those which were not. Engels, in particular, engaged in a series of private 'literary' correspondences in which he repeatedly employs the category of 'realism' as a criterion of aesthetic value. Engels argues that: 'Realism, to my mind, employs, besides truth of detail, the truthful reproduction of typical characters under typical circumstances.'[88] On the basis of this criterion, Engels criticises Margaret Harkness on the grounds that 'your characters are typical enough, to the extent that you portray them. But the same cannot be said of the circumstances surrounding them and out of which their action arises.'[89] Similarly, he praises Lassalle on the grounds that his 'characters are in fact representative of definite classes and tendencies and hence definite ideas of their time'.[90] Now Engels is here employing the literary conventions of one particular school, the nineteenth-century realist school, and is advocating, to both Harkness and Lassalle, the use of that school's particular methods. Were we merely concerned with the details of Engels's own biography, then this preference would present no real problem; it was, in fact, entirely appropriate for Engels to judge Harkness's and Lassalle's works in terms of the conventions of nineteenth-century realism. However, we are not merely concerned with Engels's own literary critical judgements. In Stalin's Russia, Lukács and others erected on the basis of Engels's notion of realism a theory of literary dogmatism which was used in order to stifle all genuine artistic creativity. Soviet artists were, in effect, instructed to write in the style of nineteenth-century realism, to 'Be like Tolstoy— but without his weaknesses! Be like Balzac—only up to date!'[91] as Brecht mockingly commented. Thus Lukács argued that great art is always realistic in the precise sense that it is always an accurate reflection of objective social reality: 'Great literature of all ages, from Homer to the present day has, in the final analysis, "contented itself" with showing how a given social condition, a stage of development, a developmental tendency, has intrinsically influenced the course of human existence, human development.'[92] Clearly, such a literature can in fact only be possible if the writer is in possession of a scientifically correct account of the social world. And Lukács does not shun this implication; for him the 'objectivity of the artistic reflection of reality depends on the correct reflection of the totality'.[93] The great writer must, then, express in his work 'the organic, indissoluble connection between man as a private individual and man as a social being, as a member of a community'.[94] Such a representation of the nature of the social totality is possible, argues Lukács, here clearly following Engels, only if the writer creates *typical characters in typical situations*. 'The central category and criterion of realist literature', he writes,

is the type, a peculiar synthesis which organically binds together

the general and the particular both in characters and situations.
What makes a type a type is not its average quality, not its mere
individual being, however profoundly conceived; what makes it a
type is that in it all the humanly and socially essential determinants
are present on their highest level of development, in the ultimate
unfolding of the possibilities latent in them.[95]

Now this notion of the typical as incorporating the ultimate
unfolding of latent possibilities is, in fact, central to Lukács's later
aesthetic. For in capitalist society the indissoluble connection between
man as a private and as a public being is obscured; market society
gives rise to a progressive detotalisation of both the social world and
the human personality. There devolves, therefore, upon the writer
the task of asserting the value of totality in the face of the detotalising
effects of capitalist reality. 'The true great realists,' argues Lukács,
'. . . knew that this distortion of reality . . ., this division of the
complete human personality into a public and a private sector was a
mutilation of the essence of man. Hence they protested not only as
painters of reality, but also as humanists, against this fiction of
capitalist society.'[96] This defence of the value of totality operates at
two levels. In the first place, it must be expressed in the content of the
work: in great realist literature 'beauty rescues man from the
dehumanisation of capitalist society and class domination and does so
by portraying the whole personality with immediacy and not by
implication'.[97] And secondly, the work of art must itself constitute a
totality, a totality which provides 'a picture of reality in which the
contradiction between appearance and reality, the particular and the
general, the immediate and conceptual, etc. is so resolved that the two
converge into a spontaneous integrity in the direct impression of the
work of art and provide a sense of inseparable integrity'.[98] Thus the
great realist writer must resolve in his work those social and personal
disharmonies which are in reality unresolved: 'The unresolved social
or personal disharmony in the subject matter can indeed be resolved,'
writes Lukács, 'when the social issue and its solution are correctly
posed.'[99] Lukács, then, identifies artistic greatness with the defence of
the humanistic ideal of totality against the encroachments of capitalist
reality. For him, 'Great art, genuine realism and humanism are
inextricably united. And the unifying principle is what we have been
emphasising: concern for man's integrity.'[100] It follows, then, that
the great artist must be ideologically committed to humanism. And
indeed, Lukács argues that such *partisanship* is essential to all great art,

that 'a writer who has no enthusiasm for progress, *who does not love good and repudiate evil*, cannot exercise the discrimination essential for great literature'.[101] 'There is a victory of realism', argues Lukács, 'only when great realist writers establish a profound and serious, if not conscious, association with a progressive current in the evolution of mankind.'[102]

In the contemporary world, this criterion of partisanship implies not that the great writer must actually be a socialist, but that: 'It is enough that a writer takes socialism into account and does not reject it out of hand. But if he rejects socialism . . . he closes his eyes to the future, gives up any chance of assessing the present correctly, and loses the ability to create other than purely static works of art.'[103] A great writer can then today be either a 'critical realist', that is, a writer such as Thomas Mann who, although not a socialist, does not actually reject socialism, or alternatively, a 'socialist realist', that is, a genuinely socialist writer, such as, for example, Sholokhov. Ultimately, of course, 'society will eventually achieve a condition which only socialist realism can adequately describe',[104] but in the meantime, critical realism and socialist realism can 'coexist' alongside one another. Both critical realism and socialist realism base themselves on the premises of humanist ideology and on a commitment to the cause of progress. Both express the indissoluble link between man as a private and as a public being through the creation of typical characters in typical situations. And together they constitute the corpus of great literature in the contemporary world (although one might add that neither is actually very evident in that world). Elsewhere, there is only the literature of 'decadence', the literature of Joyce, Kafka and Musil which 'connives at that modern nihilism from which both Fascism and Cold War ideology draw their strength'.[105] These, then, are the rules. Let us now consider their application.

The whole of Lukács's later writings are built about one all-embracing Manichean dualism, that is, the central opposition between *realism* and *modernism*, or, as Lukács concretises it, between Thomas Mann and Franz Kafka. Realist literature, is, according to Lukács, that literature which grasps the interconnectedness of subjectivity and objectivity within the totality of social reality. To this he counterposes both the 'false objectivity' of *naturalism* which rests on the creation, not of the socially typical, but rather of 'a lifeless average',[106] and the 'false subjectivity' of *psychologism*, which rests on 'an individual principle which dissolves its own self into nothingness'.[107] Thus, for example, Lukács sees the development of Zola's naturalism as a process in which 'a mechanical average takes the place of the dialectical unity of type and individual; description and analysis is substituted for epic situations and epic plots'.[108] Such a naturalism, argues Lukács, 'results from the direct, mechanical mirroring of the humdrum reality of capitalism',[109] and from the corresponding failure to assert the ideal of totality against that humdrum reality. Conversely, those psychologistic writers, such as James Joyce, whose work is concerned with a 'punctilious probing into the human soul', and a 'transformation of human beings into a chaotic flow of ideas'[110] are, according to Lukács, equally unable to express the humanistic ideal of totality. Both naturalism and psychologism are incapable of a literary presentation of the complete human personality, and both, ultimately, consist in a capitulation to the detotalising effects of capitalist society. Indeed, argues Lukács, naturalism and psychologism are inextricably interrelated. Thus, for example, whilst the dominant tendency in modernist literature is in fact subjectivist, this very subjectivism gives rise, in Joyce's work, to a use of descriptive detail which is essentially naturalistic.[111] Modernism is then, at one and the same time, both psychologistic and naturalistic. The essential unifying thread in all modernist writing is the refusal to defend the ideal of totality. 'The modernist writer,' writes Lukács, 'is uncritical towards many aspects of the modern world.'[112] This lack of critical perspective, a perspective which, as we have seen, can only be attained if the writer views reality from the standpoint of the totality, is, in Lukács's view, the source of all manner of literary deviations, ranging from, on the one hand, the morbid preoccupation with abnormality to, on the other hand, the obsessive use of allegory. But this lack of perspective gives rise, above all, to the ideology of *angst*, the ideology of despair in the face of a permanent, essentially tragic, human condition. And Kafka, argues Lukács, 'is the classic example of the modern writer at the mercy of a blind and panic-stricken *angst*'.[113] Thomas Mann, by contrast, is a great critical realist writer who 'For all his fascination with the dark regions of modern existence, . . . always shows up distortion for what it is, tracing its roots and its concrete origins in society.'[114] 'Between these methods,' writes Lukács, 'between Franz Kafka and Thomas Mann, the contemporary bourgeois writer will have to choose.' He must choose 'between social sanity and morbidity', between 'the great and progressive literary traditions of realism', on the one hand, and 'formalistic experimentation', on the other.[115]

Lukács's aesthetic consists, then, in little more than an extended eulogy to the literary methods of nineteenth-century realism. In precisely the same way in which Szeliga constructed the category of mystery out of the real world, and then constructed the real world out of that category, Lukács constructs the category of realism out of the writings of the nineteenth-century realists, and especially Balzac and Tolstoy, and then constructs 'great literature' out of that category. It is, in fact, an exercise in speculative aesthetics. It is, indeed, *idealistic* precisely in the sense that it erects 'realism' as a universal ahistorical *ideal*. This is precisely the point which Brecht made when he argued that Lukács's work is characterised by an 'element of capitulation, of withdrawal, of utopian idealism' which 'gives the impression that what concerns him is enjoyment alone not struggle, a way of escape, rather than a march forward'.[116] Lukács sees the total man, in essentialist terms, as a permanent unchanging ideal. But as Brecht pointed out: 'The masses cast off their loss of humanity and thereby men become men again—but not the same men as before. This is the path that literature must take in our time.'[117] Brecht did himself subscribe to a notion of 'realism'. But Brechtian realism is not so much a set of particular literary conventions, as a general injunction upon the artist to tell the truth by whatever means appear as necessary. Such a conception of realism clearly demands that, as reality changes, the literary methods which are employed to invoke reality must change also.[118] It is 'realism' in this wider, and more profound, sense, and not the realism of Lukácsian metaphysics, which Brecht advocates when he argues that:

With the people struggling and changing reality before our eyes, we must not cling to 'tried' rules of narrative, venerable literary models, eternal aesthetic laws. We must not derive realism as such from particular existing works, but we shall use every means, old and new, tried and untried, derived from art derived elsewhere to render reality to men in a form they can master. We shall take care not to describe one particular form of novel as realistic—say that of Balzac or Tolstoy—and thereby erect merely formal literary criteria for realism.[119]

As a creative writer himself, Brecht was easily able to detect the anti-aesthetic dynamic which informs Lukács's writings. But Brecht was unable to locate with precision the central philosophical weaknesses which underlie that dynamic. It is to that task which we must now turn our attention. During the *Symposium on the Question of Decadence*, Jean-Paul Sartre confessed that:

> I think that it was my reading of Freud, Kafka and Joyce . . . among other things, which led me to Marxism. But when certain Eastern intellectuals in Leningrad condemn all three indiscriminately as 'decadent' because they belong to a decadent society, I am led to think that I must therefore excuse myself before my Soviet friends for having read these three authors, for having known and loved them.[120]

Sartre went on to argue that 'We Western radicals cannot accept that certain authors moulded by the same society that has shaped us, and whom we shall not renounce, for example Proust, Kafka or Joyce, be considered decadent, because this is at the same time a condemnation of our past and a denial of any value of our participation in the discussion.'[121] The gist of Sartre's argument need not concern us here; what is significant is the sincerity and force of his commitment to the cause of, to use Lukács's phrase, modernist literature. In this respect, and perhaps *only* in this respect, Sartre does speak for a whole generation of western intellectuals. Lukács could, of course, merely dismiss this as symptomatic of the decadence of the western intelligentsia. But on Lukács's own account, Sartre should be a supporter of 'critical realism' rather than of 'modernism'. How is it possible, in the face of all Lukács's attempts to will it otherwise, that precisely those western writers who are sympathetic to socialism are also often extremely sympathetic to modernism? The answer, of course, consists in the fact that modernism expressed in literary form one of the most fundamental problems which confronts men in advanced capitalist societies, that is the problem of *alienation*. As Alan Swingewood has noted: 'Alienation and reification now inform the basic structures of contemporary literature.'[122] Now alienation is not, in fact, an illusion, an ideological distortion of the nature of reality. On the contrary, alienation is a constituent process within the structure of capitalist reality. In capitalist society, men do not merely *think* that they are alienated from the product of their labour, from their labour itself, and from their 'species being'; they *are* in fact thus alienated.[123] This is, of course, the whole point of Marx's theory of alienation. It is this objective fact of alienation which explains why, in Swingewood's words, 'The theme of man's alienation from a world his own activity has created . . . constitutes the basic structure informing much of the creative literature of the past fifty years.'[124] But Lukács's theory of literature has no use for the concept of alienation. Lukács, in fact, defines the reality of alienation as mere illusion, and his own illusory ideal of the total man as reality. Once again we are faced with mere speculative metaphysics; the concrete is made abstract, and the abstract concrete.

Lukács's later aesthetic is, then, essentially *idealistic*. It is idealistic in its content in that it seeks to establish the methods of a particular literary school as permanently and universally valid aesthetic categories. And it is idealistic in its fundamental underlying philosophical premises in that it seeks to counterpose the humanistic ideals of the total man and of the work of art as a totality, to the nature of capitalist reality. Both in its content and in its philosophical underpinnings, Lukács's aesthetic is more akin to the speculative aesthetics which Marx criticised in *The Holy Family*, than to Marx's own writings. Moreover, one only has to attempt to apply Lukács's categories to the analysis of any literary form other than that of the nineteenth-century realist novel in order that the patent inadequacy of those categories to the general problem of understanding aesthetic enjoyment should be demonstrated. Those categories are as irrelevant to the understanding of modern Soviet literature as they are to the understanding of modern western literature. Thus, when Lukács himself is pressed to find a great contemporary socialist realist writer, he is obliged to choose, of all people, Alexander Solzhenitsyn![125] Lukács's aesthetic is indeed characterised by the remarkable fact that almost the whole of the twentieth-century artistic achievement manages to pass it by. And if Lukács's aesthetic is inappropriate to the twentieth century, it is most certainly wholly inappropriate to our own particular project in hand, an analysis of Milton's epic poetry. It could only lead us in one of two equally inapposite directions. Either we would be forced to the conclusion that *Paradise Lost* is totally without literary merit—on the absurd grounds that it fails to give an accurate portrait of seventeenth-century English society, or alternatively, we would be forced into the equally absurd search for parallels between 'events' in the literary·text and real historical 'events'. We would find ourselves, for example, discussing Satan, not in terms of his place in the structure of *Paradise Lost*, but in terms of such irrelevancies as whether he 'reflects' Cromwell, or Milton, or Charles Stuart, or perhaps even Lilburne. An aesthetic such as Lukács's, which is obsessed with content, to the expense of virtually all formal considerations, is obviously inappropriate to the study, not only of Milton's epic poetry, but also of poetry *in general*.

We have already noted that Lukács's theory of socialist realism involves an almost total subordination of sociology to 'aesthetics'. But in so far as the theory does involve a sociology at all, in what does that sociology consist? Lukács's later sociology of literature is, in fact, built around a simple periodisation, in which capitalist development is seen as falling into two main phases: firstly, the period up to 1848, when the bourgeoisie was a 'progressive' class, and secondly, the period after 1848, when the bourgeoisie becomes a 'declining' class. The earlier period is seen as essentially favourable to the development of great realist literature. This is so, in the first place, because in the earlier stages of capitalist development, the contradiction between the bourgeoisie and the proletariat has not yet become manifest. Thus, Lukács writes that 'Balzac and Stendhal . . . had lived in a society in which the antagonism of bourgeoisie and working-class was not yet the plainly visible hub around which social evolution moved forward. Hence Balzac and Stendhal could dig down to the very roots of the sharpest contradictions inherent in bourgeois society.'[126] A second contributory factor to the development of great realist literature in the pre-1848 period is the low level of development of the division of labour. In early bourgeois society the writer is not, in fact, a literary specialist; rather he is an active participant in the social life of his time. The creative methods of different writers vary, argues Lukács, 'according to the degree to which they are bound up with the life of the community, take part in the struggles going on around them or are merely passive observers of events'.[127] Thus, for example, 'Balzac himself had to go bankrupt in order to depict Cesar Birotteau . . . he had to know from his own experience the whole underworld of Paris in order to create such characters as Rastignac and old Goriot.'[128] One cannot help but wonder whether or not Sophocles was equally obliged to murder his father, sleep with his mother, gouge out his own eyes and finally wander around the countryside wailing for his own ill-conceived offspring. In the period after 1848, 'the resistance of daily life to the deeper tendencies of literature, culture and art, has grown ceaselessly stronger'.[129] As the contradiction between the bourgeoisie and the proletariat becomes increasingly manifest, it becomes increasingly difficult for the humanist intellectual to identify his own aspirations with those of the bourgeois class as a whole. Genuinely realistic art is no longer possible since 'such merciless candour, such sharp criticism would have driven them (i.e. the writers) to break the link with their own class'.[130] At the same time, the writer's position in society changes such that 'The writer no longer participates in the great struggles of his time, but is reduced to a mere spectator and chronicler of public life.'[131] This twofold development gives birth, on the one hand, to naturalism, and on the other, to psychologism. Thus we find, at the core of Lukács's sociology, a simple schematisation which divides the development of bourgeois society and bourgeois literature into two main phases: firstly that of the period before 1848, in which the social preconditions for great realist literature existed; and secondly, that of the period after 1848, when the changed structure of society mitigated against the development of realist literature and allowed only for the development of naturalistic and psychologistic literature. Whilst this pattern prevails for the majority of capitalist societies, Lukács's sociology allows of two main exceptions: Scandinavia and Russia. 'In Scandinavia and Russia', Lukács argues, 'capitalist development began much later than in western Europe and in them, in the seventies and eighties of the nineteenth century, bourgeois ideology had not as yet been driven to apologetics. The social conditions which favoured realism and which determined the development of European literature from Swift to Stendhal were still in existence in these countries.'[132] It is thus the very backwardness of these societies which allows for the flowering of late-nineteenth-century Scandinavian and Russian realism and, in particular, for the development of Tolstoy's literary art.

Now this sociology is essentially deterministic. Lukács, in fact, argues for the existence of a direct *causal* relationship between the stage of development of a particular society (cause), and the stage of development of that society's literature (effect). This is particularly true of *The Historical Novel*, in which for example, Scott's realistic historical novel is seen as a direct consequence of, firstly, 'the French Revolution, the revolutionary wars and the rise and fall of Napoleon, which for the first time made history a *mass experience*',[133] and secondly, the 'relative stability of English development during this stormy period', which 'made it possible to channel this newly-awoken historical feeling artistically into a broad, objective, epic form'.[134] Furthermore, the theory allows of no mediating agencies between the structure of society as a whole and the literary works of particular writers, such as is provided, for example, by Goldmann's concept of the social class world vision. In so far as Lukács does make use of the concept of the world vision, he sees it as an *individual* rather than as a *social* construct. Thus, for example, the difference between the world visions of Balzac and Stendhal is explained in entirely individual terms: whereas Balzac took note of the rise of utopian socialism, Stendhal did not.[135] Similarly, Flaubert's world vision is contrasted to that of the majority of later bourgeois writers in that: 'While in most other writers of the time, a negative attitude towards the contemporary prose of bourgeois life was simply a matter of aesthetic amusement, or, frequently, of reactionary feeling, in Flaubert it is an intense disgust, a vehement hatred.'[136] This idealistic voluntarism is, of course, a logical consequence of the initial deterministic framework. Since the structure of a *whole* literature is determined by the structure of a *whole* society, it follows necessarily that differences within the structure of that literature can only be explained in individual terms. As Colin Sparks quite rightly points out: 'the precise social mechanism, which leads different writers to quite contradictory positions within one general ideology is dealt with simply in personal terms . . . Any oversimplified view of materialism leads to idealism.'[137]

The contradictions in Lukács's sociology of literature become most apparent in his *Essays on Thomas Mann*. Lukács's historical periodisation clearly precludes the development of any genuinely realist literature in late bourgeois society. But, at the same time, Lukács recognises in Thomas Mann 'the last great bourgeois writer'.[138] Indeed:

Thomas Mann is a realist whose respect, indeed reverence, for reality is of rare distinction. His detail, still more his plots, his intellectual designs may not stay on the surface of everyday life; his form is quite unnaturalistic. Yet the content of his work never finally leaves the real world. What we are offered in Thomas Mann's work is bourgeois Germany (together with genesis and antecedent paths). And of this we are offered the inner problems, deeply seized, so that while they point dialectically ahead, they do not conjure a Utopian future perspective into a present-day reality.[139]

How can it possibly be that late capitalist Germany could give birth to such a writer? Lukács's deterministic sociology is quite incapable of offering a solution to this problem. He does attempt some sort of 'sociological' explanation when he makes the extremely unconvincing suggestion that Mann was, in fact, moving towards the adoption of a socialist perspective. But even Lukács is obliged to admit that Mann's supposed socialism is essentially 'abstract' and that the 'abstract character of his socialist perspective separates Mann's work from socialist realism'.[140] What, then, is Lukács's solution to the problem? The answer is to be found in his astonishing assertion that Mann's world 'is a bourgeois world, seen by a bourgeois, but by one who looks with an unprejudiced eye and who, in his judgement of the present, his grasp of its essential character and in his understanding of the future, transcends his own class limitations'.[141] In this way Lukács's deterministic sociology reduces itself to a voluntaristic non-sociology. All a writer needs in order to 'transcend his own class limitations' is 'an unprejudiced eye'. This proposition is not only in itself non-sociological, but it also, in effect, reduces the prior structure of Lukács's sociology to the level of utter irrelevancy. If all that Zola, Joyce, Kafka and Musil required in order to attain the heights of great realism was 'an unprejudiced eye', then in what lies the value of Lukács's sociology? What remains for Lukács's sociology to explain? In the final analysis, Lukács's theory collapses into a simple idealistic voluntarism. Now, Alan Swingewood has pointed out that this particular idealistic conception of the relationship between the writer and society necessarily leads to *eclecticism*.[142] Whereas Goldmann is able, on the basis of his theory of mediation, to treat the literary text as a whole, and to relate the text as a whole to the appropriate social class world vision, Lukács's method obliges him to compare individual scenes, characters, etc., in a writer's work with the equivalent phenomena in real life. As Swingewood notes: 'Lukács' theory of literature is non-dialectical and built on a concept of reflection, which brings it close to 19th century positivism. As in positivism the literary elements are always compared with *real* social features and not set in their own, specific literary context; their meaning is fixed outside this context.'[143] This has far-reaching implications. Goldmann's work is based on respect for the integrity of the literary text, and he derives his hypotheses directly from the structure of the text as a whole, thus allowing the minimum room for his own subjectivity to impose itself upon the text. By contrast, Lukács's approach allows him to arbitrarily impose his own organising principles upon the work in question. It should be obvious that whilst such a critical method can be of value as a weapon in the arsenal of a dogmatist aesthetic, it has no real relevance to a scientific sociology of literature.

5   *Leavis and English Literary Criticism*

We have argued that the central task encumbent upon the sociology of literature is that of specifying the precise pattern of mediations which exists between the literary artifact and the total social structure. We have suggested that Goldmann's theory of mediation, his theory of the world vision, represents a considerable advance in the direction of greater methodological rigour. And we have identified the absence of such a conception of mediation as one of the central weaknesses of Lukács's socialist realism. Nonetheless, a number of other possible solutions to the problem of mediation are available. Raymond Williams has pointed to two such solutions which have, in practice, been adopted primarily by orthodox literary criticism rather than by sociology, but which, presumably, still remain theoretically available to the latter. These are respectively the 'false totalities' of 'tradition' and ' "kinds" or "genres" '.[144] In literary critical practice each of these is normally analysed in radically ahistorical and unsociological fashion. Such an approach is not completely without validity: Tillyard's attempt, for example, to relate Milton's epic poetry to an English epic tradition does have some point to it.[145] But in itself it merely registers the fact of the existence of a tradition. To explain *why* that tradition emerged and, more importantly for our purposes, *why* Milton chose to make use of it, some sort of sociological perspective is required. Such a perspective could take the form of a simple society-genre/tradition-literary work relationship such as that which is postulated by both F. R. Leavis and T. S. Eliot. We have already referred to the literary-critical work of these two writers in our earlier discussion of the general problem of aesthetic value. But, in fact, both Eliot and Leavis, and in particular the latter, were concerned to analyse problems which were not only 'literary' in the conventional sense of the term, but also genuinely sociological. This insistence on the relevance of sociological and historical themes to the discipline of literary criticism undoubtedly derives, on Leavis's part at least, from his earlier exchanges with the English Marxist school which developed during the inter-war period.[146] Leavis himself has clearly specified the extent to which his own critical methodology was developed as a response to the Marxist challenge: 'We were anti-Marxist—necessarily so . . . an intelligent, that is a real, interest in literature implied a conception of it very different from any that a Marxist could expound and explain . . . . Marxist fashion gave us the doctrinal challenge.'[147] In the debate between the Marxists and the

Leavis school during the 1930s, the former position was characterised by a more or less rigid adherence to the notion of economic determinism. The Leavis school emphasised, on the contrary, the importance of understanding literature as literature. 'The critic's aim', argued Leavis, 'is, first, to realize as sensitively and completely as possible this or that which claims his attention.'[148] It was precisely their superiority in this vital area of understanding what it is that a literary work actually conveys which ultimately secured for the Leavis school a widespread acceptance of, at least, their more general principles, and correspondingly, the almost total demise of Marxism as an intellectually acceptable approach to the study of literature. The collapse of English Marxism was, of course, partly a consequence of the relative stabilisation of the capitalist economic system during the post-war period. But this collapse was also a result of the theoretical inadequacies of English Marxism itself. As Raymond Williams observed: 'Marxism, as then commonly understood, was weak in just the decisive area where practical criticism was strong: in its capacity to give precise and detailed and reasonably adequate accounts of actual consciousness: not just a scheme of generalisation but actual works, full of rich and significant and specific experience.'[149]

The English Marxist school brought forward, then, as its own antithesis, an intellectual response in the shape of the *Scrutiny* school, centred round the person of Leavis, which took as its central principle the rejection of all attempts to reduce the literary to the non-literary. This reaction against Marxism occurred not only in Britain, but also in the United States. Scott Saunders has described this development of an anti-Marxist 'new orthodoxy' in the following terms: 'If the thesis was a criticism which emphasised politics, ideology and history, which stressed the connection between literature and society, the antithesis was a criticism which emphasized aesthetic form, neglected history and divorced literature from society.'[150] Now whilst this account may be perfectly adequate as a description of the American 'New Criticism', it is most certainly inadequate as a description of English 'practical criticism'. Leavis, in fact, neither neglected history nor divorced literature from society. On the contrary, he aimed not only to establish an aesthetic capable of dealing with literature *as literature*, but also to develop an explicitly non-Marxist *sociology* of literature. Leavis did not reject the global, 'totalising', aspirations of Marxism; rather he aspired to construct an alternative, equally global, theory of literature and society. Leavis's literary criticism represents, as Perry Anderson observed, 'the second, displaced home of the totality'[151] in the British national culture (the first being English social anthropology). And it is precisely the 'total' nature of Leavis's response to the Marxist challenge which makes of it such a significant cultural phenomenon.

Leavis's aesthetic is built around his commitment to the value of 'life', by which he means not reality, but rather a fundamental essence to be pitted against many aspects of reality. Perhaps the most precise statement of what Leavis meant by 'life' is to be found when, citing Blake with approval, he asserts that: 'To be spontaneous, and in its spontaneity creative, is of the essence of life, which manifests itself in newness that can't be exhaustively reduced to the determined.'[152] For Leavis, all great art is characterised precisely by this commitment to 'life' in the sense of non-determined spontaneous creativity. It follows, then, that great literature is not a passive response to reality, but rather an active agent influencing reality such that 'the major novelists . . . count in the same way as the major poets, in the sense that they are significant in terms of that human awareness they promote; awareness of the possibilities of life'.[153] Far from advocating an exclusive emphasis on aesthetic form, Leavis resolutely opposes the notion of art for art's sake. For him, the defining characteristic of the great English novelists is that 'they are all distinguished by a vital capacity for experience, a kind of reverent openness before life'.[154] Leavis's assessment of English poetry runs along similar lines so that the central weakness of nineteenth-century poetry is seen as its other-worldliness, its flight from reality and, correspondingly, the strength of T. S. Eliot's writing is to be found in his ability to 'invent techniques . . . adequate to the ways of feeling, or modes of experience, of adult, sensitive moderns'.[155] Great literature is, according to Leavis, characterised by its capacity to render a *form* adequate to the expression of this value of 'life'. Leavis is, indeed, quite clear in his own mind that the moral commitment to 'life' which lies at the heart of the English novel is inextricably related to the form of the novel. He writes, for example, of Lawrence thus: 'He is a most daring and radical innovator in "form", method, technique. And his innovations and experiments are dictated by the most serious and urgent kind of interest in life.'[156] Leavis shares little of the enthusiasm of the New Criticism for the work of the contemporary *avant-garde*. Indeed, his criticisms of the writing of James Joyce are couched in terms such as those which Lukács might have employed: 'it seems plain to me that there is no organic principle determining, informing, controlling into a vital whole, the elaborate analogical structure, the extraordinary variety of technical devices, the attempts at an exhaustive rendering of consciousness'.[157] Leavis's aesthetic is, in fact, in many ways analogous to that of the later Lukács. Like Lukács, he demands that the writer defend the value of *totality* against the detotalising effects of reality. And, as with Lukács, this defence of the value of totality operates at two levels: firstly, at the level of content, in that the great writer must be committed to 'life' as a value; and secondly, at the level of form, in that the work of art must itself constitute a totality, or, in Leavis's phrase, 'a vital whole'. We have already seen, in our discussion of Lukács, that this conception arises from an essentially idealist philosophical tradition. But Leavis, unlike Lukács, explicitly endorses that tradition when, for example, he recommends Collingwood's writings as necessary reading for the students of his model English school.

Just as there are certain affinities between Leavis's aesthetic and that of the later Lukács, there are also affinities between their respective sociologies. Leavis's criticisms of Marxism had nothing in common with psychologistic individualism. On the contrary, Leavis strongly emphasises the social nature of literary production: 'A literature . . . must be thought of as essentially something more than an accumulation of separate works: it has an organic form . . . in relation to which the individual writer has his significance and his being.'[158] Nor did he subscribe to the idealistic notion of the absolute autonomy of cultural forms. Rather, he merely insists that 'enormously . . . as material conditions count, there is a certain measure of spiritual autonomy in human affairs'.[159] Indeed, Leavis was acutely concerned with the problem of explaining sociologically the preconditions for literary creativity. The cer.tral notion in Leavis's sociological theory is that of the break-up of the old pre-industrial 'organic community'. Leavis draws heavily, and uncritically, on George Sturt's *The Wheelwright's Shop*, both in *Culture and Environment*, which he wrote with Denys Thompson, and in *Nor Shall My Sword*, a much more recent collection of essays. He describes the organic community in the following way: 'Sturt's villagers expressed their human nature, they satisfied their human needs, in terms of the natural environment; and the things they made . . . together with their relations with one another constituted a human environment, and a subtlety of adjustment and adaptation, as right and inevitable.'[160] The destruction of this organic community and its replacement by a more recent non–organic industrial society remains one of Leavis's central preoccupations: 'Its

destruction . . . is the most important fact of recent history.'[161] To
C. P. Snow's account of the industrial revolution as an essentially
beneficent process, Leavis replied that: 'This, of course, is mere brute
assertion, callous in its irresponsibility . . . the actual history has
been . . . incomparably and poignantly more complex than that.'[162]
Leavis regards the existence of an organic community, such as that
which existed in pre-industrial society, as one of the major preconditions for cultural health and prosperity. The breakdown of the
organic community produces, according to Leavis, a rupture between sophisticated and popular culture. In the work of Shakespeare,
Marvell and Bunyan there exists a cultural unity between the
sophisticated and the popular. The literary achievements of such
writers were only possible, argues Leavis, because 'there is, behind the
literature, a social culture and an art of living'.[163] But the process of
industrialisation results, firstly, in the almost total elimination of
popular culture, and secondly, in the eventual divorce of sophisticated culture from 'life' and in a corresponding obsession with the
construction of 'dream worlds'. For Leavis, then, as for Lukács, the
prevailing trends in contemporary western society tend towards
the destruction of art. Already, he argues, 'Poetry matters little to the
modern world'[164] and 'the present age does not favour the growth of
poets'.[165] But the future bodes even worse: 'the finer values are
ceasing to be a matter of even conventional concern for any except
the minority capable of the highest level. Everywhere below, a
process of standardization, mass production, and levelling-down goes
forward . . . So that poetry, in the future, if there is poetry, seems
likely to matter even less to the world.'[166] Lukács, of course,
recognised in Thomas Mann a writer capable of resisting this general
tendency towards cultural barbarism. In a somewhat similar manner,
Leavis, too, opts for an essentially voluntaristic escape-clause from his
general sociological determinism. The implicit logic of industrialisation can be countered if it is 'met by creative intelligence and
corrective purpose'.[167] Both T. S. Eliot and D. H. Lawrence are
awarded the heroic accolade which, in Lukács's system, went to
Thomas Mann. This contradiction between determinism and voluntarism is, admittedly, not as sharp in Leavis's system as it is in Lukács's.
For Leavis's sociology is, in fact, much more aware of the relative
autonomy of cultural forms than is that of the later Lukács.
Nonetheless, the prevalent tone in Leavis's writings is that of a last
heroic rearguard action in the face of the almost inevitable triumph of
barbarism.[168] Leavis, indeed, concedes the logic of sociological

determinism in the very act of denouncing its consequences. We can see, then, that just as his aesthetic was built around an ideal of totality, Leavis's sociology also posits an ideal totality, in this case the organic community, situated in a mythical past, by which to judge and condemn subsequent historical developments. Of course, Leavis's organic community is not a complete myth. Pre-capitalist society did, indeed, entail a direct relationship with nature such as the one Leavis describes. But the corresponding notion that pre-capitalist social relationships were equally natural is entirely false; it ignores the realities of exploitation and oppression, and of consequent social conflict, which are present in all class societies. Similarly, Leavis is quite right to emphasise the human costs of industrialisation, which are glossed over in the establishment account of history as a process of linear progress. His own account, however, ignores the genuinely progressive features of capitalism and the enormous liberating potential of industrial society. Again, many of Leavis's comments on the cultural consequences of industrialisation reveal a very keen insight. But it is only in the light of the idealistic notion of a 'total' art that it becomes possible to condemn almost the whole of the contemporary artistic effort as mere 'barbarism'. Leavis's system is indeed, as Anderson pointed out, a 'home of the totality', but each of these ideal totalities, both that of the aesthetic and that of the sociology, is a totality *without internal contradictions*, a Kantian rather than a Hegelian totality. Leavis's 'total' theory of literature and society is only 'total' in the Lukácsian sense of the term. We have already pointed to the Weberian origins of much of Lukácsian theory. Interestingly enough, Alan Shuttleworth has expressly pointed to the affinity between Leavisian literary criticism and Weberain sociology. [169] Leavis was not, of course, in any way open to the direct influence of the Weberain school. But he did arrive quite independently at similar conclusions to those which, in Lukács's work, are derived directly, though no doubt unconsciously, from the work of Max Weber.

Leavis himself defined his opposition to Marxism in terms of his rejection of economic determinism. But, in fact, a genuinely Marxist theory of literature will allow for the relative autonomy of cultural forms. There thus exists no necessary contradiction between a Marxist and a Leavisian view of the relationship between culture and society. But there is a deeper, more profound incompatibility between Leavis and Marxism. And this incompatibility can be located around the absence of a concept of *contradiction* in Leavis's system. The absence of such a conception explains why, for Leavis, the central mediating agency between the writer and society is 'literary tradition'. This concept of tradition, which Leavis takes over from Eliot, entails the notion of a continuous literary culture which is essentially the product of the whole 'community'. Leavis's literary criticism is, in fact, centred around the attempt to establish the existence of two such traditions—the English poetic tradition and the tradition of the English novel. Such a conceptual apparatus allows room neither for radical discontinuity nor for the notion that social class is a crucial mediating agency between the writer and society. Thus, when Leavis is faced with the work of a writer, such as Milton, who represents a radical break with 'the tradition', he has no alternative but to reject his work almost in its entirety. Now Perry Anderson's account of Leavis's system is peculiarly uncritical at precisely this point. Indeed, he writes of Leavis that: 'The rigour and intelligence of his discrimination established entirely new standards: *Revaluation* and *The Great Tradition* alone reconstructed the very order of English poetry and the novel.'[170] It would appear, then, that Anderson accepts Leavis's literary judgements virtually *in toto*. But once one has identified the absence of a concept of contradiction as the central weakness of Leavis's system, it becomes possible to explain the weaknesses of his literary criticism. Anderson is clearly aware of the peculiar inadequacy of Leavis's critical method to the treatment of contemporary *avant-garde* literature. But he is content to explain this in terms of the fact that Leavis's criticism depends upon the existence of a set of shared stable values, values which are irrelevant to the literature of the *avant-garde*. A more complete explanation would have been possible if only Anderson had elaborated upon his own acute comment that for Leavis, as for other leading British intellectuals, 'the twentieth century itself becomes the impossible object. The era of revolutions is, necessarily, unthinkable.'[171] The twentieth century is, indeed, an impossible object for Leavis, and it is so simply because there is no room in his world vision for contradiction. It is precisely the fact that the twentieth century is an era of revolutions, that its social systems are torn by violent contradictions and that, in consequence, its art forms negate the traditional ideals of the perfectly coherent, integrated artistic whole, which makes both it and its culture such an impossible object for Leavis to come to terms with.

This point becomes even clearer when we note that the twentieth century is, in fact, only one of *two* impossible objects in Leavis's system; the other is, of course, the revolutionary England of the mid-seventeenth century. Perhaps the most striking feature of Leavis's literary criticism, and certainly the one which has aroused the most vehement opposition, is his dismissal of the work of John Milton, the poet of that revolution. The terms with which Anderson describes Leavis's rejection of foreign and *avant-garde* literature, are almost equally applicable to his treatment of Milton: 'Blank prejudice and bafflement were the predictable products of his disorientation before them.'[172] Milton's poetry is self-consciouslessly poetic; it is 'mechanical', in Leavis's phrase, rather than 'organic'. Furthermore, it is concerned with ideas rather than with 'the emotional and sensory texture of actual living'.[173] Indeed, *Paradise Lost* is deliberately conceived as a massive 'theoretical' edifice, the prime purpose of which is to expound a system of ideas, to:

> assert Eternal Providence,
> And justify the ways of God to men.[174]

Leavis can have no sympathy with any of this; it is outside the tradition, and hence beyond redemption. Leavis's attempt to explain how it is that Milton should somehow have slipped through the net of tradition is even more significant. Leavis cannot admit that seventeenth-century England, far from representing an organic community, was, in fact, a society ravaged by violent class conflict. Milton's 'deviance' has, therefore, to be explained entirely in individual rather than social terms. To Tillyard's[175] suggestion that Milton's poetic achievements can be situated within the context of the society in which he lived, Leavis can only assert in reply 'the traditional notion of Milton as a lonely genius'.[176] Shakespeare, Marvell, Bunyan can all be understood in terms of the 'social culture' which lies behind the literature. But to admit that this is true also of Milton would imply a recognition of the simple fact that Milton's England in no way resembled an 'organic community'. John Milton, the political activist who held a post in Cromwell's government and who only barely escaped the fate of the regicides, thus becomes John Milton, the 'lonely genius' who is, despite his 'character', 'disastrously single-minded and simple-minded'.[177]

The tradition/genre approach to literary analysis, or the 'in-fluences' approach as Goldmann dubs it, is inadequate to the explanation of literary phenomena, even if it does contain an added sociological dimension, quite simply because, as Goldmann points out, it fails to account for either *choice* or *distortion*.[178] It fails to provide any answer to the questions: why was one influence (tradition/genre) chosen, and why was it distorted in a particular way? To return to the example of Milton's epic poetry: why did Milton choose the epic tradition, rather than, say, the tradition of Elizabethan drama, and why did Milton distort that tradition in the way in which he did, for example in adopting an ethical theme, rather than the more conventional patriotic themes? Such questions cannot possibly be answered if we focus our attention exclusively on either the literary context in isolation or the total social system. In fact, we can only deal with them by attempting to understand the ideas, aspirations and feelings, in short the world vision, of the social class to which Milton belonged. To anticipate the argument a little, Milton's adoption of the epic form has to be understood in terms of the moral didacticism inherent in the revolutionary Protestant rationalist world vision. Only a writer who was also a member of the army of the saints could possibly have created either *Paradise Lost* or *Samson Agonistes*. And what of Milton's 'distortion' of the English epic 'tradition'? It will hardly suffice to suggest, as Tillyard does, that Milton abandoned the patriotic theme simply because of the inconvenient association of the Arthurian legend with royalism.[179] Such an analysis rests at the level of content rather than that of structure, and in any case it ignores the existence of alternative patriotic themes. The adoption of a moral theme can be seen to be related to the general ethical preoccupations of Protestant rationalism. But, to consider more specifically Tillyard's opposition between politics and ethics, it is clear that Milton's apparent concern with ethical rather than overtly political themes in *Paradise Lost* is a product of that reassessment of the efficacy of political action forced upon the revolutionary Protestants, initially by the disintegration of the Commonwealth, and finally by the Restoration of 1660. Goldmann's conclusion that analyses of 'influences' 'have no explanatory value'[180] may very well be a little too harsh. But it is certainly true that such an approach can only attain any real explanatory power when it is situated within the context of an analysis of the objective demands of the world vision of the particular social class to which the writer belongs.

6   *Conclusion*

We have rejected both those theories, such as Lukácsian socialist realism, which perceive the relationship between literature and society as essentially unmediated, and those theories, developed by both Eliot and Leavis, which perceive that relationship as mediated through purely 'literary' factors, such as 'tradition' and 'genre'. And we have argued in favour of Goldmann's notion of the social class world vision as the key mediating agency between writer and society. There is, however, a fourth possible alternative solution to the problem of mediations. It is, in fact, possible to consider social class not as *the* mediating agency between the writer and society, but rather as *one* of a whole series of such agencies. There is a sense in which Sartre's 'regressive–progressive' method[181] points in this direction, and certainly his study of Flaubert focuses its attention on family rather than on class.[182] But this approach is rather more obviously exemplified in conventional biographical literary criticism. Such attempts to understand literature in terms of biography (whether existential or otherwise) have a certain obvious appeal. They appear capable of dealing with the totality of influences which come to bear upon a writer, rather than with only one particular aspect of that totality. At this point it becomes necessary to establish with some precision the identity of the subject of literary creation. Now there is an obvious sense in which the individual writer is the subject of literary activity; *Paradise Lost* was, after all, written by John Milton, and not by a select committee of defeated Protestant revolutionaries. But, in Goldmann's view, and we would concur with this, great art takes on cultural significance in so far as it becomes significant *for others*, in addition to the writer, and it thus has a trans–individual, rather than an individual, subject. Given this general proposition, Goldmann's specific identification of the trans-individual subject with the social class follows from the elementary proposition of Marxian sociology that social classes are the key actors in human history. In the opening words of *The Communist Manifesto*: 'The history of all hitherto existing society is the history of class struggles.'[183] Goldmann is particularly scathing in his opposition to 'psychological' explanations of literary phenomena, such as those propounded by Sartre. Thus he writes that 'psychological explanations . . . have never succeeded in accounting for any notable portion of the text, but merely for a few partial elements or a few extremely general features',[184] and that, even where they do account for certain aspects of a work, 'these are always aspects and characteristic features which in the case of literature are not literary'.[185] Let us be more specific. It is reasonable enough to suppose that Milton's unhappy experience of marriage accounts somewhat for his early polemical divorce pamphlets.[186] And it is certainly possible that that experience colours his account of Adam's fall; there is certainly something *personal* in, for example, Adam's grim warning at the end of Book IX:

> Thus it shall befall
> Him whom to worth in women overtrusting
> Lets her will rule; restraint she will not brook,
> And left to herself, if evil thus ensue,
> She first his weak indulgence will accuse.[187]

But despite Milton's personal spleen, *Paradise Lost* is not, in fact, a misogynist work. On the contrary, the essential features of the Adam/Eve relationship imply a sustained eulogy to married love. It is quite impossible to explain the structure of the peculiar Miltonic version of the myth of the Fall, *seen as a whole*, in such biographical terms. It can only be fully understood in terms of the general Protestant rationalist conception of the relationship between reason and passion. It is this general conception, a product of the Protestant rationalist world vision, rather than of Milton's own personal prejudices, which gives substance to the myth of the Fall, and, indeed, to the whole of *Paradise Lost*. And yet Milton did write *Paradise Lost*; not Cromwell or Ireton, but Milton. As Sartre writes: 'Valéry is a petit bourgeois intellectual . . . But not every petit bourgeois intellectual is Valéry.'[188] Of course, Sartre is right. Milton's own individual experiences, as opposed to, say, Cromwell's do explain *why* Milton became an epic poet, and not Protector of England. But given that, they do not explain what Milton wrote. We are here dealing with two quite distinct problems: on the one hand, the problem of explaining why one individual rather than another becomes a great writer, which can indeed be approached in biographical terms; and on the other, the problem of explaining the content of a writer's work, which can only be approached sociologically. Not every petit bourgeois intellectual is Valéry . . . but Valéry's *work* is significant in so far as it deals with the preoccupations of the petit bourgeois intelligentsia as a whole. We should add that our second problem is by far the more important of the two, since Milton's significance derives not from the fact that he was a *writer*, but from the nature of his *writing*. It is this problem which will act as the focal point for our further investigations.

   The conclusion of our discussion of methodology permits us, at last, to define the object of our inquiry with some precision: we shall be concerned to elucidate the precise pattern of relationships which exists between the literary and philosophical writings of John Milton, the social situation of the seventeenth-century English bourgeoisie, and the world vision of Revolutionary Independency.

2 The World Vision of Revolutionary Independency

We have already noted that Goldmann's sociology of literature has, as one of its main aims, the establishment of an ideal typology of possible world visions, and we have rejected the formalistic implications of such a typology. Nonetheless, it remains possible to retain Goldmann's central categories, on the condition that we understand the world vision as a concrete form of consciousness, rather than as a formal maximum possible consciousness. Goldmann points to the existence of five main world visions which have dominated human thought since the break-up of feudalism: dogmatic rationalism, sceptical empiricism, the tragic vision, dialectical idealism, and dialectical materialism.[1] What primarily concerns us here are the two main world visions of classical bourgeois thought, the rationalist and the empiricist. In a sense both rationalism and empiricism form part of a wider world vision, that of bourgeois individualism, in that they each posit as their central category the isolated individual; this is as true of Locke and Hume as it is of Descartes and Leibniz. But whereas rationalism constructed a system of universal mathematics, of logical necessities, empiricism based itself, much more pragmatically, on the observed contingencies of the sensible world. Thus, for example, Hume attacked the whole concept of cause and inserted in its place the mere fact of empirical correlation.[2] Goldmann's sociology contrasts the growth of continental rationalism with that of English empiricism, so much so that empiricism almost becomes the English disease. And indeed it is a truism that the English national culture has been characterised by an all-pervading empiricism, an ideological preoccupation with what is, to the exclusion of all consideration of alternative possibilities. Goldmann explains the genesis of English empiricism in terms of three main factors: firstly, that English bourgeois society was born out of a class compromise between the bourgeoisie and the nobility, and that such circumstances necessarily gave birth to a more pragmatic and less radical world vision than did those which prevailed, for example, in France, where a long class struggle kept the bourgeoisie in radical opposition to the nobility; secondly, that the consequent absence of rationalist traditions itself militated against the emergence of rationalist philosophies; and thirdly, that the great English philosophers, Locke, Berkeley and Hume, wrote in a situation in which the bourgeoisie had already effectively assumed power, and that, in consequence, their work becomes the expression of a world vision based on the facts of bourgeois society, rather than on the *a priori* necessity for its creation.[3] In general terms, we would accept this analysis, though we should add that the English class compromise between the 'bourgeoisie' and the 'nobility' occurred on the basis of the transformation of the English nobility into a landed bourgeoisie. Thus English bourgeois ideology is characteristically pragmatic and empiricist, but it is nonetheless a genuinely *bourgeois* ideology, and not, as Perry Anderson suggests, an ideological capitulation to the aristocracy. To argue, as Anderson does, that utilitarianism is a 'crippled caricature' of a bourgeois ideology, and that the 'hegemonic ideology of this society was a much more aristocratic combination of "traditionalism" and "empiricism", intensely hierarchical in its emphasis, which accurately reiterated the history of the dominant agrarian class'[4] is patently false. Utilitarianism was, and in many respects still is, the hegemonic ideology in English society. And what ideology could be more 'bourgeois' than that of utilitarianism? What possible role could there be for the rational utility-maximising individual in a traditional feudal society?

We have, then, accepted the general characterisation of the English bourgeois world vision as empiricist. However, we must add that the predominance of empiricism in English bourgeois thought only dates from the Restoration in 1660, and more especially the Glorious Revolution in 1688, and that the revolutionary crisis of the mid-seventeenth century witnessed the creation and subsequent destruction of an indigenous English rationalism. The social basis of English empiricism was, as we have noted, the coincidence of an already established bourgeois economic power with a gradual, pragmatic growth of bourgeois political power (in the sense of an increasing bourgeoisification of the political system, in which the constitutional monarchy became progressively more 'constitutional' and the House of Commons became progressively more important than the House of Lords). But the mid-seventeenth-century revolutionary crisis witnessed an alternative pattern of development. Whole sections of the bourgeoisie turned to the task of a revolutionary transformation of the English feudal state machine into a fully-fledged bourgeois republic. And this conflict gave rise to a rationalist world vision, which contrasted the irrational present with the perfect rational institutions, modes of behaviour, etc., to which the revolutionary bourgeoisie aspired. That world vision found political form in Revolutionary Independency, and it was, of course, the failure of the Independent enterprise which led the English bourgeoisie to the political strategy of gradualism and the world vision of empiricism. Nonetheless, the decades of the revolutionary crisis and its immediate aftermath do indeed witness the emergence of an indigenous English rationalism which has, as its major intellectual spokesman, the poet John Milton. This is not, of course, an entirely original proposition. The association between Protestantism, capitalism, and rationalism is almost as old as sociology itself. It is to be found, for example, in both Engels's Introduction to *Socialism: Utopian and Scientific*[5] and, of course, Weber's *The Protestant Ethic and the Spirit of Capitalism*.[6] But both of these works can be criticised on two major counts. In the first place, they each fail to understand the full extent to which revolutionary Protestantism can be viewed as a fully-fledged *rationalist* world vision. Certainly, Weber recognises the 'rationalization of conduct within this world'[7] as one of the main consequences of Protestantism. But he is primarily concerned with Protestantism *per se*, considered as a religion, rather than with its nature as a rationalist philosophy, and its relationship to other rationalisms. And secondly, they each radically overestimate, indeed misunderstand, the importance of Calvinism in the general Protestant undertaking. We shall seek to demonstrate below that the genuinely revolutionary dynamic in Protestantism comes to fruition *precisely* in so far as a *rejection* of Calvinism is effected. The recognition of the importance of Protestantism in shaping the form of Milton's poetic achievement is equally commonplace. But again, the rationalist core of Milton's Protestantism is rarely recognised.[8] We intend to show, then, that the English revolutionary crisis did, in fact, produce a rationalist world vision. Furthermore, we intend to demonstrate that this world vision can be seen to develop in two stages: the first of these is the period of revolutionary victory and the programme of reason triumphant, the second the period of reaction and the problematic of reason embattled. And in each of these stages in the development of

English rationalism, John Milton towers over his contemporaries, as the intellectual embodiment of the maximum real consciousness of the English revolutionary bourgeoisie.

Let us attempt a brief sketch of the structure of the rationalist world vision. As we have already noted, rationalism is, in the first place, a form of *individualism*. For the rationalist the central datum is the discrete individual, and it is he, and he alone, who decides what is true and what is untrue. If this is so, then it follows that the individual must be, in the most profound sense, in possession of his own freedom, for if the individual's behaviour is in any sense determined, or contingent, then the centrality of the individual must give place to the centrality of some other determining agency. The rational individual must, then, be free from all forms of constraint, whether they be external (institutions, etc.) or internal (non-rational elements within the individual personality, i.e. the passions). This implies, politically, an *opposition to privilege and tradition*, ontologically, a conception of man based on a radical *dualism between reason and passion*, and ethically, *an opposition to passion*. Since we are dealing with revolutionary Protestantism, a specifically Christian form of rationalism, it would seem legitimate enough to ask where *God* stands in this system. The answer is surprising: since the discrete individual is the central datum of the system, there is logically no independent place for God whatsoever. And this is precisely what we find in revolutionary Protestantism: certainly, the existence of God is never doubted, but God is conceived as having no practical independent existence other than through the medium of the discrete individuals of which the universe is practically composed.

Let us elaborate on each of these categories at a little more length. The central datum of the rationalist world vision, we have said, is the discrete *individual*. Revolutionary Protestantism asserted this doctrine, centrally and primarily, in its insistence on the individualistic interpretation of the Bible. For medieval Catholicism, the interpretation of truth was the function of the church; for Luther, Calvin and Knox it was the function of the individual. Hence the demand for an English translation of the Bible was one of the first posed by English Protestantism. But Revolutionary Independency went much further than any previous form of Protestantism in its insistence of the primacy of the individual. In the conflict between the Presbyterians and the Independents, the latter argued for religious toleration and against the re-establishment of a monolithic state church, whether Anglican or Presbyterian. And the theoretical basis of this tolerationism was a belief in the capacity of the individual, free from the tyranny of the state church, to distinguish truth from error. The most famous of the tolerationist tracts is, of course, Milton's *Areopagatica*.[9] But there were many others.[10] And perhaps the most succinct statement of the Independent position is to be found in *The Ancient Bounds*:

> There are two things contended for in this liberty of conscience: first to instate every Christian in his right of free, yet modest, judging and accepting what he holds; secondly, to vindicate a necessary advantage to the truth, and this is the main end and respect of this liberty. I contend not for variety of opinions; I know there is but one truth. But this truth cannot be so easily brought forth without this liberty; and a general restraint, though intended but for errors, yet through the unskilfulness of men, may fall upon the truth. And better many errors of some kind suffered than one useful truth be obstructed or destroyed.[11]

On the question of toleration, the Levellers and Independents were in full agreement: both the Independent *Heads of Proposals* and the Leveller *Agreement of the People* call for toleration of religious dissent.[12] The Parliamentary Independents were as committed to the cause of toleration as was the Army—witness Vane's amendment to the League and Covenant which sought, at a time of Presbyterian predominance, to retain some way open to toleration by insisting that reformation was to be carried through 'according to the Word of God', rather than simply according to the principles of Pres-byterianism.[13] This insistence on the individual's right to in-terpret the Bible may appear, superficially at least, more akin to the scholastic emphasis on authority (in this case Biblical authority) than to rationalism. But such an assessment ignores the practical *social* logic of the argument. In asserting the individual's right to interpret the Bible, Independency in fact denied the validity of all other auth-orities, and firmly located the source of all truth, all knowledge, in the individual reason. Thus the Protestant appeal to Scripture becomes, in effect, an appeal to the individual reason. As Basil Willey observed, in an astute comparison between Protestantism and more orthodoxly 'rationalist' philosophies: 'The "inner light" of the Quakers ranks with the "Reason" of the Platonists, the "clear and distinct ideas" of Descartes, or the "common notions" of Lord Herbert of Cherbury, as another of the inward certitudes by means of which the century was testing the legacies of antiquity and declaring its spiritual independence.'[14]

Our second major rationalist category was that of *freedom*; freedom, firstly, from external (that is, political) constraints, and secondly from the internal constraints imposed by passion. Let us consider each in turn. That Revolutionary Independency, as a political force, was committed to a far-reaching *attack on privilege and tradition* is almost self-evident. From the initial Parliamentarian opposition to the power of the bishops, and to the abuses of monarchical power, the Independents went on to launch a full-scale attack on the traditional institutions of England. They swept aside the traditionalist structure of the Parliamentarian Army and created the New Model Army, an army which, in its career structure, came as near to establishing 'equality of opportunity' as has any subsequent English army; they abolished both the House of Lords and the monarchy (and in the process executed a king), and 'purged' or dissolved parliaments as it pleased them; they broke the power of the industrial monopolies and smashed aside the constraints on improving landlordism which the old feudal state machinery had imposed.[15] Perhaps the most famous of all Cromwell's words, 'I tell you, we will cut off his head with the crown upon it', expressed this mood with the utmost clarity. The Independents accepted no institution, no law, no tradition, as valid in itself; everything was tested against the criteria of reason and justice, and that which was found wanting was discarded. Indeed, one of the central features of Independency, which distinguishes it both from Presbyterianism on the right, and from the Levellers on the left, is its disregard for legality. Thus, for example, when the Independents set about the task of bringing the king to 'justice', they were attacked by both Presbyterians and Levellers for the unconstitutional manner in which they acted. The Levellers, of course, were no friends of the king, but they had persistently maintained, as had the Presbyterians, that many necessary liberties were already enshrined in English law: a central mode of argument in many of Lilburne's pamphlets is the reference to ancient law. And Lilburne had no doubts whatsoever that both Pride's Purge and the subsequent trial of the king were illegal acts. The Levellers, Lilburne tells us, 'objected against their (i.e. the Independents) total dissolving or breaking the House and the illegality of their intended and declared trying of the King'.[16] And he goes on to contrast the Independents unfavourably with the grand rebels of the past, Korah, Dathan,

Abiram, the Anabaptists, John of Leyden and Knipperdolling, Jack Straw and Wat Tyler,

For did any or all of them forementioned ever rebel against their advancers, promoters, and creators, as these have done several times? Did ever any or all of them chop off (without all shadow of law) a king's and nobles' heads, ravish and force a parliament twice, nay raze the foundation of a parliament to the ground, and under the notion of performing a trust, break all oaths, covenants, protestations, and declarations, and make evidently void all the declared ends of the war?[17]

The Independent apologists did half-heartedly attempt to argue that Charles's execution was in accord with the law. But the main drift of their argument was to sweep aside the question of legality and to concentrate on the question of whether or not the execution was just. In Milton's words: 'What if the greater part of the senate should choose to be slaves, or to expose the government to sale, ought not the lesser number to interpose, and endeavour to retain their liberty, if it be in their power.'[18] Thus did the Revolutionary Independents deal with the majesty of the law.

In the rationalist view of the world, the rational individual must be free, not only from external constraints, but also from the tyranny of his own passions. At the core of all rationalisms rests an ontology which sees in man a radical dualism between reason and passion. This dualism is no mere contingent factor in rationalism; rather, it is an essential component of any rationalist world vision in that it provides an explanation for the existence of unreason in the world. We have noted that rationalism takes as its central datum the discrete individual, and allows of no other factor in its interpretation of the world. It follows, then, that the existence of irrationalities (and to the bourgeois rationalist, the whole of previous human history is essentially irrational) must also be explained in terms of the faculties of the discrete individual. Hence, the category of 'passion', the principle of the anti-rational within the individual man, is essential to the explanatory credibility of a rationalist system. And it fulfils precisely this role in the world vision of Revolutionary Independency. The Independents were characterised by a consistent soul-searching, a preoccupation with personal morality, and by a tendency to explain political behaviour, whether their own or that of their opponents, in purely personal terms. Thus, for example,

Thomas Collier contrasted the old political order with the new order coming into being in the following terms: 'in respect of the persons ruling, they shall be such as are acquainted with, and have an interest in, the righteous God; that as formerly God hath many times set up wicked men to rule and govern . . . so he will give it into the hands of the Saints'.[19] Or again, consider Adjutant Allen's account of the Independents' decision at Windsor in 1648 to discontinue negotiations with the king:

> And in this path the Lord led us not only to see our sin, but also our duty; and this so unanimously set with weight upon each heart that none was able hardly to speak a word to each other for bitter weeping, partly in the sense and shame of our iniquities; of our unbelief, base fear of men, and carnal consultations (as the fruit thereof) with our wisdoms, and not with the Word of the Lord.[20]

When the Independents accused their enemies of sin (for example, the Leveller Walwyn was accused of being a drunkard and whoremaster)[21] this was no mere propaganda ploy; since they themselves were in possession of reason, it had to follow that their opponents were under the sway of passion. Milton's explanation of popular opposition to republicanism is thus characteristically Independent:

> If men within themselves would be governed by reason, and not generally give up their understanding to a double tyranny, of custom from without, and blind affections within, they would discern better what it is to favour and uphold the tyrant of a nation. But, being slaves within doors, no wonder that they strive so much to have the public state conformably governed to the inward vicious rules by which they govern themselves.[22]

We noted, in our earlier brief sketch of the structure of the rationalist world vision, that rationalism is, in a strong sense, logically *atheistic*. Now atheism would seem a very strange charge indeed to level at men such as Cromwell, Vane, Ireton, Harrison and Milton. And, of course, we do not mean to suggest that any of them ever doubted the existence of God. However, what they did do was to deny the independent presence of God in the world. Rather, God is present in the world only through the *Elect*, that is through the medium of certain discrete individuals. Divine plans are achieved only through the exercise of the rational free wills of men, and not through any direct intervention of God in the world. We would argue that any genuine theism must maintain some sort of tension, some sort of separation, between man and God. For once God is liquidated into the reasons of particular individuals, then what remains of God? And in revolutionary Protestantism this tension, this separation, is abolished. In effect, Milton and Cromwell, and the Independents generally, identified themselves with God, and identified God with history. To quote Collier again: 'This is the great work . . ., that God calls for at your hands, . . . It is the execution of righteousness, justice and mercy, without respect of persons. It is to undo every yoke. And this being the great work in hand, *and that which God calls for; and will effect*, give me leave to present amongst many national grievances, some few unto you.'[23] He then proceeds to list such oppressions as denial of freedom of conscience, the use of the French language in legal proceedings, tithes, and free-quartering! Only a rationalist God could object to tithes—and, we might add, only a rationalist poet would presume to justify the ways of God to man. When James Nayler, an ex-member of Cromwell's Army, declared himself God, he did little more than carry the doctrine of election to its logical conclusion. We have here dealt with the problem of the status of God in the Protestant rationalist system in only a cursory fashion. A more detailed analysis must await our discussion of the theory of election, in both its Calvinist and non-Calvinist forms, and of the general significance of Calvinism in the Protestant enterprise, to which we shall turn in the following chapter.

Thus far we have been concerned to elucidate the structure of the Revolutionary Independent world vision as it developed in the years of triumph. But the break-up of the Protectorate and the Restoration in 1660 imposed upon the former Independents a new problematic: how to explain the triumph of unreason. Here we are faced with the problem that censorship effectively prevented any public articulation of the revolutionary Protestant response to the Restoration. And not only censorship; the execution of the leading regicides was an even more effective obstacle to the articulation of opposition. But in Milton's great poems we do indeed find a systematic working out of such a response. In fact, there developed two alternative, but not incompatible, genuinely rationalist solutions to the problem of unreason triumphant. The first of these is the personal individualist response, which found its religious expression in the quietism of, for example, the Quakers. It is important to remember that this quietism was not an original feature of Quaker religion. As Alan Cole observed: 'Pacifism was not a characteristic of the early Quakers: it was forced upon them by the hostility of the outside world.'[24] This theme of personal redemption, of stoic resistance to the irrationalities of the world, is central to that great literary monument to the Protestant conscience, written by an ex-soldier in Cromwell's Army, John Bunyan's *Pilgrim's Progress*. It is also of central importance in Milton's later poems but there it is combined with a second alternative response to the victory of unreason, the *politico-historical* response, which counterposes the future triumph of reason to its present defeat. We shall argue that it is this theme which becomes progressively more important in Milton's later work so that, ultimately, he is obliged to work out a conception of history. The final expression of the revolutionary Protestant world vision, as it appears in Milton's work, is, then, embodied in a sense of the tension between *particular* defeats and the epic victory of the *historical-universal*. And this notion of the tension between the particular and the historical-universal, we will argue, represents a considerable advance beyond the simple dualisms of the earlier optimistic rationalism. But before we turn to a detailed examination of Milton's work, we must consider first the precise details of the English revolutionary crisis which produced both the world vision of Revolutionary Independency and the literary and philosophical writings of John Milton.

3 The English
Revolutionary Crisis

In the previous chapter we attempted a rough sketch of the structure of the Protestant rationalist world vision as it developed during the course of the seventeenth-century English revolutionary crisis. We suggested that this world vision, which found political expression in Revolutionary Independency, reveals certain structural affinities with other rationalist philosophical systems, affinities which can be explained by reference to their common sociological origins in specifically bourgeois social groupings. And finally, following Goldmann, we pointed to the contrast between rationalist philosophical systems which are the product of *critical* bourgeois thought, and empiricist philosophical systems, which are the product of *apologetic* bourgeois thought. This theoretical opposition between critique and apologia cannot, of course, be understood in terms of the merely subjective orientation of particular thinkers, or even of particular social groups, towards the 'social system' conceived in the abstract. On the contrary, it has its origins in the objective differences between different points on that trajectory which the various bourgeois classes have followed through history, and in particular, in the difference between the bourgeoisie's experience as subordinate class and as superordinate class. For the object of critical bourgeois thought is not bourgeois but feudal society. And conversely, the object of apologetic bourgeois thought is bourgeois society proper. This is not to suggest that each bourgeois class necessarily produces in turn a rationalist and then an empiricist world vision. In fact, the different modes of intellectual practice possess such a degree of autonomy, or, which is another way of saying the same thing, they are subject to such a pressure of inertia, that a philosophical system once established exercises considerable influence over subsequent intellectual development. The nature of a particular bourgeois world vision at any given time will be determined not so much by the point in history at which the bourgeoisie stands, as by the point at which that class's independent world vision *initially emerged*. Now we have suggested that the seventeenth-century English revolutionary crisis marks the initial moment of transition from critique to apologia in English bourgeois thought. Such a reading of English intellectual history remains tenable only on the basis of the assumption that the English Revolution was very definitely a bourgeois revolution, and that it was, moreover, a *successful* revolution in so far as it succeeded in installing the bourgeoisie as a superordinate class. Each of these two propositions is necessary to explain the emergence of empiricist thought. But at the same time, we are obliged to explain the destruction of English rationalism, a process which occurred despite the inertial properties of intellectual practice which we have pointed to. This defeat of rationalism can only be explained by reference to the Restoration and the subsequent emergence of a *class compromise* between bourgeois and landed classes. Thus, in the case of English empiricism, the apologetic nature of the world vision is, as it were, overdetermined, in Althusser's phrase, by the nature of the 150-year-long class truce which followed on the 1688 Settlement. This set of propositions is not particularly original. It is hinted at, for example, in Hill's observation that: ' "The Puritan Revolution" failed . . . The economic and political revolution succeeded to a much greater extent.'[1] Nonetheless, it remains essentially controversial. It is to that particular controversy that we now turn.

1   The Nature of the Revolutionary Crisis

The notion that the English Revolution was a bourgeois revolution is one of the commonplaces of contemporary Marxist thought, a commonplace that derives from Marx's and Engels's own work. Certainly, no major Marxist historian has ever suggested otherwise. It should be noted, however, that the proposition that the English Revolution was a bourgeois revolution is only a specific hypothesis within the Marxist science of history, and that the science as a whole in no sense stands or falls on the correctness or otherwise of this particular hypothesis. It would be perfectly possible, for example, for a Marxist historian to interpret the Revolution as a particularistic, aristocratic counter-revolution, directed against the emerging ab-solutist state, somewhat analogous to the *Fronde* in France. It should also be emphasised that it is in no way incumbent upon contemporary Marxism to defend every one of Marx's and Engels's propositions lock, stock and barrel. Any science which adopts an uncritical approach towards its own history will of necessity be debarred from intellectual advance, and must ultimately degenerate into ideology. We must state very clearly, then, that the English revolutionary crisis is part of the object of our enquiry and that its character cannot, therefore, be assumed in advance. Having cleared the decks of ideological clutter, we can now turn to the central problem of determining, firstly, what exactly is involved in a bourgeois revolution, and secondly, whether or not it remains appropriate to so designate the English Revolution.

Perhaps we might best begin by establishing precisely what is *not* involved in a bourgeois revolution. In an otherwise quite successful critique of Eric Hobsbawm, Hugh Trevor-Roper argued that, since a bourgeois revolution results in a triumph of capitalism, for the English Revolution to be understood as such: 'It must be shown either that the men who made the revolution aimed at such a result, or that those who wished for such a result forwarded the revolution, or that such a result would not have been obtained without the revolution.'[2] The first two of Trevor-Roper's 'tests' of the validity of the bourgeois revolution thesis are quite simply irrelevant. Hobsbawm himself pointed out in reply that: 'The gap between men's intentions and the social consequences of their actions is wide enough to make this proposition avoidable.'[3] In fact, Trevor-Roper here betrays an adherence to a form of naïve subjectivism which would only have been intellectually tenable in a world in which sociology had never developed. For the recognition that social action has unintended consequences is the common intellectual property of both Marxism and the best of academic social science.[4] But there is more to be said. The transition from feudalism to capitalism is, in fact, neither an intended nor an unintended consequence of subjectively determined social action. On the contrary, it is a structural process, which operates at the level of the total social system, and, as such, both its causes and its consequences can only be analysed at the level of *structural determination*. In other words, in order to demonstrate that the English Revolution was a bourgeois revolution we have to show that the structure of English society was essentially feudal at some time prior to the Revolution; that it ultimately became essentially capitalistic; that the specific reforms achieved by the Revolution *decisively facilitated the movement from the one form of social organisation to the other*; that the revolutionary crisis itself arose out of a set of contradictions between the older feudal structures and the emergent

capitalist structures; and finally, that this set of structural contradictions worked itself out through a process of class conflict in
which social groupings affiliated to the emergent capitalist structures
emerged triumphant over other social groupings affiliated to the
older feudal structures. We can see then that Trevor-Roper's third
'test' is, in fact, relevant to the problem at hand, but not in the form in
which he poses it. It is unnecessary, and indeed impossible, to
demonstrate that capitalism could not have emerged triumphant in
England without this *particular* revolution. Obviously, another
revolution, or perhaps even invasion by a foreign capitalist power,
would have attained the same result. Our problem is not to compare
the reality with other hypothetical alternative futures, but rather to
discover whether or not this *particular* revolution, which actually
happened, did in fact contribute decisively to the successful movement from feudalism to capitalism. We have defined our problem.

The vast majority of historians would readily accept the propositions that English society was at one time essentially feudal, say in
the thirteenth century, prior to the commutation of services, and
that it ultimately became essentially capitalist (or 'industrial'), say in
the nineteenth century. The point at issue is the relative significance of
the English Revolution in this total process of movement from the
earlier to the later mode of social organisation. But in order to
understand this problem we must first establish what exactly is meant
by the terms 'feudalism' and 'capitalism' In general, Marxist
historians have tended to view the central opposition between
capitalism and feudalism as that between wage-labour and serfdom.
Thus, for example, Takahashi writes that:

> In capitalist society the means of production, as capital, are
> separated from labor, and the characteristic law of development is
> that productivity develops . . . as if it were the productivity of
> capital. In feudal society, on the other hand, the means of
> production are combined with the producer, and productivity
> develops . . . as the productivity of the direct producer himself.[5]

This opposition between free wage-labour separated from the means
of production, and serf labour tied to the means of production,
obviously implies the existence of quite distinct modes of exploitation. Whereas under capitalism the exploitation of labour is effected
through the unequal exchange of the labour market, under feudalism
we find, in Maurice Dobb's words, the 'exploitation of the producer

by virtue of direct politico-legal compulsion'.[6] The surplus thus extracted need not, of course, take the form of direct labour services. On the contrary, it can equally well consist in either rent in kind or money rent.[7] Such then has been the general consensus amongst Marxist historians.

Such a definition of feudalism poses certain problems, and in particular the problem of distinguishing between feudalism and other forms of pre-capitalist social organisation. Perry Anderson has recently pointed out that *all* pre-capitalist social formations are characterised by the extraction of surplus through the means of extra-economic coercion, and that in consequence, in all such societies, the various superstructures necessarily constitute part of the structure of the mode of production.[8] It follows then that if we are to distinguish between the different pre-capitalist modes of production, we must take into account the forms of these various superstructures. Anderson thus proceeds, on the basis of Marx's criticisms of the work of Kovalevsky, which have only been published in Russian, to offer the following definition of feudalism: 'feudalism typically involves the juridicial serfdom and military protection of the peasantry by a social class of nobles, enjoying individual authority and property, and exercising an exclusive monopoly of law and private rights of justice, within a political framework of fragmented sovereignty and sub-ordinate fiscality, and an aristocratic ideology exalting rural life'.[9] Elsewhere, Anderson defines feudalism, rather more pithily, in terms of 'an organic *unity* of economy and polity, paradoxically distributed in a chain of parcellized sovereignties throughout the social for-mation'.[10] Now there is a peculiar contradiction in Anderson's work at precisely this point. For whilst he is concerned to emphasise the importance of the politico-legal superstructure as constitutive of the feudal mode of production itself, he is, at the same time, equally concerned to emphasise the *feudal* nature of the absolutist state. Not once does he move from a view of absolutism as essentially '*a redeployed and recharged apparatus of feudal domination*'.[11] But of course, the formation of the absolutist state involved, as Anderson himself stresses, a considerable centralisation of sovereignty, in other words a change in the politico-legal superstructure. Anderson's justification for regarding the absolutist state as a form of feudal state is itself interesting: 'so long as aristocratic agrarian property blocked a free market in land and factual mobility of manpower—in other words, as long as labour was not separated from the social conditions of its existence to become 'labour-power'—rural relations of production remained feudal.'[12] In this way, Anderson is forced back towards a definition of feudalism which leaves out of account the form of the politico-legal superstructure, and which emphasises, above all, precisely that combination of the producer with the means of production which Takahashi and Dobb have pointed to. And rightly so. In fact, Anderson's entirely commendable attempt to lay the basis for a systematic differentiation between the different pre-capitalist modes of production fails precisely because of its overemphasis on superstructural factors. Any future analysis which will seek to establish a typology of pre-capitalist social formations will have to derive its classificatory criteria from the mode of production itself and not from any supposed superstructural intrusions into the mode of production.

We have defined both capitalism and feudalism. The problem remains of assessing the significance of the English Revolution in the movement of transition between the two modes of production. It would, of course, be quite mistaken to suggest that classical feudalism remained completely intact until 1640, and that it was suddenly overthrown, as a result of the Revolution, and replaced by an alternative capitalist mode of production. Such an interpretation, which has never been seriously held by any Marxist historian, but which is often passed off by non–Marxists as an account of the Marxist theory of the genesis of capitalism, is false on two main counts. In the first place, no society contains one and only one mode of production; rather, all societies contain a multiplicity of modes of production of which only one is dominant. Thus feudal society always contained within itself urban enclaves which encompassed the essentially capitalist relations of production constituted by merchant capitalism. This form of capitalism was in no sense in contradiction with the predominant feudal mode. On the contrary, it was, as both Marx and Weber recognised, a necessary corollary of the latter.[13] And secondly, it should be emphasised that it is precisely the progressive dissolution of feudal relations of production and the concomitant development of capitalist relations within feudalism which provide the preconditions for the Revolution: for there to be a bourgeois revolution, there has to be a bourgeoisie. In England, the central dynamic towards the emergence of capitalism as the dominant mode of production arose from the various forms of productive capitalism unleashed by the dissolution of feudalism. The prime mover in the feudal mode of production is the struggle for rent. In feudal society, 'the owners of the means of production, the landed proprietors, are constantly striving to appropriate for their own use the whole of the surplus produced by the direct producers'.[14] In the case of England, this process stimulated the peasantry to increases in production, achieved either through technical innovation or through the spread of cultivation to previously uncultivated areas. The resultant increase in the absolute value of surplus over subsistence requirements gave rise, on the one hand, to social differentiation within the peasantry and, on the other, to the rise of production for the market.[15] And increasingly the demands of the market, rather than those of the process of rent extraction, became the main stimuli to production. This process was well under way centuries before the Revolution of 1640; indeed, its beginnings date from the early fourteenth century. But in the century preceding the Revolution the process quickened rapidly, partly as a result of its inherently exponential character, and partly as a result of the Henrician Reformation. In the short run, of course, the Reformation strengthened both the old landed ruling class and its state machine. But in the long run, the transfer of monastic lands from church to lay ownership contributed to both the extension of enclosure for sheep farming and the development of the coal, iron, metallurgical and salt industries.[16] By the seventeenth century the subordinate capitalist mode of production had developed to the point at which it came into clear contradiction with the dominant feudal mode.

The resultant social crisis was, as are all such revolutionary crises, a total crisis, a crisis of the whole of society, and not merely an 'economic' crisis in the narrow sense of the term. There *was* a short-term economic crisis, a product of the poor harvests of the 1630s, but far more important is the long-term process of economic growth which had marked the century preceding 1629. An historian not noted for his sympathy with the Marxist account of the Revolution has commented on this century of growth that 'these economic developments were dissolving old bonds of service and obligation and creating new relationships founded on the operations of the market, and . . . the domestic and foreign policies of the Stuarts were failing to respond to these changing circumstances'.[17] And this economic crisis, a product of the structural contradiction between two modes of production, gave birth to a whole series of other crises: the crisis in the church fought out between the Laudian hierarchy and the Puritan ministers; the constitutional crisis embodied in the struggle between the monarchy and the House of Commons; the crisis of values which underpins the conflict between Ancient and

Modern in intellectual thought; and, yes, Stone's own crisis of the aristocracy, a crisis of power and prestige as much as of income.[18]

Above all else, of course, it was a crisis of the *state*. Indeed, it is precisely this factor which makes of it a revolutionary crisis. There is a tendency, amongst both Marxist and non-Marxist historians, to counterpose 'political' and 'economic' explanations of the Revolution as if the two were mutually exclusive. This notion underlies much of the altercation between Hobsbawm and Trevor-Roper. Both of these writers subscribe to the theory that the English Revolution was merely one facet of an international 'general crisis' of the seventeenth century. Whilst Hobsbawm's Marxist version of the theory points to a general crisis of production in the feudal economy, the solution to which could only be found in the emergence of genuinely capitalist relations of production, Trevor-Roper's 'Namierist' version points, by contrast, to the existence of a general crisis in the relations between society and state, between 'court' and 'country'. We should note, in the first place, that the very notion of a general crisis is somewhat suspect. Certainly, there are certain features of seventeenth-century history which suggest such a crisis. As Hobsbawm points out, the middle decades of the century saw not only the English Revolution, but also Catalan, Neapolitan and Portuguese revolts against the Spanish Empire, the *Fronde* in France, and peasant risings in Switzerland, the Ukraine, Hungary, Russia and Bohemia. But to infer from this some sort of general crisis is surely unwarranted. The existence of such a crisis would imply either a high degree of homogeneity in the economic development of different societies, or alternatively, a high degree of integration in the international economy (and, hence, responsiveness to changes in the level of economic activity in other societies). Neither of these conditions is met in the seventeenth century. In fact, what we observe is not a general crisis, but rather a set of particular crises, often quite different in kind, and only very tenuously related to each other. Thus the East European peasant revolts are examples of a phenomenon which is normal to feudalism, and which punctuates its history at regular intervals. The *Fronde* in France, by contrast, are aristocratic, particularistic revolts against the centralising monarchical state, and represent a hostile response by sections of the ruling class to the specific conjuncture of the construction of the absolutist state. *Only in England* do we find a situation in which, as Perry Anderson writes,

Absolutism was brought to a crisis by aristocratic particularism and clannic desperation on its periphery: forces that lay historically behind it. But it was felled at the centre by a commercialized gentry, a capitalist city, a commoner artisanate and yeomanry: forces pushing beyond it. Before it could reach the age of maturity, English Absolutism was cut off by a bourgeois revolution.[19]

The weakness of Hobsbawm's approach derives from his adherence to a form of economic determinism which sees the general political crisis as a simple consequence of the supposed general economic crisis. In opposition to this, Trevor-Roper argues for a complete separation of economic and political analysis, and for a theory of the general crisis of the European state. Much of what has been said of Hobsbawm's theory of the general crisis obviously also applies to this alternative version. E. H. Kossmann points out that there was nothing at all resembling a struggle between court and country in either France or the Dutch Republic, and goes on to observe, quite rightly, that Trevor-Roper's general crisis is, in fact, merely the English crisis projected on to a wider, inappropriate, European canvas.[20] Furthermore, Trevor-Roper's analysis consistently rests at the level of *form* rather than of content. Thus, for example, we are offered a theory couched in general terms about 'the state' and 'society', without any analysis of what specific states actually do, of whose interests they actually serve. Similarly, we are told that there is a return to mercantilism, without any attempt to distinguish between the old mercantilism of the medieval communes and the new mercantilism of the centralised states in terms of their content, that is in terms of what sort of specific interests are furthered by these policies. There is, however, one great merit in Trevor-Roper's approach, that is in his insistence on the conflict between the state institutions and the institutions of the wider society as one of the central sources of the revolution. This theory should, of course, be set in the context of the thesis advanced elsewhere by the same writer[21] that the English Revolution was a product of the strengthening of the Crown and of the state bureaucracy at the expense of the declining gentry, a thesis for which there is little or no reliable evidence, and which is contradicted by Tawney's figures which demonstrate that land passed from the Crown to the gentry during the century preceding 1640.[22] Nonetheless, Trevor-Roper's insistence that the locus of conflict rests around the institutions of the state is extremely valuable, far more so than is Hobsbawm's spurious insistence on the importance of the supposed crisis of production. The English revolutionary crisis was, indeed, a crisis 'of the state, or rather, of the relation of the state to society'.[23]

It could not be otherwise. All revolutions are, in fact, fought in order to determine which class will control the state and, which is the same thing, what form the state will take. As Marx himself wrote: 'Every revolution breaks up the *old society*; to this extent it is *social*. Every revolution overthrows the *existing ruling power*; to this extent it is *political*.'[24] The English Revolution was indeed fought, as Trevor-Roper suggests, in order to destroy English absolutism, but the absolutist state, like all other states, is a particular form of the collective power of a particular social class. Contemporary Marxist historians have generally demonstrated rather more clarity and consistency in their treatment of the absolutist state than did either Marx or Engels.[25] With a few rare exceptions, such as Paul Sweezy, they have generally subscribed to the view that: 'The absolute monarchy was a different form of feudal monarchy from the feudal-estates monarchy which preceded it; but the ruling class remained the same.'[26] The prime function of the feudal state was, of course, the repression, not of the bourgeoisie, but rather of the peasantry. And the development of the absolutist state out of the old estates-monarchy represents a response, on the part of the landed ruling class, not to the rise of merchant capital, but rather to the changed circumstances of the peasantry, and in particular to the substitution of money rents for labour services and rent in kind. Anderson describes the process thus:

> With the generalized commutation of dues into money rent, the cellular unity of political and economic oppression of the peasantry was gravely weakened, and threatened to become dissociated (the end of this road was 'free labour' and the 'wage contract'). The class power of the feudal lords was thus directly at stake with the gradual disappearance of serfdom. The result was a *displacement* of politico-legal coercion upwards towards a centralized, militarized summit—the Absolutist State.[27]

This process has a somewhat paradoxical effect upon the conditions of existence of the subordinate capitalist mode of production. On the one hand, its rationalising and centralising dynamic, which results for example in the abolition of internal customs, makes for the expansion of production for the market. But on the other hand, that self-same centralism sweeps aside the relative immunity from feudal power which the medieval merchant bourgeoisie enjoyed in its safe urban enclaves. And as the contradictions between the two modes of production heighten, as a direct consequence of the expansion of the capitalist mode, so the state apparatus becomes more repressive.

This opposition between the policies of the absolutist state and the needs of the developing capitalist mode of production informs the whole of early seventeenth-century English history. Thus, for example, the Crown supported both internal monopolies and monopolistic trading companies, such as the Merchant Adventurers, so much so that in 1621 some 700 of them were in existence.[28] Parliament, on the other hand, generally opposed these restrictions on both internal and external free trade. In 1601 it declared free trade with France, Spain and Portugal; in 1624 its Statute of Monopolies declared all monopolies not granted to corporations illegal; and in the same year it specifically abolished the Merchant Adventurers' monopoly on the cloth trade. Significantly, this monopoly was restored by Charles I during the period of personal government. Stuart governments regularly sought to prevent enclosures and, during the period of personal government, enclosers were prosecuted. At the same time, the retention of the feudal right of wardship allowed the Crown or royal courtiers to plunder the estates of the landed gentry. The underlying dynamic behind Stuart government policy was the perennial search for revenue, and this, in turn, follows on as a necessary consequence from the progressive dissolution of English feudalism. The medieval estates-monarchy was, of course, an extremely cheap form of government; the feudal monarch was, in fact, simply the largest and most powerful landowner, and the primary sources of governmental revenue were his own estates. The levying of taxation to supplement these revenues generally necessitated the summoning of the Estates of the realm, the medieval parliaments. But in the late sixteenth and early seventeenth centuries, such methods of financing governmental expenditure became increasingly untenable. At a time of both generally rising prices and a general move towards economic rents the Crown continued to lease land on favourable terms as a source of patronage, thereby unwittingly impoverishing itself.[29] The situation was compounded by the generally inefficient management of Crown property, and by the profligacy with which Tudor monarchs had sold off Crown lands. This contraction in government revenue coincided with increasing demands on government expenditure, in particular those posed both by the cost of the expanding state machine and by the rising price of warfare, itself a consequence of technical innovation. In such circumstances the Stuart monarchy was obliged either to turn to Parliament for funds or to explore alternative sources of revenue. But the early seventeenth-century House of Commons, increasingly under the sway of a bourgeoisie and a bourgeoisified gentry, was totally opposed to the entire direction of royal policy. Thus the early Stuart monarchs were obliged to embroil themselves even further in that complicated maze of restrictions on trade which was the very source of Parliamentary oppositionism. The same dynamic underlies much of the conflict over foreign policy: quite simply, the Crown could not *afford* war with Spain without making itself financially dependent on Parliament.

In the decade preceding the Revolution, during the period of Charles I's personal rule, the contradictions between the demands of state policy and the needs of the increasingly capitalist economy finally come to a head. Lawrence Stone has summarised the history of this decade as the history of the Crown's involvement in a fourfold reaction: a religious reaction in which the monarchy bound itself to the Laudian hierarchy and an Arminian theology in opposition to Puritanism; a political reaction, which found its most obvious expression in the institution of personal government itself, but which also informs both the search for alternative sources of revenue and the attack on the autonomy of the Justices of the Peace; a social reaction, which took both trivial forms, such as the increasing aristocratic concern with coats of arms and family genealogies, and rather more consequential ones, such as the recourse on the part of the nobility to long-forgotten feudal dues; and an economic reaction, which manifested itself in the imposition of guild organisation on a number of trades and crafts, in the increased government support for monopolies, and in the fining of enclosing landlords.[30] Stone is, of course, one of the very few historians of this period whose work has been radically influenced by the development of modern academic sociology, and, as such, his analysis of the causes of the English Revolution evidences many of the weaknesses which are endemic to contemporary functionalism. Robin Blackburn has pointed out that functionalist theories of revolution tend to overestimate the import-ance of the particular decisions taken by governing elites. Thus, in Chalmers Johnson's analysis, revolution is seen as a consequence, on the one hand, of 'multiple dysfunction' in the social system and, on the other, of 'elite failure'.[31] Such an approach suffers from two main weaknesses. In the first place, as Blackburn notes, it defines conscious action as the sole prerogative of the ruling elite and thereby denies any capacity for initiative to the revolutionaries. And secondly, the functionalist emphasis on social structure as integrative leads to a disjuncture between the structural level of analysis, which deals only with the preconditions for revolution, and the conjunctural level of analysis, which becomes exclusively concerned with various forms of voluntaristically conceived social action. In this manner, functionalism fails to perceive the structural determinants of the conjuncture. In fact, Stone is not entirely uncritical of functionalist sociology. Indeed, in his own discussion of contemporary academic sociology, Stone notes that Johnson 'is a victim of the fallacy of intended consequences'[32] in so far as his analysis overstresses the capacity of elite action to remedy dysfunction. But Stone himself falls victim of that self-same fallacy. In his treatment of the monarchy's involvement in reaction, he argues that: 'The main emphasis must be placed upon the folly and intransigence of the government, its blind refusal to respond constructively to criticism, and its obstinate departure upon a collision course.'[33] Such an assessment at once concedes too much and too little to Charles Stuart, the individual. It confers upon him a power to influence events which in reality he did not possess, and in so doing attributes to him a portion of blame which he does not deserve. The real circumstances of Charles I are better grasped in Marx's observation that: 'Over and above their personal prejudices, the princes' hands are tied by a whole civil, military and ecclesiastical bureaucracy—constituent parts of the absolute monarchy which by no means desire to exchange their ruling position for a subordinate position under the bourgeoisie.'[34]

We have outlined the set of structural contradictions between the capitalist mode of production, on the one hand, and the feudal absolutist state, on the other, which led to the revolutionary crisis. But if we are to demonstrate not only that the English Revolution was a bourgeois revolution, but also that it was a *successful* bourgeois revolution, then we are obliged to attempt some assessment of the permanent achievements of the revolutionary period. Perhaps the most obvious achievement of the Revolution is the abolition of the absolute monarchy itself. For the restored monarchy was, of course, a constitutional monarchy, restored by the summons of Parliament, rather than by any royal fiat. The prerogative courts, abolished during the Interregnum, were never revived. Nor were royal pretensions to rule by divine right. Furthermore, government finance was made permanently dependent upon the House of Commons; in return for the abolition of feudal tenures, another of the irreversible achievements of the Revolution, the Crown received £100,000 per annum and the promise of a fixed regular income *voted on by Parliament*. The Crown's right to grant industrial monopolies was another permanent casualty of the Interregnum, although some commercial monopolies persisted, in the field of non-European trade. But, even without these financial checks on monarchical power, the new constitutional monarchy was established on a firm political basis. The English bourgeoisie had disposed of one recalcitrant king, and it was to prove perfectly capable of disposing of another in 1688. A parallel fate awaited both the restored House of Lords and the restored Episcopacy: resolutions of the Commons passed in 1661, 1671 and 1678 denied the Lords the power to amend money Bills; ecclesiastical courts, abolished by the Revolution, were never restored; and the tolerationist aspirations of the Independent revolutionaries achieved final confirmation in the Toleration Act of 1689. In this manner, the whole structure of the feudal absolutist state was abolished and replaced by the *quite different* set of political institutions which composed the constitutional monarchy.[35]

The abolition of the absolutist state implied, above all else, the abolition of that complex matrix of restrictions on trade which had served both to finance absolutism and to hinder the development of capitalism. This process has been summarised thus by Lawrence Stone: 'Many things were restored at the Restoration, but it is surely significant that among those which were not were feudal tenures, restraints upon enclosure of land, such monopolies and economic controls as did not suit the convenience of influential interest groups, and a foreign policy which gave little weight to commercial objectives.'[36] Indeed, the remarkable continuity of government economic policy as between the Interregnum and the restored monarchy stands in sharp contrast to the radical disjuncture between that of the Interregnum and the old absolutist monarchy. This permanent and irreversible sundering of the old fetters on commercial and industrial activity coincided with the enormous mobilisation of rural capital which followed on as a product of the revolutionary land seizures. During the Interregnum, Crown, Church, and Royalist lands had been subject to the three-fold process of sequestration, composition, and sale. At the Restoration many of these lands were returned to their original owners, although not those sold privately to finance sequestration fines. But, in any case, returning Royalists were as much obliged as Interregnum carpet baggers to adopt the new managerial techniques dictated by the needs of the market economy. The dynamics of this process have been ably summarised by Christopher Hill:

> During the interregnum, capital was mobilised either by short-term 'spoiling' or by long-term improvements in the technique of management, whether by sequestration committee, purchaser, or returned delinquent. In all three cases a capital sum passed through the hands of the state into the possession either of capitalist contractors and creditors, or of soldiers, most of whom were bled by officers speculating in debentures. Moreover, when lands were transferred they either remained in the hands of purchasers anxious to recoup themselves, or after improvement at their hands were resold at a higher price to others, or returned to delinquents whose own impoverishment made it necessary for them to turn improving landlords.[37]

The victory of relatively large-scale capitalist farming was also, of course, secured in part by the defeat of the copyholders' movement to secure their own economic independence during the Interregnum period. We may reasonably conclude, then, that the English Revolution was a successful bourgeois revolution in so far as its specific reforms can be demonstrated to have contributed *decisively* to the long-term movement from an essentially feudal form of social organisation to an essentially capitalist.

2   Class and Class Conflict in the Revolutionary Period

Thus far we have analysed the revolutionary crisis in terms of the structural contradictions present in early seventeenth-century English society and their ultimate structural resolution. But to confine ourselves to this level of analysis would be to fall prey to a fetishism of 'structures' such as is conventionally found in formalistic structuralism. Such structural contradictions are, in fact, only resolved through the conflictual interaction of opposed social groupings, that is through the dynamics of class struggle. And it is to the problem of the various social class alignments of the revolutionary period itself that we must now turn. The problems of such an analysis allow of no easy solution. There are no readily available, and easily recognisable, distinct bourgeois and noble classes which provide the immediately discernible social bases of, respectively, Parliamentarism and Royalism. Let us note, in the first place, that there are distinct problems of classification involved in any recourse to seventeenth-century data. For the men of that time did not view themselves through the conceptual framework of modern scientific Marxism. In consequence, such terms as 'gentleman', which are essentially status rather than class designations, conceal as much as they reveal about the social class backgrounds of those whom they describe. We should also be wary of expecting to find any one-to-one correlation between social class position and political allegiance. Such neatness is not the stuff of which history is made, and for a number of reasons. In the first place, social classes are rarely homogeneous; rather there are always fissures within them which set up particularistic, rather than class-wide, loyalties. Secondly, any class conflict which reaches the point of revolutionary war must become more than a simple sordid struggle for gain; it will involve a clash of opposed world visions, and it is perfectly possible, indeed normal, that each world vision will attract to itself individuals and even social groups which fall outside the compass of its class of origin. Finally, we may note that all revolutionary crises involve a whole series of subsidiary class conflicts in addition to the dominant, ultimately determining, opposition of class forces. But these are merely cautionary notes which the historian must bear in mind when approaching-the study of each and any social revolution. There are further problems posed by the specific features of the development of English capitalism and, in particular, by its largely rural nature, which followed as a direct consequence of the relative absence of powerful urban enclaves from the medieval English polity.[38] As Engels observed, 'ever since Henry VII, the English "aristocracy", far from counteracting the development of industrial production, had, on the contrary, sought to indirectly profit thereby; and there had always been a section of great landowners willing, from economical or political reasons, to co-operate with the leading men of the financial and industrial bourgeoisie'.[39] The result was not only the relative ease with which the compromise of 1689 was achieved, which Engels himself points to, but also a certain lack of clarity in the class boundaries of 1640. Indeed, the initial lack of support for Charles I from even the titular aristocracy strongly attests to the full extent to which the old feudal nobility had fallen under the sway of the developing market society.

The above qualifications have been offered not in order to hedge our bets, but rather in order to establish what should be obvious, that Marxism is as easily capable of, and just as much under an obligation to, the analysis of complexity and diversity as is any other sociological theory. Oversimplification renders as little service to the science of history as it does to any other science. What evidence can, then, be gleaned from the available data? Let us note, first of all, that a clear majority of the titular nobility supported the King; that, as might be expected, the great majority of the ruling class ultimately rallied to the defence of their state. But a considerable minority, some 25 per cent[40] in all, initially sided with Parliament. There are probably two quite distinct elements within this pro-Parliamentarian nobility: firstly, an essentially reactionary and particularistic revolt against absolutism characterised, in Stone's words, by 'a traditional, medieval hostility to royal constitutional autocracy';[41] and, secondly, the more genuinely bourgeois element constituted by the peculiar combination, on the one hand, of the increasing aristocratic involvement with capitalistic farming and capitalistic trading enterprises, and on the other, of the enormous inflation of honours under Buckingham.[42] Nonetheless a clear majority of the nobility did side with the Crown, despite whatever business connections they may have possessed. The reasons for this should be obvious. As Hexter notes: 'What concerned most of the peers most constantly was the advancement of themselves and their families in prestige and wealth. In its command of their time and energy, and perhaps in its potential for yielding the advancement they sought, "business" ran a bad fourth to office at court, marriage, and estate management.'[43] In other words, although this is an inference which Hexter himself refuses to make, they were still a predominantly feudal class. With the nobility, of course, went the majority of their tenants and retainers. At the opposite extreme, the small merchants, tradesmen, shop-keepers, artisans, and apprentices of the towns sided overwhelmingly with Parliament. Indeed, with only one or two exceptions, such as Oxford and Chester, the whole of urban England opted for the Parliamentarian cause. These, then, are the more obvious lines of division.

When we turn to the merchants and the gentry, however, the contour lines become rather less clear. Perhaps the most interesting available data on the social composition of Parliamentarian and Royalist MPs is to be found in Brunton and Pennington's *Members of the Long Parliament*, which concludes that 'the greater and lesser gentry were not on different sides . . . merchants . . . were to be found on both sides, and in such proportions as to make it doubtful whether there was any general hostility to the King amongst provincial merchants'.[44] Brunton and Pennington themselves readily admit that their analysis suffers from the major weakness that it confines itself to an enquiry into the political and social affiliations of MPs, rather than into the social bases of the two sides outside Parliament. We have only to turn our attention to the social class backgrounds of, respectively, MPs and voters in modern British society, somewhat less opaque objects of study than their seventeenth-century equivalents, to recognise the inadvisability of inferring the one from the other. Nonetheless, the extent to which the political dividing lines run through, rather than between, these two social groupings strongly suggests the need for a coherent account of the lines of fission which existed within them. Brunton and Pennington's detailed analysis of the merchants is itself suggestive. They point to a three-fold division within the merchant MPs between, respectively, the great national figures with close court connections, the monopolists, who sided to a man with the Crown;[45] the London merchants, who with one exception sided with Parliament, and who tended towards the more radical wing of the Parliamentarian side; and the provincial merchants, a clear majority of whom supported Parliament, and who, again, tended to support the more radical Independents against the Presbyterians.[46] Clearly, the dividing line appears to run between those, on the one hand, who were tied to, and profited from, the institutions of the absolutist state, and those, on the other, who did not. Now this distinction allows of a more general theoretical formulation than is possible within English empiricist historiography. We noted earlier that both Marx and Weber recognised the importance of the distinction between merchant and productive capital to the theory of the rise of capitalism.[47] Merchant capital proper is, in fact, a normal component of feudal social formations. Indeed, the traditional merchant oligarchies were often organically linked to the feudal landed classes; as Manning notes, 'cliques of merchants . . . ruled the towns and commerce on behalf of the aristocratic and absolutist system'.[48] These groups were necessarily bound to the absolutist state which was the source of their power and privileges. By contrast, the small merchants and their equivalent in the countryside, the yeomanry, who were excluded from the system of monopolies, and who actually provided the dynamic behind the growth of industrial capital, tended to support

Parliament. As Takahashi observes, the Revolution was, in part, 'a strenuous struggle for the state power between a group of the middle class . . . and a group of the *haute bourgeoisie* originating in the feudal landed aristocracy, the merchant and financial monopolists'.[49]

Brunton and Pennington's discovery that there was no significant division between the greater and lesser gentry is valuable in itself in that it constitutes a final refutation of Trevor-Roper's declining gentry thesis. Whatever divisions existed within the gentry, they were not those which run between an embittered Independent declining country gentry and a prosperous Royalist court gentry. There is evidence elsewhere for this conclusion: of the 55 certain or possible Independent gentlemen, which Yule identifies, 31 were greater gentry and only 24 were lesser gentry.[50] Brunton and Pennington themselves offer no real explanation of the divisions within the gentry other than the tentative suggestion that 'the parliamentary history of the seventeenth century can only be written in terms of families, of local rather than national affairs',[51] a conclusion which has been much echoed elsewhere.[52] Now, of course, kinship and 'connection' systems are obviously important in delineating the internal organisation of the two sides. But to take them as given, as the starting point for analysis, is, in fact, to empty them of any real content. Unless we offer some explanation of *why* particular families fought on different sides, we effectively reduce their political allegiances to the level of pure caprice. Fortunately, possible explanations of the pattern of division within the gentry are available. The most fertile source of such an explanation is surely the distinction between the Royalist gentry of the north and west, and the Parliamentarian gentry of the south and east, which Hill points to.[53] Indeed, the English Civil War can be seen as almost as much a conflict between the north and the south as the American, although the respective geographical locations of the advanced and backward sectors of the economy are reversed. Brunton and Pennington note the distinction between the two areas, but conclude that the 'unprogressive' gentry can hardly be considered a social class.[54] But, of course, they can be considered as such once we understand the full extent to which the contemporary status term of 'gentleman' binds together social groupings which, in fact, stand in quite different relationships to the means of production. There is a world of difference between a southern gentleman, actively involved in trade and capitalist farming, and a northern gentleman still committed to the older, essentially. feudal patronage systems. Brunton and

Pennington do touch upon this distinction. They note, for example, that: 'Among county families it is easier to find Parliamentarian than Royalist members who were exploiting local assets and opportunities. More characteristic of the Royalists are the supplementary sources of income that could be picked up through connections at Court and in the capital.'[55] Here then lies the solution to our problem: just as the status term 'merchant' obscures the crucial distinction between merchant and industrial capital, so too the status term 'gentleman' obscures the equally crucial distinction between the new rural bourgeoisie and the older essentially feudal, landed classes. Such an understanding of the divisions within the merchants and the gentry renders the whole seventeenth-century English social structure into rather more transparent form and indicates the irretrievably bourgeois character of the revolutionary upheaval itself.

But what, then, of the divisions which arose within the Parliamentarian camp subsequent to the short reign of King Pym, the divisions between Presbyterians, Independents and Levellers? There has been much dispute, in recent decades, over the reliability of traditional interpretations of the pattern of party alignments in the early years of the Interregnum, and in particular over the relative significance of the split between the Independents and the Presbyterians. Much of the recent emphasis on the non-religious aspects of the party conflict has provided a salutary corrective to the traditional notion of a nation divided simply over rival conceptions of church government. Undoubtedly, the Independents were as much, or even more so, the party that stood for a more vigorous prosecution of the war and a stronger line in negotiations with the King, as the party of religious Independency proper. And conversely, the political moderation of the Presbyterians is as least as significant as their Calvinist religion. But Hexter's attempt to brush aside the religious question altogether and to reduce the label 'Independent' to a mere term of political abuse is misconceived.[56] As Yule points out, Hexter's list of political Independents, that is of Rumpers and regicides, who were, in fact, Presbyterian in religion is weighted towards the more moderate wing of the party. Whereas something like 40 per cent of the whole Independent parliamentary party participated in the King's trial, only 14 per cent of those in Hexter's list did so.[57] Elsewhere, the same writer has demonstrated a clear correlation between political and religious radicalism in respect of the hard core of the revolutionary wing of the party: of the 65 readily identifiable leaders of this group whose religious affiliations are known, 55 were Independents and only 10 Presbyterians.[58] And the reasons for this should be obvious; as Yule observes: 'Religion for the Puritan was not an addendum to the rest of life but the vehicle for giving one "a world view". Consequently, radicalism in religion was itself radicalism.'[59] This attempt to question the significance of religious issues in the dispute has often formed a constituent part of a wider critique of the relevance of the notion of party itself. Thus, for example, Underdown argues that the Independent party was nothing more than 'a loose and temporary alliance of distinct groups',[60] which lasted for little more than the two years 1646 and 1647. In this interpretation of the early years of the Interregnum, not only is 'religion' supplanted by 'politics', but politics is, in turn, converted into mere issue politics, devoid of any consistent principled content. Once again, Yule's comments are instructive. He points out that the split between the Independents and the Presbyterians had emerged as early as 1644 and that, whilst the party terms fell into disuse after Pride's Purge, quite simply because the Presbyterian parliamentary party had been forcibly dissolved, there is nonetheless considerable continuity of both personnel and policy between the old Independent party and the Rump Parliament.[61] The most obvious feature of this policy continuity is, of course, the issue of religious toleration, which Underdown is able to overlook only because of his general devaluation of religious questions. We may conclude, then, that there was a party conflict between the moderate Calvinist party, on the one hand, and the radical Independent party on the other, that this conflict was only resolved by the Independents' use of their influence in the Army to purge the Parliament of its Presbyterian members, and that the governments of the 1650s were, in effect, Independent party governments.

The problem remains of attempting an analysis of the respective social bases of the Presbyterian and Independent parties. In general, both Marxist and non-Marxist historians have proved singularly unsuccessful in developing such an analysis. Trotsky, for example, hazarded the bold, but almost certainly false, suggestion that: 'The Presbyterians were the party of the bourgeoisie, the party of wealth and education. The Independents and the Puritans in general were the party of the petty bourgeoisie, and the petty independent land-owners.'[62] Now if there is anything at all of which we can be certain in respect of the class alignments of the 1640s, it is that the haute bourgeoisie, the merchant monopolists, were not Parliamentarians at all, but Royalists, and that the urban petty bourgeoisie constituted the social base, not of Independency, but of the Leveller Party.[63] It does not even seem possible to associate the Presbyterians, rather than the Independents, with wealth. Indeed, both Royalist[64] and Leveller[65] observers at times characterised Independency precisely by its association with wealth. But if Trotsky's few brief suggestions are somewhat misleading, then Trevor-Roper's fully developed analysis of Interregnum party alignments must constitute a veritable compendium of error. Trevor-Roper's account is, of course, well-known; the social basis of Independency is, quite simply, 'the backwoods gentry who, in 1640, sat on the back benches of Parliament, but who, as war and revolution progressed, gradually broke through the crumbling leadership which had at first contained them'.[66] In this view, the opposition between Presbyterians and Independents is merely a special form of the old opposition between court and country, in which the capital city itself comes to substitute for the Crown in the demonology of the rural gentry. The central weakness of this theory is its total failure to account for the group of London Independents, amongst whom Isaac Pennington, who had initially secured the City of London for Parliament, was the single most prominent figure.[67] Nor was this group of wealthy London Independents apparently without support in the capital; the adhesion of a number of suburbs, such as Southwark, to the Army's cause when it marched on London to defeat the attempted Presbyterian coup, in August 1647, is indicative of some considerable body of sympathy with the London Independents. It would seem, then, that the notion of a sharp cleavage between a Presbyterian capital city on the one hand, and an enraged Independent country gentry on the other, is, to say the least, somewhat untenable.

The failure of a whole series of often quite diverse attempts to establish a readily definable sociological basis to the political conflict between Presbyterianism and Independency probably derives, not from an inadequate conceptualisation as such, but from the very nature of the object of study itself. For it would seem that there is little difference in the social composition of the two groups. Brunton and Pennington's comparison between the Independent members of the Rump Parliament and the secluded Presbyterian members does, in fact, show that the more radical counties, that is, those which were over-represented in the Rump, were the areas in which open-field agriculture predominated—Yorkshire, the Midlands, Kent, Somerset, and Sussex.[68] They also note that 'Independency was strong among members from the clothing counties, old and new'.[69]

Certainly, this is indicative of some correlation between the degree of political radicalism and the general level of economic development. But the overall sociological similarity between the Presbyterian and Independent parties suggests that we are dealing with differences of degree, rather than of kind, with divisions *within* a class rather than *between* classes. There is a looseness to this conclusion which makes it appear almost inherently unsatisfactory. But we should surely be wary of attempting to impose upon history an order to which it will not easily submit. Indeed, we only have to turn to the history of the modern labour movement to appreciate the folly of assuming that each social class is necessarily so internally homogeneous that it is able to articulate its political aspirations through the medium of one, and only one, political grouping. The division between 'moderates' and 'radicals' within social classes, and indeed within political parties, is such a familiar feature of the contemporary political landscape that we should find little cause for surprise at its presence in seventeenth-century England. We may readily admit that Presbyterianism, as the more moderate and conciliatory of the two groupings, constituted in part a subordination of the bourgeois class to the feudal ideology of the old absolutist state. But nonetheless it remained, as much as Independency, an essentially bourgeois political party. The very nature of the emergence of the split between the two groups is indicative in itself of their underlying social unity. It is generally accepted that, as late as 1643, the majority of MPs, and perhaps even of ministers, were neither decidedly Presbyterian nor decidedly Independent, and that they were progressively forced towards partisanship only after the entry of the Scots into the war. Even John Milton, ultimately the most hardened of Independent supporters, only moved gradually from a conditional support for Presbyterianism in 1642 to the strident advocacy of Independency which we find in the *Areopagatica* of 1644. We may conclude, then, not that Independency and Presbyterianism derived their support from quite distinct social groupings, as both Trotsky and Trevor-Roper have, in different ways, suggested, but rather that they are both bourgeois political groupings; and that the difference between the two consists in this: that, at each successive state in the class struggles of the 1640s and 1650s, the Independent, rather than the Presbyterian, programme is that which embodies most fully the class interests of, and which expresses at the highest level the class consciousness of, the English bourgeoisie.

If the division between the Presbyterians and the Independents was essentially a conflict within a class, that between the Independents and the Levellers was most certainly one between classes. Whereas the Independents were essentially a bourgeois political grouping, the Levellers were, in Brailsford's words, 'a third force, drawn from the lower middle class, the skilled craftsmen and the small farmers'.[70] At each successive stage during the political struggles of the period 1640–9, in the course of both the war between King and Parliament and the later conflict between Presbyterians and Independents, the revolutionary bourgeoisie were obliged to mobilise the masses in order to defeat their opponents. But in so doing, they unleased a political force which ultimately came to articulate its own independent political aspirations and which, in consequence, came into conflict with the central dynamic of the Revolution. Engels described this process in the following terms:

> although, upon the whole, the bourgeoisie, in their struggle with the nobility, could claim to represent at the same time the interests of the different working classes of that period, yet in every great bourgeois movement there were independent outbursts of that class which was the forerunner, more or less developed, of the modern proletariat. For example, . . . in the great English Revolution, the Levellers.[71]

We should be wary of an unqualified endorsement of Engels's judgement in this matter. The social basis of the Leveller Party was 'the forerunner of the modern proletariat' only in the special sense that it crystallised out of a social class, the seventeenth-century petty bourgeoisie, which was ultimately to be subject to a process of proletarianisation. But the Levellers do not appear to have drawn their support primarily from the proletariat itself. On the contrary, their franchise proposals, which specifically exclude all wage earners from the suffrage, strongly indicate the essentially petty bourgeois nature of their social basis.[72] The Levellers did not, in fact, demand the extension of the suffrage to include all adult males, as has been suggested by a number of writers, including, of course, Brailsford himself.[73] Rather, they advocated, as Petty expressed it at Putney, 'that all inhabitants that have not lost their birthrights should have an equal voice in elections'.[74] Brailsford's interpretation of this statement as a demand for manhood suffrage[75] is somewhat misleading. For those who have 'lost their birthrights' include, again in Petty's words, 'apprentices, or servants[76] or those that take alms[77]. . .

because they depend upon the will of other men and should be afraid to displease them'.[78] The class content of the debate on the franchise at Putney has been aptly summarised by Macpherson in these terms:

> Cromwell and Ireton held that only freeholders and freemen of corporations, . . . had the property basis upon which they could live as free men without dependence. The Levellers thought that all men except servants and alms-takers were free men. For both Levellers and army leaders franchise was properly dependent on freedom, and freedom meant individual economic independence. But the two groups, with different class roots, had different views of the property basis of economic independence.[79]

The Levellers were, then, a specifically petty bourgeois grouping, whose political theory centred on the characteristically petty bourgeois value of individual economic independence, and who, indeed, had very little sympathy with any form of *economic* 'levelling'.[80]

3   The Nature of Independency

We have argued that the Independent party, which triumphed over the Presbyterians at Pride's Purge on 6 December 1648, and over the Levellers on the night of 14/15 May 1649, represented the political expression, at the highest level, of the class consciousness of the English bourgeoisie. But in what did this class consciousness consist? What were the major points at issue between the political programmes of the three parties? The differences between the Levellers and the Independents are both better documented and more readily discernible than those between the latter and the Presbyterians, and therefore allow of a more summary consideration. In the first place, they were divided, as we have seen, over the suffrage question: whilst the Independents supported the existing franchise, which was restricted to owners of freehold land worth 40 shillings a year or more and freemen of trading corporations, the Levellers advocated the extension of the franchise to include all adult men except wage servants, apprentices and alms-takers.[81] The Leveller position on the franchise was itself a constituent part of a wider political theory which vested ultimate political sovereignty in 'the people', rather than in Parliament, a proposition which neither the Presbyterians nor the Independents could ever have accepted. The Levellers opposed, too, the Independents' war of conquest in Ireland.[82] Finally, of course, the Levellers and the Independents engaged in a bitter battle for control over the Army, in the course of which the Levellers counterposed their relatively democratic theory of rank and file control, through the election of Agitators, to the Independents' conception of a professional army essentially subject to the discipline of its commanding officers. The outcome of this particular battle and, with it, the fate of the Leveller Party as a whole, was finally decided by the crushing of the Leveller mutiny at Burford.[83] The class basis of this political opposition is readily discernible. For whilst the Levellers, unlike the Diggers, affected no opposition to private property as such, indeed were positively in its favour, they were strongly susceptible of the dangers of a tyranny of large property-holders over small property-holders. At Putney, on 29 October 1647, Colonel Rainborough ably articulated the Levellers' fears in a phrase which stands, almost, as a premonition of the future of the English petty bourgeoisie: 'Then, I say, the one part shall make hewers of wood and drawers of water of the other five, and so the greatest part of the nation be enslaved.'[84] The Leveller political vision was essentially that of a society of free, independent small producers and, as such, it was fundamentally incompatible with both the immediate objectives of the propertied Independents and the long-term historical future of English capitalism. Engels once commented that 'in all three great bourgeois risings, the peasantry furnishes the army that has to do the fighting; and the peasantry is just the class that, the victory once gained, is most surely ruined by the economic consequences of that victory. A hundred years after Cromwell, the yeomanry of England had almost disappeared.'[85] Perhaps a similar realisation prompted the Leveller pamphlet, probably written by Walwyn, which directed to the Army, ordered to Ireland by an Independent government, this question: 'Will you go on still to kill, slay and murder in order to make them (your officers) as absolute lords and masters over Ireland as you have made them over England?'[86]

The conflict between the Presbyterians and the Independents is rather less clear cut than that between the latter and the Levellers, but in general it takes the form of an opposition between moderation and extremism. The Presbyterians were acutely aware of the threat to the whole social order posed by a civil war which had necessitated the political mobilisation of the masses and, whilst they aimed to secure the sovereignty of Parliament against monarchical tyranny, they sought to situate this achievement within the context of a general maintenance of traditional institutions. Thus, for example, the Presbyterians opposed the abolition of both the monarchy and the House of Lords, and each of these gains were only effected after Pride's Purge. Indeed, as Woodhouse observes:

> The monarchy, shorn of its power, they would cherish in the interests of a lasting settlement—an assurance that the revolution had not been so revolutionary after all, and a guarantee that it should go no further . . . The King was indeed essential to their scheme, and the time was to come when they would sacrifice almost anything but the church settlement to gain him. He refused their terms and ruined himself and them.[87]

The Independents initially shared these Presbyterian intentions, but in the face of continuing Royalist intransigence, they ultimately determined on nothing short of the execution of the King and the abolition of the monarchy. They were divided also over the question of the revolutionary land settlement. The Presbyterians were prepared to agree to sequestration, which imposed upon the 'delinquent' Royalists the loss of the income from their estates, but not to the seizure of property itself. The Independents and the Levellers, on the other hand, representative as they were of an Army whose pay was consistently in arrears, demanded the confiscation and sale of Royalist lands. As Hill notes:

> Opposition to sale came throughout from the House of Lords and the 'Presbyterian' section of the House of Commons, from motives of social conservatism. They were prepared to sacrifice bishops' lands as an additional insurance against the restoration of the hierarchical power. . . . Further than that they refused to go, and there were no more state sales until after Pride's Purge.[88]

There is, of course, a strong sense in which the ultimate outcome of the Revolution represented a triumph for the Presbyterian, rather than the Independent, programme: in 1660 the monarchy, the House of Lords, and most of the Royalist estates were all restored, and in very much the form in which the Presbyterians had intended. And whilst the Independent leaders went to the scaffold, Presbyterians such as Prynne became the trusted servants of Charles II. This end result of the revolutionary process has led many conservative historians into an unwise deprecation of the significance of the

Revolution itself. Perhaps the most succinct formulation of this view is contained in Trevor-Roper's judgement that:

Socially, as politically, the Revolution had been a failure, and the history of England after 1660 was a continuation of its history before 1640. The Interregnum was merely an untidy interruption. The only permanent changes were a few constitutional changes that could have been, and sometimes had been, achieved by peaceful legislation, and certainly did not require civil war, revolution and military dictatorship.[89]

There is surely a certain disingenuousness in this verdict. The Independents did not, after all, *set out* to destroy the monarchy: the *Heads of Proposals*, the clearest statement of the Independent programme, specifically states, in Section XIV, that 'the things here before proposed being provided, for settling and securing the rights, liberties, peace, and safety of the kingdom, His majesty's person, his Queen, and royal issue, may be restored to a condition of safety, honour and freedom in this nation'.[90] Rather, they were *driven* to republicanism by the continued Royalist resistance to their intentions, that is by the very fact that their political aims *could not be achieved* without civil war, revolution, and military dictatorship. The Presbyterian triumph in 1660 was, in fact, conditional upon the Independent victories of 1648 and 1649. Perhaps the dynamics of this process are best grasped in Engels's suggestion that:

As a rule, after the first great success, the victorious minority divided; one half was satisfied with what had been gained, the other wanted to go still further, and put forward new demands, . . . the more moderate party would regain the upper hand, and what had last been won would wholly or partly be lost again; the vanquished would then shriek of treachery or ascribe their defeat to accident. In reality, however, the truth of the matter was largely this: the achievements of the first victory were only safeguarded by the second victory of the more radical party; this having been attained, . . . the radicals and their achievements vanished once more from the stage.[91]

But in one significant respect, and that perhaps one of the most important, that is the religious settlement, the laurels of victory went finally, not to the Presbyterians, but to the vanquished Independents.

Between the tolerationist policies of the 1650s and those of the 1690s
it is the period of the Stuart Restoration which appears as an 'untidy
interruption'. And this brings us to the central ideological difference
between the two parties, that is the nature of their religious beliefs.
The Presbyterians were, of course, the party of Calvinist orthodoxy.
They adhered, on the one hand, to the grim doctrine of predestination which asserts that, in Prynne's words, 'God from all eternity
hath, by his immutable purpose and decree, predestined unto life, not
all men, not any indefinite or undetermined, but only a certain select
number of particular men (commonly called the Elect, invisible true
Church of Christ), which number can neither be augmented nor
diminished; others hath he eternally and perpetually reprobated unto
death;'[92] and, on the other, to the belief in one single state church,
possessed of true Calvinist doctrine, and in the use of state power to
suppress all rivals to that church. In both respects, they were loyal
disciples of the Genevan tyrant. These, then, were the new forcers of
conscience whose doctrines provoked Milton to the judgement that
'New Presbyter is but old Priest writ large'. Initially, religious
Independency had been little more than 'a form of decentralized
Calvinism'[93] which sought merely to substitute the local congregation for the presbytery as the locus of power in church government. But as Independency crystallised into a major political force,
rather than a small religious grouping, its doctrines underwent some
considerable transformation. And, in particular, the Independents
moved towards the acceptance of a much more generally tolerationist
position than that adhered to by their Presbyterian opponents.

The precise extent and limitations of Independent tolerationism
have often been a matter of some controversy. Yule, for example,
comes very near to defining Independency as the party of toleration.[94] But for Brailsford, whose sympathies are self-evidently
with the Levellers, the Independents were merely the party of
'Puritan intolerance'.[95] In practice, the Independent position varies
from time to time. In August 1647, their political programme
outlined in the Heads of Proposals included, in Section XI, a demand
for general religious toleration: 'An Act to be passed to take away all
coercive power, authority, and jurisdiction of bishops and all other
ecclesiastical officers whatsoever, extending to any civil penalties against
any persons so censured.'[96] But only two months earlier, Ireton's
Representation of the Army had included the qualification that 'it is not
intended that this liberty shall necessarily extend to Popery or
Prelacy'.[97] The record of the Independent governments of the 1650s

can be summarised thus: they created what was, in effect, an Independent state church, but tolerated, and indeed believed as a matter of principle in the toleration of, Presbyterians and sectaries; they secured a *de facto* toleration of the London Jewish community; but on the other hand, they effected a very real persecution of the Quakers, and of the Irish Roman Catholics, and denied legal toleration to both the Episcopalians and the English Roman Catholics, although in each case this intolerance fell short of an active campaign of persecution.

The Independents, then, never accepted that degree of general toleration, extended to include even atheists, advocated by the Levellers.[98] But, nonetheless, they stand in sharp contrast to the radical intolerance of both the pre-revolutionary Royalist governments and the Presbyterian party. Whereas both Royalists and Presbyterians agreed on the necessity for a single, monolithic state church, the Independents believed *as a matter of principle* in the toleration of groups outside that church. Indeed, the more radical amongst their number, including both Vane and Milton, actually agreed with the Leveller proposals for a complete separation of state and church, but not, however, with those for the legal toleration of Catholics. The limitations of Independent tolerationism are readily comprehensible: both the Quakers, who included amongst their ranks many ex-Levellers, and the Episcopalians and Catholics, who were Royalist almost to a man, were always either actual or potential enemies of the revolutionary state. This is not to suggest that Independent intolerance was subjectively perceived simply as a matter of political tactics; religious ideas, once born of political necessity, take on a certain dynamic of their own. But Milton, at least, was prepared to admit, of the Catholics, that 'if they ought not to be tolerated, it is for just reason of state, more than of religion'.[99] And it is doubtful that it could have been otherwise. In times of war, whether between states or between classes, no government can readily afford to allow its opponents the freedom to actively propagandise. The implications of this situation have been effectively grasped in a recent, perceptive, but at the same time radically flawed, Marxist commentary on Milton's *Areopagatica*: 'Milton, like every humanist revolutionary from St. Paul to Fidel Castro, is indeed a libertarian: but the counter-revolution, religious or political, is outside the limits of reason and tolerance, for to every revolutionist, the revolution is reason and salvation, purpose and morality, the threatened tabernacle which alone preserves genuine human freedom.'[100] The significance of this Independent tolerationism, limited though it may be, is its break with the feudal notions of a co-extensive state and church, and of authority as the source of all knowledge. In each respect, in its advocacy both of institutional pluralism and of epistemological individualism, Independency is peculiarly consonant with the needs of the developing market society.

The second major feature of Presbyterian orthodoxy which we pointed to was its adhesion to the doctrine of predestination. We should note that in seventeenth-century England this doctrine was in no sense the exclusive property of Presbyterianism as such; it was shared too by many Independents and even by Episcopalians, such as Bishop Joseph Hall.[101] But whereas Calvinism was an essential feature of Presbyterianism, this was never true of Independency. The very nature of the Independent church itself, as a decentralised church, permitted considerable doctrinal heterodoxy. Thus, whilst the religious Independents did, indeed, formally adopt the predestinarian doctrine at the Savoy Conference of 1658, there were many amongst their number who were always firmly opposed to it. John Goodwin, for example, perhaps the most famous of the Independent divines, a representative of the party in its debates with the Levellers at Whitehall,[102] the author of the influential *Independency God's Verity*[103] and of *Right and Might Well Met*, a defence of Pride's Purge,[104] was most certainly an Arminian opponent of Calvinism.[105] Presumably so, too, was Isaac Pennington, the effective leader of the Independent party in the City, one of the King's judges, and also a member of Goodwin's congregation.[106] And many of the leading figures in the Independent political party were not, in fact, religious Independents at all. The party in Parliament included: Baptists, such as John Carew and Colonel Hutchinson, both of whom were regicides, Robert Bennett, Henry Danvers, Henry Lawrence, Samuel Moyer, and William Steele; theists, such as Thomas Challoner and Henry Marten, both regicides, and Henry Nevil; and Erastians, such as Henry Parker, Sir Robert Reynolds, Oliver St. John, who with Vane jointly led the party in Parliament, and Bustrode Whitelocke—all of whom were presumably hostile to Calvinism's theology as well as its mode of church government.[107] And, of course, Milton's verdict on the doctrine of predestination is well known: 'The Calvinist is taxed with predestination, and to make God the author of sin; not with any dishonourable thought of God, but it may be over-zealously asserting his absolute power, not without plea of scripture.'[108] Trevor-Roper's observation that the struggle between Presbyterians and Independents 'is in one sense—the intellectual sense—a struggle between Calvinists and Arminians',[109] marred as it is by a tendency to over-statement customary in that writer, does point to the general direction in which Independent theology moved.

Now this presents something of a problem in that it stands in sharp contradiction to that commonplace association of Calvinism with capitalism and revolution which has become so firmly entrenched in modern sociology. Indeed, both Marxist and non-Marxist sociologists are generally in agreement as to the decisive importance of Calvinism in the process of transition from feudalism to capitalism. Weber's views on the subject are too well known to bear much repetition. The doctrine of predestination, he argues, gives rise to a doctrine of proof in which successful labour in a lay calling is seen as as indispensable sign of election, and which demands of its adherents 'a systematic self-control which at every moment stands before the inexorable alternative, chosen or damned'.[110] The consequent rationalisation of conduct gives rise to an ethic which is, in Weber's view, essential to the 'spirit of capitalism' in which accumulation, devoid of hedonism, becomes an end in itself. Engels's analysis of Calvinism runs along remarkably similar lines. In his view, the doctrine of predestination 'was the religious expression of the fact that in the commercial world of competition success or failure does not depend upon a man's activity or cleverness, but upon circumstances uncontrollable by him'.[111] Both Weber and Engels point to Calvinism's superiority over Lutheranism as a thorough-going bourgeois ideology.[112] But this supposed correlation between capitalism and Calvinism is, in fact, extremely suspect. We have seen that the English Revolution was carried through to its climax, not by the Calvinistic Presbyterians, but by their Independent opponents. This, in itself, suggests a certain inadequacy in the theory. But, as Trevor-Roper has demonstrated, the Weber thesis, which is also in some respects the Engels thesis, is open to even further criticisms. In general, he points out, Calvinism's strength was located, not in the capitalistic centres of southern England and Amsterdam, but in their politically and economically retarded hinterlands—Scotland and Gelderland.[113] Trevor-Roper concedes that most sixteenth and seventeenth-century capitalists adhered to the notion of a lay calling, and that this notion was crucial to their practice as capitalists, but adds that it was Erasmian, rather than Calvinist, in its origins. In the transition from the Renaissance to the Enlightenment, which was also, although Trevor-Roper would not concede this point, the transition from absolutism to capitalism, 'the new philosophy was forwarded in successive Calvinist societies, if it was forwarded, in each instance, not by Calvinism, but by the defeat of Calvinism. . . . Calvinism, that fierce and narrow re-creation of medieval scholasticism, was its enemy.'[114]

Let us consider this doctrine of predestination in rather more detail. In the first place, let us note that it need not give rise to a doctrine of proof; Weber himself admits that this latter notion follows, not from the internal logic of Calvinism, but from the demands of practical pastoral work, in which the radical uncertainty of election, inherent in Calvin's Calvinism, has to be *overcome*.[115] In fact, the concept of rational practice in a lay calling derives *more readily* from non-predestinarian Baptism, with its emphasis on *individual* conscience, than it does from Calvinism as such. It should not surprise us, then, to find Baptists, theists, and Erastians, rather than Presbyterians, in the vanguard of the English Revolution. Engels's analysis appears as equally misconceived as Weber's. In so far as the doctrine of predestination can have had any value to the early bourgeoisie, it would have derived from its provision of an alternative basis for legitimate authority to those of 'tradition' and 'hereditary right'. But Calvinism only went half way; that basis still resided outside the discrete rational individual. In fact, an essential component of any developed bourgeois ideology is surely, the converse of what Engels suggests, the proposition that success in bourgeois society is *precisely* a consequence of 'merit', of effort, hard work, etc., and that it does indeed depend upon a man's activity or cleverness. And it is non-Calvinist (and non-Lutheran) protestantisms, and later secular rationalisms, which most readily yield up such propositions. In this context it seems appropriate to refer briefly to the political implications of Milton's theory of election, although its detailed consideration must await the next chapter. In Milton's system, the world is made up of discrete individuals, each of which possesses the capacity to exercise free will, but only some of whom actually achieve their freedom, that is, actually subordinate their passions to their reasons. Those who do freely receive Christ into themselves, who are governed by reason, come to constitute an elect which is freed 'FROM THE BONDAGE OF SIN, AND CONSEQUENTLY FROM THE RULE OF LAW AND OF MAN,'[116] an elect which is entitled, indeed obliged, to undertake the government of sinners. It should be noted that the elect attain their positions neither by hereditary right nor by predestination, in the orthodox Calvinist sense of the term, but rather by merit. This conception provides a theoretical articulation for the practice of the English bourgeois revolutionaries in a twofold sense. In the first place, it establishes an 'equality of opportunity' model of human behaviour, in which each man is given the opportunity to achieve election, but only some actually succeed, and they through their own merit. This type of model, rather than a predestinarian one, exactly describes the structure of an ideally functioning bourgeois society. And secondly, of course, it provides a rationale for the Independents' ruthless seizure of power, since, as an elect, they are both free from the rule of law and entitled to rule over sinners. The strength of the Miltonic theory of election is that, unlike Calvinism, it both provides an alternative basis for legitimate authority to that of hereditary right *and* emphasises that success is a product of individual merit. *Here, then, resides the second central locus of the theoretical superiority of Independency over Presbyterianism.* Of course, not all Independents would have acquiesced in Milton's heresy; many of them were orthodox Calvinists. But as the leading Independent intellectual, Milton was able to articulate theoretically and coherently those notions, often only half-formed and dimly perceived, which actually underlie the political practice of Independency. As Goldmann would have it, Milton's work is 'the *coherent* exceptional expression in great works of philosophy or art',[117] of the world vision of his social class. We turn, in the next chapter, to a detailed analysis of the internal structure of Milton's philosophical and political vision.

4 Reason Triumphant

In the course of our earlier discussion of the structure of the Revolutionary Independent world vision, we suggested that that structure should be understood, not as a single entity to be grasped synchronically, but rather as a changing entity best grasped in terms of its movement, its central pattern of development. We pointed to the existence of an initial set of rationalist categories, which are premised upon, and indeed contain within themselves, a set of essentially optimistic ideological assumptions. And we suggested that this system developed, under the impact of the shock of the Restoration, two alternative, but not incompatible, responses to the triumph of un-reason over reason, the one personal and quietistic, the other political and historical. This presents us with a relatively straightforward framework for the analysis of Milton's life-work: a schematisation which is concerned, firstly, with the works of the pre-Restoration period, which express the world vision of an emergent triumphant rationalism, and secondly, with the works written under the Restoration, which express the world vision of reason embattled. Alternative schema are, of course, available. Professor Grierson, for example, claimed to detect a disjuncture in Milton's thought between, as he viewed it, the prophetic writings of the period 1641 to 1654, and the artistic, non-prophetic, writings prior to and antecedent from that period. [1] It seems to us that this particular distinction is somewhat misleading in that it ignores the genuinely political (and prophetic) content of both the three later poems and some, at least, of the earlier poems. Grierson's decision to date the shift from prophecy back to artistry from 1654 also seems to us to be mistaken. Certainly, there is an increasing disillusionment with the revolutionary movement, but, as late as 1660, Milton rallies to its defence in his *The Ready and Easy Way to Establish a Free Commonwealth*. [2] And even here there is evidenced a rationalistic optimism which makes the proposals outlined seem, in the given historical context, hopelessly utopian. But, in particular, it seems to us that *A Treatise on Christian Doctrine*, which was almost certainly written after 1654, is, in effect, a summing up of the whole of Milton's previous intellectual development. The real shift in Milton's view of the world comes, we would argue, with the Restoration in 1660, and receives artistic expression in the three longer poems, *Paradise Lost, Paradise Regained,* and *Samson Agonistes. Paradise Lost* was, of course, probably begun before the Restoration, but it was not published until 1667 and, almost certainly, the bulk of it was composed after 1660. Furthermore, the work must have entailed a great deal of revision, and so it would seem legitimate to treat it as essentially a post-Restoration work. I intend, therefore, to consider Milton's works as falling into two main phases: those which express the world vision of reason triumphant, and those which express the world vision of reason embattled.

In considering each of these two main phases we will necessarily employ slightly different analytical techniques. For, in so far as we are concerned with a sociology *of literature,* and not merely with a sociology of seventeenth-century English thought, our prime object of study must be the three longer poems. It is the last poems which, in fact, constitute Milton's major *literary* legacy. Who, after all, apart from professional scholars, today reads *L'Allegro* or *Il Pensero?* We shall therefore attempt to develop, in the next chapter, an account of these three poems which, following Goldmann's methodological prescriptions, conceives of *each* of them as a *literary totality.* By contrast, our analysis of the pre-Restoration writings, in this chapter, will be concerned not so much with an account of each particular work as with a 'reading' of the whole of those writings intended at elucidating the underlying categories which inform the whole system. And the reasons for adopting these differing approaches should be clear. We are involved, in this chapter, with, to use Goldmann's terms, the process of explanation rather than that of comprehension. The literary objects which we are concerned ultimately to *comprehend* are *Paradise Lost, Paradise Regained,* and *Samson Agonistes.* But in order to effect that comprehension it becomes necessary to develop, out of an analysis both of Milton's pre-Restoration works and of the central pattern of development of seventeenth-century English history, a model of the Miltonic world vision, the function of which is primarily *explanatory.* Since our purposes in this chapter are essentially those of sociological explanation, rather than those of literary comprehension, our attention will be mainly focused on the prose writings of the revolutionary period itself (1640–60), for it is there that the structure of the world vision is elucidated in its most comprehensive form. The poetry of both the pre-revolutionary and the revolutionary periods, and in particular the former, is certainly interesting from the standpoint of understanding Milton's *individual* poetic development (i.e. his increasing mastery of problems of poetic technique, etc.). But it does not allow us that same access to Milton's view of the *world* which is provided by the prose writings. The earlier poems are almost all short poems. In the work of an as yet intellectually immature poet, we could not reasonably expect to find any clear articulation of the complex structure of a world vision in poetry of such length. Furthermore, they are often intended primarily as experiments in form, and, as such, reveal very little of Milton's own deeper beliefs. The transparent absence of any real emotional commitment to his subject matter in the early *On the Death of a Fair Infant*, written when Milton was only nineteen, has often been commented on. Many of the earlier poems are simply exercises in the art of poetry, and often unsatisfactory ones at that. Milton himself discarded his unfinished *The Passion* with the wry observation that its subject was 'above' his years. [3] And his seventh sonnet, written as late as 1632, indicates Milton's own dissatisfaction with his early poetic achievements:

> How soon hath Time, the subtle thief of youth,
>   Stol'n on his wing my three and twentieth year!
>   My hasting days fly on with full career,
>   But my late spring no bud or blossom shew'th [4]

Since, then, we are concerned with Milton's early writings only in order to construct an account, in this chapter, of the fundamental underlying categories which are essentially those developed prior to 1660, and, in the next chapter, of the specific conjunctural organisation of those categories necessitated by the specific problem of the Restoration, we would argue that a fairly 'cavalier' treatment of the early poetry is here appropriate.

In our earlier discussion of rationalism as a world vision, we defined its central categories as, firstly, the discrete rational *individual*, secondly, *freedom from external constraint*, and thirdly, *freedom from passion*. We added that, in the case of Protestant rationalism, *God* is present in the world only through the medium of the discrete rational individuals who actually inhabit the world. I intend now to proceed to an examination of the way in which these categories inform and order Milton's system as it developed in the prose writings of the period 1640—60. The earlier poetry will enter into our analysis only in so far as it sheds some direct light on the nature of that system. We shall, however, also attempt an explanation of both the epistemological and aesthetic principles which derive from Milton's rationalist world vision. Clearly, such an explanation will be of some considerable value to our analysis of the three longer poems. There remains, of course, the obvious danger that an exclusive concern, in this chapter, with the prose works of the revolutionary period will result in a partial and therefore necessarily distorting account of the pattern of Milton's intellectual development. It might well be objected, for example, that the earlier poetry, rather than merely inadequately articulating the same world vision as that expressed in the prose works, actually articulates a different world vision altogether. If this were the case then Milton's rationalism would be a product of the 1640s, and of the Revolution itself, rather than of the pre-revolutionary period. Some form of 'check' on our hypothesis therefore becomes necessary. We shall, then, conclude this chapter with an account of *Comus*, the longest of the earlier poems and thus the one which permits the clearest expression of Milton's underlying value-system, an account designed to test for the presence or absence in the early poetry of those rationalistic categories which inform the prose writings of the revolutionary period. *Comus* will be, as it were, the litmus paper for this the first part of our experiment in sociologically informed textual analysis.

1 The Discrete Rational Individual

As a Christian, Milton, of course, subscribes to the belief that in the beginning there was God, and that God subsequently created man. But the man which God created is characterised, in Milton's view, by his possession of *individual reason* and *free will*. This particular conception of man is central to the whole of Milton's polemical writings. It underlies much of his attack on the powers of bishops and presbyters, of regal tyrants and censors. In the *Areopagatica*, for example, he explicitly argues for promiscuous reading on the grounds that God has entrusted man 'with the gift of reason to be his own chooser'.[5] And this gift is in no sense arbitrary or accidental. Rather, it is of the very essence of man as man: 'Many there be that complain of divine Providence for suffering Adam to transgress. Foolish tongues! when God gave him reason, he gave him freedom to choose, for reason is but choosing; and he had been else a mere artificial Adam'.[6] The most serious and sustained account of Milton's doctrine of the essential nature of man is to be found, however, not in the earlier polemics, but rather in the work which the poet came to regard as his theological masterpiece, the later *Treatise on Christian Doctrine*. There Milton attempts to define the precise relationship between divine necessity and human freedom. His solution to this problem needs to be situated against the background of current Presbyterian and Calvinist accounts. As we saw earlier, Prynne had maintained, in conventional Calvinist fashion, that the whole of human history, including the election or reprobation of each and every individual, had been predestined by God at the beginning of time. This notion led Prynne necessarily to the conclusion that 'there is not any such free will, any such universal or sufficient grace communicated unto all men, whereby they may repent, believe, or be saved if they will themselves'.[7] Thus, for the Calvinistic Presbyterians, man ceased to be an effective moral actor. For Milton, however, such a solution is entirely unacceptable; were it true, it 'would entirely take away from human affairs all liberty of action, all endeavour and desire to do right'.[8]

The problem is nonetheless a serious one: in the face of an omnipotent and omniscient God, there would appear to be very little room for human freedom. Milton's solution is contained in the notion that the omnipotent God deliberately willed human freedom into being, that 'the Deity purposely framed his own decrees with reference to particular circumstances, in order that he might permit free causes to act conformably to that liberty with which he had endued them'.[9] Such a conclusion is only tenable, of course, if one postulates a radical distinction between certainty, on the one hand, which follows from divine omniscience (i.e. prescience), and necessity, on the other, which would follow from divine determinism (i.e. predestination). And Milton explicitly endorses that distinction: 'nothing happens of necessity, because God has foreseen it; but he foresees the event of every action, because he is acquainted with their natural causes, which in pursuance of his own decree, are left at liberty to exert their legitimate influence. Consequently the issue does not depend on God who foresees it, but on him alone who is the object of his foresight.'[10] For Milton, then, the outcome of human action, both in this world and the next, is a direct consequence of that action itself and not of any external agency. The divine decree of salvation/damnation is 'universally conditional'[11] upon human endeavour. In this manner, Milton is able to reconcile his belief in

God with the characteristically revolutionary-bourgeois, and Enlightenment, notion of man as agent, as the maker of his world, the shaper of his own destiny, a notion which still finds faint echoes in modern sociological 'action theory'. At one point in the argument, the specifically bourgeois nature of this conception is precisely articulated. In so far as it professes a belief in predestined salvation and damnation, Calvinism, Milton notes, 'cannot avoid attributing to God the character of a *respecter of persons*, which he so constantly disclaims'.[12] Here Milton expresses the central notion contained within the conception of bourgeois right, the notion of free and equal individuals standing in the face of impersonality, the impersonality of God, of the law, of the democratic process, of the market. It is not God, but bourgeois society, and more particularly the ideal society as conceived by bourgeois revolutionaries, which is no respecter of persons, which sweeps aside the particular personal privileges of the feudal order, and erects in their stead the ideal of impersonal rationality. Thus Milton rescues the notion of the individual man as rational agent from the clutches of Calvinistic determinism. But only at a price, the price paid by God who is reduced to the level of first cause, an all-knowing spectator, rather than an all-determining participant, in human history.

Milton is obviously aware of the dangers inherent in this rationalistic individualism, and he attempts to absolve himself from the charge of detracting from God's grace by suggesting that 'the power of willing and believing is either the gift of God, or, so far as it is inherent in man, partakes not of the nature of merit or of good works, but only of natural faculty'.[13] Thus salvation is the product, not of human merit *per se* but of the effective operation of those faculties which God (or 'nature') planted in man. This particular formula is perfectly adequate to Milton's purposes: it keeps God in the picture. But, nonetheless, it clearly fails to redress the balance between activity and passivity in the conception of God's role in the God–man relationship. Whether or not God endowed man with his natural faculties, it remains true for Milton that *man's fate* is determined by the use to which *man* puts those faculties. And although this strongly anti-Calvinist emphasis on the importance of human activity in the attainment of salvation is only explicitly formulated in the un-published, and heretical, *Christian Doctrine*, it is nonetheless present in his thought even in the early 1630s. The closing lines of *At A Solemn Music*, for example, are indicative of such a belief:

O may we soon again renew that song,
And keep in tune with heav'n till God ere long
To his celestial consort us unite,
To live with him, and sing in endless morn of light.[14]

As in the *Treatise*, reconciliation with God is here seen as conditional upon human activity, which is represented, in the poem, both symbolically and literally, as a renewal of pre-lapsarian harmony, which 'we' humans may 'soon' achieve. Despite his regular disavowals, Milton is actually committed to an essentially meritocratic theology: the world is made up of discrete rational individuals whose achievements are conditional upon their own efforts.

Thus far, we have been concerned with rationalistic individualism as a general philosophical category, and at this level Milton's system reveals a remarkable formal similarity with later explicitly atheistic or agnostic rationalisms. But of course Milton was a Protestant. And, as we have already noted, rationalistic individualism finds expression in Protestantism generally, and in Milton's work in particular, primarily in the emphasis on individual scriptural interpretation. In his attacks on episcopacy, for example, Milton asserts the right of the individual to personally interpret the scriptures, without any mediation between himself and God. For Milton, the bishops are merely 'a tyrannical crew',[15] the customary practices which they point to in self-justification merely 'the old vomit of your traditions',[16] and the scholastic authorities whom they cite merely whatever 'time, or the heedless hand of blind chance, hath drawn down from of old to this present, in her huge drag-net, whether fish or sea-weed, shells or shrubs, unpicked, unchosen'.[17] Against all of these Milton pits only this: 'The testimony of what we believe in religion must be such as the conscience may rest on to be infallible and uncorruptible, which is only the word of God.'[18] Milton's precise phrasing is here extremely revealing. He argues, not simply that Scripture must be believed in, but rather that our beliefs must be determined by our consciences, and that our consciences can only really rely upon Scripture. In other words, it is the individual conscience, rather than authority, or even indeed Scripture itself, which is the final arbiter of truth. And, in fact, Milton is actually prepared to discard, or at least to go to extraordinary lengths to explain away, pieces of Scripture to which his conscience cannot subscribe. Thus, for example, in the course of his strenuous advocacy of a liberalisation of the divorce laws, Milton warns that Christ mustn't be taken too literally and suggests, somewhat unconvincingly, that Christ often argues in favour of one excess (in this case, excessively stringent marriage laws) in order to correct another (excessively loose marital behaviour).[19] Finally, Milton is driven to the remarkable conclusion that the 'incoherence of such a doctrine',[20] the doctrine in question being the Biblical account of the Mosaic divorce laws, cannot stand 'against so many other rules and leading principles of religion, of justice, and purity of life'.[21] Just as Scripture is pitted against authority, so conscience is pitted against Scripture. And in the *Treatise on Christian Doctrine* Milton provides a systematic rationale for such a procedure. 'Under the gospel,' writes Milton,

> we possess, as it were, a twofold Scripture; one external, which is the written word, and the other internal, which is the Holy Spirit, written in the hearts of believers . . . although the external ground which we possess for our belief at the present day in the written word is highly important . . . that which is internal, and the peculiar possession of each believer, is far superior to all.[22]

His conclusion could not be more explicit: 'everything', including Scripture itself, 'is to be finally referred to the Spirit and the unwritten word'.[23] Thus Milton's apparent fundamentalism collapses into a peculiar Miltonic *cogito*, the proud and lonely self-assertiveness of the new bourgeois man, a man who can take nothing on trust, since all institutions, all authorities, all doctrines, partake in part of the nature of the old feudal society, a man who is guided only by 'that intellectual ray which God hath planted in us'.[24]

The earlier of Milton's polemical pamphlets, in particular, abound with a sense of the almost unlimited capacities of the individual reason. Thus, in *An Apology for Smectymnuus*, for example, Milton maintains that matters of church government in no way 'exceed the capacity of a plain artisan'.[25] A congregation will easily be able to determine the competence of its minister, he argues, since 'there will not want in any congregation of this island, that hath not been altogether famished or wholly perverted with prelatish leaven; there will not want divers plain and solid men, that have learned by the experience of a good conscience, what it is to be well-taught'.[26] These early pamphlets in fact evidence an uncharacteristically democratic tone, which is almost certainly the product of a very specific conjuncture, that of the all-embracing Parliamentarian alliance. But, for the main part, Milton's understanding of individual reason and free will in no way implies a democratic conception of society. Milton believed that all men possess free will, but he did not believe that all men exercise their free will. For Milton man is only free when his actions are governed by reason:

> know that to be free is the same thing as to be pious, to be wise, to be temperate and just, to be frugal and abstinent, and lastly, to be magnanimous and brave; so to be the opposite of all these is the same as to be a slave . . . You, therefore, who wish to remain free, either instantly be wise, or, as soon as possible, cease to be fools; if you think slavery an intolerable evil, learn obedience to reason and the government of yourselves.[27]

Milton held that, in practice, most men choose not to be governed by reason and that: 'It is not agreeable to the nature of things that such persons ever should be free.'[28] In Milton's system, then, the sinner, the man who freely chooses to subordinate his reason to his passions, thereby loses his freedom. Thus the world is made up of discrete individuals, each of whom possesses the capacity to exercise free will, whilst at the same time it is factually the case that only some men actually do achieve their freedom, that is, do subordinate their passions to their reason. We find, then, at the core of Milton's system a structure of thought which is essentially that of a characteristically bourgeois 'equality of opportunity' model, in which all men have the same opportunities, but only some take advantage of them. This notion gives rise, as we shall see, to the Miltonic version of the theory of election.

2   Freedom from External Constraint

Our second major category was that of *freedom from external constraint*. Since the rational free man will act justly, it follows that any constraints imposed upon him must necessarily deflect him from the path of righteousness. Thus Milton is led to a profoundly libertarian conception of the nature of social institutions in general, and of three particular institutions especially, the *church*, the *state*, and *marriage*. Let us consider each of these in turn. In his initial attacks on prelatical power, Milton had confined himself to a modest advocacy of Presbyterianism as 'the only true church government'.[29] In this context, Milton's 'Presbyterianism' appears to imply little more than a preference for decentralised, as opposed to centralised, church government. Certainly, he shows no sign of sympathy with the centralised Presbyterianism of the Scottish church. But as the party conflict between Presbyterians and Independents began to gather momentum, Milton found himself obliged to define his position more explicitly. In the face of the Presbyterian campaign to establish a Calvinist state church in succession to the old episcopalian one, Milton argued the radical Independent case 'that many be tolerated, rather than all compelled'.[30] Milton's opposition to Presbyterian ecclesiastical totalitarianism is, of course, the theme of his most famous 'political' poem, *On the New Forcers of Conscience Under the Long Parliament*, in which he warned that 'New Presbyter is but old Priest writ large'.[31] But his rejection of the state church also provides the subject matter for the sonnets addressed to Fairfax,[32] Cromwell,[33] and Sir Henry Vane.[34] This last sonnet, a sustained eulogy to the Independent parliamentary leader, praises him not only for his diplomatic skills, but also, and especially, for his understanding of the need for a radical separation of church and state:

> . . . besides, to know
> Both spiritual power and civil, what each means,
> What severs each, thou hast learnt, which few have done.[35]

It should be emphasised that Milton's anti-Presbyterianism represents not so much a change of heart as an application to the particular situation of principles to which he already adhered. As early as 1637, in *Lycidas*, Milton had delivered his verdict on those priests who

> . . . for their bellies' sake
> Creep and intrude and climb into the fold!
> Of other care they little reck'ning make
> Than how to scramble at the shearers' feast,
> And shove away the worthy bidden guest.[36]

In the works of the late 1650s Milton actually elaborates a completed theory of the proper forms of church government, the most systematic account of which is given in the *Treatise on Christian Doctrine*. There he argues for the complete separation of church and state, and for a church consisting of a plurality of autonomous, internally democratic congregations. Each such congregation, 'however small its numbers, is to be considered as in itself an integral and

perfect church, so far as regards its religious rights; nor has it any
superior on earth, whether individual, or assembly, or convention, to
whom it can be lawfully required to render submission';[37] and the
choice of its ministers, of course, 'belongs to the people'.[38] The
Treatise remained unpublished in Milton's lifetime, and indeed for
many decades after. But in a *Treatise of Civil Power in Ecclesiastical
Causes*,[39] which was published in 1659, he outlines a very similar
conception of the nature of church government. Again we find the
firm denial of the state's right to interfere in matters of individual
conscience. And again we find the essentially voluntaristic notions of
particular churches as merely congregations of individuals who come
together, of their own agreement, and for their own purposes, and of
the church in general as merely a plurality of particular churches. The
philosophical basis of Milton's theory of church government is, of
course, his individualism, which leads him necessarily to the notion
that 'no man or body of men . . . can be the infallible judges or
determiners in matters of religion to any other men's consciences but
their own'.[40] But its sociological basis is clearly that essentially
bourgeois structure of thought, or world vision, which sees in the
fusion of epistemological individualism and institutional pluralism
the route to both worldly and spiritual success. We should note,
however, that in practice the limits of Miltonic tolerationism were
almost identical to those actually imposed by the revolutionary
governments: it did not extend to the point of tolerating papism.
Milton, at least, seems to have been rather more aware of the possible
inconsistencies inherent in this position than were most of his fellow
Independents. Hence his admission that the exclusion of Roman
Catholics from toleration is for 'reason of state', which we noted
earlier, and hence, too, his insistence that their religion 'the more
considered, the less can be acknowledged a religion; but a Roman
principality rather'.[41] One can readily understand the unease with
which a systematic liberal-rationalist thinker would regard these
exceptions to the general rule of tolerance. Nonetheless, they follow
necessarily, as we suggested earlier, from the logic of the revolutionary situation itself. In the face of counter-revolution, the revolution
knows no tolerance.

We have already briefly touched upon Milton's theory of *the state*
in so far as it pertains to his theory of church government. We have
noted his repeated insistence on the radical separation of the two. But
Milton's analysis of the nature of the state itself is extremely revealing
as to the central structure of his thought. Just as Milton rejects the

feudal organicist conception of the church in favour of an essentially voluntaristic notion of the church as a constructed institution, formed by individuals in order to meet their own needs, so too he rejects the feudal conception of the state as organism in favour of the notion of the state as construct: 'all nations are at liberty to erect what form of government they will amongst themselves, and to change it when and into what they will'.[42] And just as in religious matters the rational man is essentially free, so too is he in political matters. Thus any form of political government, as any form of church government, which imposes an external constraint upon the exercise of individual rationality, is to be rejected out of hand. 'Being therefore peculiarly God's own,' writes Milton 'and consequently things that are to be given to him, we are entirely free by nature, and cannot without the greatest sacrilege imaginable be reduced into a condition of slavery to any man, especially to a wicked, unjust, cruel tyrant.'[43] But, of course, states do exist, and indeed the Revolutionary Independents did themselves seize the government of a state. And so Milton was faced with the problem of reconciling political order with political liberty. In fact, this leads Milton to his own particular version of the theory of *social contract*, a theory which he discusses briefly in *A Defence of the People of England*, and which he outlines in some detail in *The Tenure of Kings and Magistrates*. There, Milton begins, as one might expect, with the notion of the free, rational individual: 'all men naturally were born free . . . and were, by privilege above all the creatures, born to command, and not to obey'.[44] But, argues Milton, as a result of violence and wrong, men are faced with the need to bond themselves together 'by common league'[45] in order to protect themselves from mutual injury, and thus with the need to create a common authority. 'This authority,' writes Milton,

> and power of self-defence and preservation being originally and naturally in every one of them, and unitedly in them all; for ease, for order, and lest each man should be his own partial judge, they communicated either to one, whom for the eminence of his wisdom and integrity they chose above the rest, or to more than one, whom they thought of equal deserving.[46]

Government established on such a basis is, of course, neither natural nor divine in origin, but rather human, and as such it remains essentially a matter of convenience. Thus it follows, argues Milton, here anticipating Locke, that 'the power of kings and magistrates is

nothing else but what is only derivative, transferred, and committed
to them in trust from the people to the common good of them all, in
whom the power yet remains fundamentally'.[47] And if such is the
case, 'then may the people, as oft as they shall judge it for the best,
either choose him or reject him, retain him or despose him . . . by the
liberty and right of freeborn men to be governed as seems to them
best'.[48]

Like Locke, Milton bases his theory of political legitimation on the
notions of consent and trust, but unlike Locke, he attaches no
particular significance to the role of property in the formation of
political order. At first sight this is somewhat surprising: one might
reasonably have expected a bourgeois theorist, and in particular a
theorist affiliated to a political party locked in mortal combat with the
Levellers, to have made property pre-eminent in his system. But, of
course, the Levellers were by no means the only political opponents
of Independency; both the Royalists and the Presbyterians have also
to be taken into account. Whereas Locke was essentially the theorist
of class compromise—that is, of the particular class compromise
between the propertied classes of England which is enshrined in the
1688 Settlement—Milton was the theorist of a small revolutionary
party which had seized power against the opposition of substantial
sections, probably the majority, of those self-same propertied classes,
and which had found itself obliged to effect an agreement of sorts
with the plebeian Levellers in order to carry through that seizure of
power. In fact, Milton could neither base his theory of legitimation
on property, which would have implied a recognition of the rights of
the Royalists and Presbyterians, nor on *simple* consent, which would
have implied a direct concession to the 'democratic' aspirations of the
Levellers. But, of course, there had to be some basis for the
legitimation of the new revolutionary government.[49] Milton's first
line of defence is the argument that all government, including
monarchical government, is subject to law. Precisely because governments cannot ultimately be trusted, argues Milton, laws were
invented, either framed or consented to by all, 'so man, of whose
failings they had proof, might no more rule over them, but law and
reason, abstracted as much as might be from personal errors and
frailties'.[50] There is one rather obvious practical weakness in such an
argument: the Independent seizure of power was, to say the least, of
somewhat dubious legality. In the *Tenure* itself, Milton merely
contents himself with the bald assertion, in the context extremely
unconvincing, that the trial of the king was indeed perfectly legal.

But in the *Defence*, Milton finally comes to grips with the question of legality: 'if any law or custom be contrary to the law of God, of nature, or of reason, it ought to be looked upon as null and void'.[51] It is not the written law, then, but rather the unwritten law of reason which is paramount. And just as the law of the land is superseded by the law of reason, so too the consent of the country is superseded by the consent, rather perhaps the active participation, of those few who are properly in possession, not of property, but of reason: 'for nothing is more agreeable to the order of nature, or more for the interest of mankind, than that the less should yield to the greater, not in numbers, but in wisdom and virtue'.[52] The legitimacy of the revolutionary government thus comes to rest, not on the consent of the propertied, still less on the consent of the masses, but rather on the consent of the rational minority, the men most *fit* to govern, in fact the Independents themselves.

To summarise: the state is an artificial construct, produced by rational men in order to meet their rational ends; in consequence, its government requires the active consent of those rational free men who live within its boundaries, but only in so far as they are indeed *rational* men and not merely 'men'. Thus Milton, like Cromwell, shows a remarkable lack of interest in the *forms* of government, constitutions, laws, and the like, since each of these merely represents yet another external constraint upon rational behaviour. He is concerned only with the rationality or irrationality of the *content* of government, that is with policies and personalities. It is a political theory which, for all its occasional incoherencies, manages to articulate the revolutionary dynamism of the new government. It also, of course, points to the central political weakness of the revolutionary regime, its failure to gather support from outside the ranks of its own adherents; for who but a rational Independent could subscribe to a political theory, and a political practice, which vested all authority in the hands of the only really 'free' men, the rational men, the Independents themselves?

The institution of *marriage* was the third major social institution to which Milton turned his attention. His divorce tracts are often viewed as mere idiosyncrasy, a simple product of his own somewhat strained domestic relations. But such a judgement is surely unwarranted. Milton's own account of his early prose writings clearly indicates the role which the institution of marriage plays in his overall conceptual framework. In the *Second Defence* Milton explains that, after the defeat of the bishops, 'I had leisure to turn my thoughts to other subjects; to the promotion of real and substantial liberty; which is rather to be sought from within than from without . . . I perceived that there were three species of liberty which are essential to the happiness of social life—religious, domestic, and civil.'[53] Having already discussed religion, Milton explains, he therefore proceeded to the analysis of domestic liberty, and produced a series of tracts on divorce, education,[54] and censorship.[55] There seems little reason to doubt Milton's account; it bears the hallmark of the rationalist thinker carefully planning out his strategy for the construction of an entirely *new*, rational, social world. As with the church and state, so too with marriage, Milton emphasises the constructed nature of the institution; it is 'not a natural, but a civil and ordained relation'.[56] Indeed, Milton deliberately likens the institution of marriage to that of the state, and emphasises that they are both contractual relationships:

> He who marries, intends as little to conspire his own ruin, as he that swears allegiance: and as a people is in proportion to an ill government, so is one man to an ill marriage. If they, against any authority, covenant, or statute, may, by the sovereign edict of charity, save not only their lives but honest liberties from unworthy bondage, as well may he against any private covenant, which he never entered to his mischief, redeem himself from insupportable disturbances to honest peace and just contentment.[57]

The institution of marriage exists for men (and women[58]), for the purposes of 'godly society', for civil ends, and for the marriage bed,[59] and if in any of these respects a particular marriage is unsatisfactory, then it should be dissolved. Given such a voluntaristic conception of the function of the institution, Milton can only object to any form of external compulsion in marriage. Thus the typically feudal practice of arranged marriages, of 'forcing marriages', is condemned as 'savage inhumanity'.[60] So, too, it is none of the church's business to interfere in purely private, domestic relations.[61] Nor is it a matter for the state: 'the law can to no rational purpose forbid divorce, it can only take care that the conditions of divorce be not injurious'.[62] We can see, then, that Milton's analysis of the institution of marriage runs exactly parallel to his analyses of the church and state. In each case, society is conceived as consisting of a set of rational individuals, who enter into voluntary, contractual, relationships with each other for their own rational ends, and who are therefore perfectly free to dissolve those relationships in the event of their proving inadequate to the satisfaction of those ends. As Milton himself writes, 'no covenant, no, not between God and man, much less between man and man, being, as all are, intended to the good of both parties, can hold to the deluding or making miserable of them both'.[63]

We began our analysis of Milton's rationalistic critique of the existing institutional framework by emphasising its essential libertarianism. But in the course of our discussion of the Miltonic theory of the state, we came to note the anti-democratic, indeed positively authoritarian, components within that critique. It is, of course, hardly surprising that this element should come to the fore in Milton's treatment of the political system. For the state is necessarily an authoritarian institution, the power of which, as Lenin aptly remarked, 'consists of special bodies of armed men which have prisons, etc., at their command'.[64] And it is precisely this authoritarianism which becomes most visible at a time of revolutionary crisis: in the wars with the Royalists, at Pride's Purge, at Burford, and during the rule of the Major-Generals, the role of special bodies of armed men was self-evidently pre-eminent. The Independents required their *own* state in order to smash the old absolutist state and the old monolithic state church. 'No army, no toleration' was equally as true as 'No bishop, no King'. It now seems appropriate to turn to a brief analysis of the philosophical basis of Milton's elitist, revolutionary politics, that is, to his theory of election, to which we referred briefly in the previous chapter.

As we have seen, Milton believed that all men are essentially free by nature, and that they cannot therefore properly be subject to the tyranny of external constraint. But as we have also noted, in Milton's view not all men remain true to their nature; many, in fact, surrender themselves up to passion and so lose their freedom. And so Milton's theory of free will gives rise to a theory of election, a theory of, as it were, spiritual aristocracy, which is profoundly anti-democratic. As we have seen in our discussion of his views on predestination, Milton believed that, through God's grace and the sacrifice of Christ, the option of salvation/damnation was made available to all, 'that there is no particular predestination or election, but only general,—or in other words, that the privilege belongs to all who heartily believe and continue in their belief,—that none are predestined or elected irrespectively'.[65] Thus those who stand and those who fall do so according to their own merits: 'the gift of reason has been implanted in all, by which they may themselves resist bad desires, so that no one can complain of, or allege in excuse, the depravity of his own nature compared with that of others'.[66] Now this 'equality of opportunity' model, as we referred to it earlier, is not a merely theological construct. It also has direct political relevance. For Milton believed that the intervention of Christ and the message of the Gospel had given birth to '*Christian liberty*', that is 'that whereby WE ARE LOOSED AS IT WERE BY ENFRANCHISEMENT, THROUGH CHRIST OUR DELIVERER, FROM THE BONDAGE OF SIN AND CONSEQUENTLY *FROM THE RULE OF LAW AND OF MAN*'.[67] Those who freely receive Christ into themselves—that is, those who are governed by reason—thus come to constitute an elect, not only for the purposes of salvation, but also for the purposes of worldly politics. And furthermore, not only is this elect free from the rule of law and of man, but it is also entitled to exercise government over sinners, for 'nature appoints that wise men should govern fools, not that wicked men should rule over good men, fools over wise men; and consequently they that take the government out of such men's hands act according to the law of nature'.[68] As we noted in the previous chapter, this particular conception of election is theoretically superior to the orthodox Calvinist version in two major respects. Firstly, it is premised upon an 'equality of opportunity' model of human behaviour. And secondly, it provides an adequate rationale for the Independent seizure of power: the contempt for law and tradition which we recognised as characteristic of the political practice of Revolutionary Independency, in fact, finds theoretical expression in this doctrine of election. Lest we should have any doubts that the elect are indeed the revolutionary bourgeoisie, Milton specifically describes the sort of men who are fit to rule both themselves and others. They are 'the middle sort, amongst whom the most prudent men, and most skilful in affairs, are generally found; others are most commonly diverted either by luxury and plenty, or by want and poverty, from virtue, and the study of laws and government'.[69]

3   *Freedom from Passion*

We have already touched upon our third major category, that of *freedom from passion*, but let us now consider it in a little more detail. The theme of a radical opposition between reason and passion is central to Milton's system; it is present in almost all of the prose writings, and, indeed, it informs the whole of the great epic poems. Milton's ontology, his doctrine of the essential nature of man, derives explicitly from Plato, but as Saurat[70] and others[71] have pointed out, Milton substitutes a simple reason/passion dualism for the tripartite Platonic distinction between reason, passion, and desire.[72] Like Plato, Milton identifies the human essence with reason *per se* and sees passion as essentially alien to that essence. Only when the passions are thoroughly subordinated to reason is man genuinely human. This particular conception of man is, in fact, one of many which exemplify Professor Gellner's theory of the 'Hidden Prince', that is, the notion of some inner self as more genuinely oneself than any merely phenomenal outer selves can be.[73] This Miltonic version is, of course, to borrow the points of reference of Gellner's own argument, Kantian rather than Darwinian. It is reason rather than passion, the mind rather than the body, which is genuinely human: 'For in human action the soul is the agent, the body in a manner passive. If then the body do out of sensitive force what the soul complies not with, how can man, and not rather something beneath man, be thought the doer?'[74] Since the reason only is properly human, since the body and the passions are essentially 'beneath man', the central ethical imperative in Milton's system becomes the effective regulation of the body and the passions by the mind. Thus: 'Righteousness towards ourselves consists in a proper method of self-government . . . From this, as from a fountain, the special virtues in general derive their origin.'[75] It should be emphasised that this notion of moral freedom as freedom from passion involves an active rather than a passive conception of the individual as moral actor. For in Milton's view this freedom can only be genuinely attained in the course of a sustained struggle with those temptations which are imposed upon the individual both from without and from within. As Milton writes in one of the finest passages of the *Areopagatica*: 'I cannot praise a fugitive and cloistered virtue unexercised and unbreathed, that never sallies out and seeks her adversary, but slinks out of the race, where that immortal garland is to be run for, not without dust and heat. Assuredly we bring not innocence into the world, we bring impurity much rather; that which purifies us is trial, and trial is by what is contrary.'[76] Milton espouses an ethic as *activist* as his politics, and indeed, as we shall see, as his poetics.

This notion of a radical opposition between reason and passion underlies much of the argument in Milton's divorce pamphlets. For

Milton defines the main ends of marriage, improbably enough, as pre-eminently intellectual. 'I suppose it will be allowed us,' he writes 'that marriage is a human society, and that all human society must proceed from the mind rather than the body, else it would be but a kind of animal or brutish meeting.'[77] Milton's ideal marriage is one in which the demands of reason and passion are harmonised, that is, in his view, one in which passion is subordinated to reason. Thus 'a meet and happy conversation is the chiefest and the noblest end of marriage'.[78] However, Milton recognised (and had, indeed, experienced) the fact that a man overtaken by passion can marry 'unwisely'. Such a marriage will not 'satisfy that intellectual and innocent desire which God himself kindled in man to be the bond of wedlock',[79] but rather will serve 'only to remedy a sublunary and bestial burning'.[80] As such it should result only in divorce. Milton's vehement denunciation of the idea that adultery alone can constitute adequate grounds for divorce, clearly follows from his initial rationalistic conception of the nature of marriage. For in Milton's system, the problem of sexual fidelity, which is a purely carnal matter, must, of necessity, be secondary to the problem of intellectual compatibility. To allow divorce only on such grounds, 'the last and meanest', 'is a perverse injury, and the pretended reason of it as frigid as frigidity itself, which the code and canon are only sensible of'.[81] Milton's opposition to this notion of adultery as the only genuine matrimonial offence proceeds in two directions. Firstly, it is expressed as an objection to the idea that sexual infidelity is in itself all that important.[82] And secondly, and for Milton more importantly, it becomes an objection to the notion that a marriage in which there is nothing more than mere sexual fidelity in fact constitutes a real marriage. In Milton's view, even a marriage in which there is complete sexual fidelity, but which also lacks everything else, which is satisfactory only to the passions, cannot be considered a proper marriage. Such a marriage, writes Milton, is one 'wherein the mind is so disgraced and vilified before the body's interests, and can have no just or tolerable contentment', that it becomes 'therefore no marriage'.[83]

Milton's disposition to see sexual passion as passion *par excellence*, which is clearly present in the divorce tracts, is, of course, characteristically Puritan. But in Milton's political writings, too, the struggle between reason and passion reappears as one of the central themes, and there passion receives a somewhat broader definition. In typically

Platonic fashion, Milton formulates a theory of politics in which the inner structure of the state is seen as analogous to that of the soul of the individual man. As Milton writes, 'look what the grounds and causes are of single happiness to one man, the same ye shall find them to a whole state'.[84] Just as reason should govern passion in the soul of the individual, so too, in the state, rational government becomes the primary criterion for political legitimacy. Thus Milton's ideal polity is one subject to the impersonal government of the rule of reason: 'The happiness of a nation must needs be firmest and certainest when no single person, but reason only, sways.'[85] The application of this essentially abstract principle to political reality always remained problematic for Milton. In the earlier pamphlets, he identifies parliament as the main institutional locus of collective rationality;[86] later, he came to view Cromwell's one-man government as the political embodiment of reason;[87] and later still, in the face of imminent counter-revolution, he proposed a 'perpetual senate' of the fittest men in the country as the best form of government.[88] But the central political principle remains constant throughout: political reason should govern over political passion. We should, of course, note that this inability to translate political principle into institutional form was a characteristic weakness, not only of Milton's own political writings, but also of Revolutionary Independency as a whole.

The philosophical basis of this central theoretical and practical weakness derives from a form of psychologism which is characteristic of individualistic rationalist world visions in general. Since the only effective political actors are the discrete individuals out of which the social world is constructed, it must follow that the source of all political virtue (and error) resides in the nature of those individuals. It is this emphasis on individual personal morality which precludes any sustained concern with institutional and/or organisational problems. Thus, for example, when Milton seeks to distinguish tyranny from just government, he does so in terms of whether the ruler is motivated by reason or by passion. A tyrant is one whose government is determined by 'his own brute will and pleasure',[89] who, 'whether by wrong or by right coming to the crown . . . reigns only for himself and his faction'.[90] Milton's critique of popular democracy is couched in similar terms: 'who would vindicate your right of unrestrained suffrage, or of choosing what representatives you liked best, merely that you might elect the creatures of your own faction, whoever they might be, or him, however small might be his worth, who would give you the most lavish feasts, and enable you to drink to the greatest excess?'[91] And his verdict on the Presbyterians, expressed in his twelth sonnet, runs along the same lines:

> Licence they mean when they cry liberty;
> For who loves that must first be wise and good:
> But from that mark how far they rove we see,
> For all this waste of wealth and loss of blood.[92]

This emphasis on the triumph of passion over reason as the source of all political error, of all political disaster, indeed of all political opposition to the views of his own party, is characteristic of Milton's general mode of argument. Milton's verdict on Charles I that 'had his reason mastered him as it ought, and not been mastered long ago by his sense and humour . . . perhaps he would have made no difficulty',[93] is thus typical. So too is his eulogy to Cromwell: 'He first acquired the government of himself, and over himself acquired the most signal victories; so that on the first day he took the field against the external enemy, he was a veteran in arms, consummately practised in the toils and exigencies of war.'[94] Many commentators have been repelled by the viciousness of Milton's polemics against his opponents. But this is no mere stylistic detail, the·product of a mere callousness of mind on Milton's part. Rather, it follows necessarily from, firstly, that psychologism which is endemic to individualistic rationalism, and secondly, the assumption, specific to the Revolutionary Independents, that their own programme represented the embodiment of reason. This latter assumption should take no one by surprise, when we situate it in the context of bloody civil war and revolution: men do not fight and die for causes that they do not believe in. Milton's ultimate explanation of the Restoration, in *Paradise Lost*, in terms of the nation's decline from virtue and reason, is already prefigured in the *Second Defence*: 'Unless that liberty which is of such a kind as arms can neither procure nor take away, which alone is the fruit of piety, of justice, of temperance, and unadulterated virtue, shall have taken deep root in your minds and hearts, there will not be wanting one who will snatch from you by treachery what you have acquired by arms.'[95] In this way all rationalisms ultimately result in the collapse of the socio-political world into the problems of individual psychology.

4 Milton's God

We turn now to what is almost certainly my most contentious point—that Milton's rationalism is logically *atheistic*. I would like now to reiterate some of the points made in our earlier discussion of the rationalist world vision. We argued that theism demands the maintenance of some sort of tension, some sort of separation, between man and God. Thus the central problem of all theologies is essentially that of establishing the correct relationship between God and man. However, if this tension is abolished, if God is liquidated into man, and man into God, then no such relationship is possible. God becomes man, and man becomes God, which implies, since man is presumably in reality unchanged by this process, that God, in effect, ceases to exist. This, we would argue, is precisely what happens in Milton's system. We have already noted the explicit secularism of much of Milton's thought, a secularism which is clearly present in, for example, his belief in the separation of state and church,[96] and in his insistence on the civil nature of marriage and divorce.[97] But this secularism is only a part of a wider world vision which interprets the fate of human beings as a consequence of their own actions, rather than of those of any divine agency, and which attributes central theoretical pre-eminence to the notion of an impersonal 'Reason', rather than to that of a personal God. The latter conception of God as, in effect, identical to reason, informs the whole of Milton's writings. When, for example, Milton seeks to justify the trial of Charles I, he argues, significantly, not that kings are subject to the will of God, but that 'justice is the true sovereign and supreme majesty upon earth'.[98] Similarly, Milton dismisses the Royalist argument that political government is subject to a special divine dispensation: God's intervention is 'visible only in the people, and depending merely upon justice and demerit'.[99]

This reason, which *is* God, is not revealed reason, but rather that reason which is discernible to the rational inquiring mind. It is this particular notion of reason which permits Milton's profoundly non-fundamentalist approach to the problem of scriptural interpretation, his belief 'that there is scarce any one saying in the gospel but must be read with limitations and distinctions to be rightly understood'.[100] In fact, Milton subjects *Christianity itself* to the critical light of reason. He rejects the doctrine of the trinity on the grounds that it offers 'violence to reason',[101] he dismisses the notion of transubstantiation as incompatible 'with reason and common sense',[102] and, of course, as we have already noted, he simply cannot reconcile the Biblical teachings on divorce with his own conception of rationality. The bar on divorce, argues Milton, is

> not only grievous to the best of men, but different and strange from the light of reason in them . . . If the law of Christ shall be written in our hearts . . . how can this in the vulgar and superficial sense be a law of Christ, so far from being written in our hearts, that it injures and disallows not only the free dictates of nature and moral law, but of charity also and religion in our hearts?[103]

All theologies are necessarily faced with the problem of determining the precise relationship between God, on the one hand, and goodness, on the other. Given that that which God wills is good, a proposition which is axiomatic to all Christianity, the problem always remains of deciding whether this is so because that which God wills is necessarily right (i.e. goodness is defined arbitrarily by divine decree), or whether it is so because God wills only that which is right (i.e. God, being good, wills only good things, goodness here being understood as independent of and antecedent to any divine decree). The typical feudal solution to the problem was, of course, located in the former option. For feudal society, based as it is on a relatively static hierarchy of pre-given relations of personal superordination and subordination, normally articulates itself theoretically in terms of political, ethical, epistemological, and hence, necessarily, theological, conceptions which emphasise the legitimacy of the arbitrary, personal commands of social, and hence, too, metaphysical superiors. But Milton's rationalism leads him inevitably to the alternative option. Thus, for example, when Milton seeks to justify the execution of tyrants on the grounds that God has so commanded, he is careful to add that: 'It was not therefore lawful to kill a tyrant, because God commanded it; but God commanded it, because, antecedently to his command, it was a justifiable and a lawful action.'[104] In Milton's system, it is reason, which is also goodness, truth and justice, which is general and allows of no exceptions, rather than God the person, which is the determining factor. And this reason is no divine mystery, but rather something which the individual man can readily apprehend. The *logical* atheism of this position should be readily apparent: a God which is *purely* internal is no God at all.

Thus far, we have approached Milton's God somewhat obliquely. Let us turn now to Milton's own explicit account of that God. It is, of

course, a common criticism of *Paradise Lost* that, whereas the portrait
of Satan is full-blooded and convincing, that of God never comes to
life. And the reason for this is that the God of Milton's theology is
equally unimpressive. Milton's attempt at a proof of the existence of
God is particularly revealing. In the first place, he points to the
evidence of the world, to 'the beauty of its order',[105] which must
testify to the presence of some ordering power. Secondly, Milton
argues that the world must be governed either by a morally
beneficent or by a morally maleficent power, and concludes that,
since the notion of the world as governed by evil is incredible, God
must exist.[106] Finally, he argues that God is necessary in order to
avoid ethical relativism: if there is no deity, then morality must
consist merely in men's opinions, a proposition which would
preclude the existence of any objective criteria of 'right' and
'wrong'.[107] We should note that Milton does not argue simply that
we should believe, that we should obey, that God exists, and that is all
there is to it. Rather, he is concerned to demonstrate that God *must*
exist in order that the truth of *other* necessary propositions (the
notions of the world as orderly, of that order as essentially beneficent,
of morality as an objective absolute) be maintained.[108] The authoritative voice of religion, the imperative command to believe, to
prostrate oneself in the face of the unknowable, is here entirely absent.
Milton's God is a logically necessary construct, an abstraction the
function of which is the justification of those other conceptions which
are actually central to the poet's belief system.

The emptiness of this God becomes apparent whenever Milton
attempts any further analysis. As is well known, Milton's anti-
trinitarianism led him to distinguish sharply between the three
persons of the Christian trinity. God the *Father*—that is, in fact,
in Milton's view, God himself—is characterised primarily by
his extreme lack of definition: he is 'WONDERFUL, and
INCOMPREHENSIBLE',[109] and he is very little else. He does, though,
in Milton's particular version of materialism, play a peculiarly passive
role as the stuff out of which the universe is made. Thus: 'the world
was framed out of matter of some kind or another . . . it appears
impossible that God could have created this world out of
nothing . . . that matter, I say, should have existed of itself from all
eternity is inconceivable . . . There remains, therefore, but one
solution of the difficulty . . . namely, that all things are of God.'[110]
Once again, God is introduced into the scheme of things because he is
logically necessary, because there remains 'but one solution'. And

once the universe has been brought into existence, God is barely active within it. The *Holy Spirit* fares even worse at Milton's hands. The chapter, 'Of the Holy Spirit',[111] in the *Treatise on Christian Doctrine*, contains little more than an embarrassed account of how little we know about this mysterious entity. Elsewhere, the Spirit enters into Milton's system in only one significant respect, that is, as the force or power which illuminates the individual reason. Milton's bewilderment in the face of this particular mystery is, to say the least, somewhat self-evident. Indeed, the notion of God as an agency within *this* world enters into Miltonic theology at only one major point. The active role of the deity is, in fact, taken by the *Son*, who is, significantly, defined in relatively limited, circumscribed terms. The Son is incarnated as Christ, and it is through the medium of Christ that God becomes truly present in the world. But Christ's significance is this—that he is continually incarnated into the elect, that is, into real men actually present in the world. Thus: 'Believers are said TO BE INGRAFTED IN CHRIST, when they are planted in Christ by God the Father, that is, are made partakers of Christ.'[112] Furthermore, as we have already noted, the major consequence of Christ's own intervention into this world is the creation of that Christian liberty which frees the elect from subservience to the laws of man. To summarise: God the Father is little more than a logically necessary moral and material first cause; God the Holy Spirit is virtually a synonym for the rational part of the individual conscience; and God the Son, the active principle in the deity, becomes present in the world only through the medium of the free wills of the individual members of the elect. And so Milton liquidates the Son into man, and man into the Son. God as agent remains merely as a justification of the behaviour of the elect, in practice of the revolutionary Independents. Trotsky's comment that 'Cromwell himself and his "holy" troops considered the realisation of divine commands to be the true end, but in reality the latter were merely the ideological conditions for the construction of bourgeois society',[113] appears extremely apposite.

5   A Note on Milton's Epistemological and Aesthetic Principles

We have outlined the central structural categories of the Miltonic world vision. In so far as these categories enter into Milton's poetry, they do so, most obviously, at the level of content. Thus, for example, the last three great poems are clearly built around the central structural opposition between reason and passion. However, Milton's rationalism also enters into the *formal* structure of his prose and poetic writings, and it does so *via* the medium of his own rationalistic aesthetic and, in so far as it bears upon the former, of his own rationalistic epistemology. It therefore becomes encumbent upon us to attempt a brief sketch of Milton's epistemological and aesthetic principles.

The problem of *epistemology* was, of course, of central significance to the seventeenth century, a century which witnessed the wholesale rejection of that medieval synthesis between pagan antiquity and Latin Christianity which was scholasticism. Scholasticism's central epistemological principle was contained in the notion that 'the "truth" of any proposition . . . depended ultimately, not upon its correspondence with any particular "state of affairs", but upon its being consistent with a body of *given* and of course unquestionable doctrine'.[114] We have already pointed to the clear structural homology between scholastic epistemology and the nature of the feudal social formation. And, as the nascent capitalist mode of production effected a progressive disruption of the older social structure, so, too, new theories of knowledge came into conflict with the older ideational structures. Milton himself fully participated in this intellectual assault upon the theoretical credibility of, to use his own succinct formulation, this 'scholastic trash'.[115] Throughout his prose writings, Milton consistently objects to the archetypically scholastic resort to authority. In *Tetrachordon*, for example, he sternly warns that 'testimony be in logic an argument rightly called "inartificial" and doth not solidly fetch the truth by multiplicity of authors, nor argue a thing false by the few that hold so'.[116] And in the *Second Defence*, he mocks the high intellectual reputation of his Royalist and scholastic opponent, Salmasius:

> Men in general entertained the highest opinion of his erudition, the celebrity of which, he had been accumulating for many years, by many voluminous and massy publications, not indeed of any practical utility, but relating to the most abstruse discussions, and crammed with quotations from the most illustrious authors. Nothing is so apt as this to excite the astonishment of the literary vulgar.[117]

Certainly, Milton himself is not exactly reluctant to cite his own authorities. But he *does* insist, repeatedly, that in themselves 'authorities' prove nothing. In the early controversy over episcopalianism, Milton explicitly defined his position with regard to scholastic 'authoritarianism':[118] 'I shall not intend this hot season to bid you the base through the wide and dusty champaign of the councils, but shall take counsel of that which counselled them . . . reason.'[119] Milton's analytical method, then, unlike that of scholasticism, bases itself, not upon authoritative doctrine *per se*, but upon the criterion of compatibility with reason, and pre-existent doctrine is introduced into the argument only in so far as it is in conformity with that criterion.

Milton's insistence that he would take counsel, not with the councillors, but with the reason which had counselled them, is significant, not only for its anti-scholasticism, but also for its clear articulation of an alternative, and essentially rationalist, epistemology. Given the rejection of authority as a guarantor of epistemological certitude, one is faced automatically with the necessity of identifying an alternative criterion of truth, an alternative platform upon which to stand in order to survey the world. Formally, there are probably an extremely large number of possible alternative criteria. But, in practice, bourgeois thought found itself faced initially with only two major options: the 'state of affairs' to which any particular proposition had to correspond in order to be considered true, could be either external or internal. In the former case, the criterion of truth becomes compatibility with the sense-impressions of external phenomena; in the latter, compatibility with the internal reason. English bourgeois thought has, of course, decisively opted for the first of these two alternatives, that is, for the empiricist option. So much so, in fact, that the seventeenth century 'battle of the books' is often interpreted *simply* as a conflict between the old scholasticism and the new empiricism. Christopher Hill, for example, concludes his work on the intellectual origins of the English Revolution with the observation that 'the ideas which we have been looking at can be linked by the emphasis on experience, experiment, rather than authority; on things rather than words, on the test of the senses and the heart as against intellectual exercises divorced from practice'.[120] Hill's notion of an underlying theoretical connection between scientific empiricism and the Puritan emphasis on 'experience', which has recently re-surfaced in his *Change and Continuity in Seventeenth Century England*,[121] has been severely criticised by, amongst others, J. H. Hexter. In a review of this last work, Hexter astutely observes that 'to link Puritanism to modern science through the term "experiment" by means of a coincidence not of sense but of sound is to establish a connexion on the treacherous sands of a pun'.[122] But Hexter himself only succeeds in adding to Hill's confusion by insisting that the crucial distinction is that between rational scientific experiment, on the one hand, and Puritan emotional experience, on the other. Such is the dead-weight of empiricism in modern Anglo-Saxon thought that Hexter is quite unable to conceive of a rationality which is *rationalist*, rather than empiricist. In fact, the key distinction to be insisted upon is that between empiricism, which is *non-rationalistic*, in that it reduces the human mind to a passive recipient of external sense-stimuli,[123] and rationalism proper, which sees the mind as essentially active, and knowledge as the deliberate construct of human reason. Of course, the Puritan emphasis on internality can result in mere emotional subjectivism. But in the hands of a Milton or a Descartes the internal becomes the rational and thereby establishes a rigorously critical criterion for the analysis of the world.

Milton's own epistemology is, in fact, explicitly rationalist and non-empiricist. Unlike Locke, indeed unlike Hexter, Milton puts no faith in 'the weak and fallible office of the senses'.[124] For Milton, the ultimate source of knowledge is not sensation, but rather reason. The two are directly counterposed to each other in the *Second Defence*, where Milton, replying to Salmasius's jeering at his blindness, writes that 'I would, sir, prefer my blindness to yours; yours is a cloud spread over the mind, which darkens both the light of reason and of conscience; mine keeps from my view only the coloured surface of things.'[125] Milton expresses a similar sentiment in his twenty-second sonnet, addressed to his friend and former pupil Cyriack Skinner, Sir Edward Coke's grandson, on the subject of his blindness:

> . . . What supports me, dost thou ask?
> The conscience, friend, to have lost them overplied
> In liberty's defense, my noble task,
> Of which all Europe talks from side to side.
> This thought might lead me through the world's vain masque,
> Content though blind, had I no better guide.[126]

This preference for the inner certitude as opposed to the external 'coloured surface of things', the 'world's vain masque', clearly follows from the initial premise of a radical dualism between reason and passion, mind and body. Since the reason and the mind are superior to the passions and the body, an epistemology which bases itself on the sense impressions received by the body must necessarily be false. At times, Milton's anti-scholasticism does indeed appear to suggest his adherence to a form of empiricism. For example, Salmasius's absurd, and typically scholastic, argument that, since the superior power is by definition kingly power, kings cannot be dislodged, earns from Milton the scathing retort that 'words ought to give place to things . . . we having taken away kingly government itself, do not think ourselves concerned about its name and definition . . . know for the future, that words must be conformable to things, not things to words'.[127] But Milton is not, in reality, here objecting to the process of definition as such, but rather to the specifically scholastic mode of definition. Elsewhere, Milton elaborates his own rationalist account of the role of definition in theoretical analysis. 'All arts acknowledge,' he writes, 'that then only we know certainly, when we can define; for definition is that which refines the pure essence of things from circumstance.'[128] It is reason, operating through the process of definition, which can alone identify the *essential* nature of things, which can alone separate out the essence from the 'circumstance' which is the beginning and the end of empiricism proper.

Milton's rationalistic epistemology runs through the whole of his prose writings; it is the key thread which runs through the fabric of his work. It shapes the typical method of exposition by which he proceeds from an initial argument according to reason to a subsequent, and secondary, citation of supportive examples. It also permits that stern intellectual rigour with which he consistently exposes the shere *illogicality* of his opponents' arguments. Thus, for example, he contemptuously dismisses the Presbyterians' 'reformist' (and empiricist/pragmatist) opposition to republicanism with the observation that 'it must needs be clear to any man not averse from reason, that hostility and subjection are two direct and positive contraries, and can no more in one subject stand together in respect of the same king, than one person at the same time be in two remote places'.[129] He rejects their 'riddling covenant' as 'seeming to swear counter, almost in the same breath, allegiance and no allegiance'.[130] This coincidence of rationalism and political extremism is by no means accidental. For rationalism necessarily demands a remorseless progression towards the single logically necessary solution to any particular problem. By contrast, the ideology of 'compromise' and 'moderation' involves the blurring of logical distinctions, the avoidance of the logical conclusion to a particular argument in

preference to the discovery of a 'happy medium' located some-
where between the different conclusions to different arguments.
Mathematics knows no compromise; there are only right and wrong
answers. And Milton's rationalist politics adopts a similar procedure.
It is, of course, extremely significant that most English intellectuals
have failed even to begin to comprehend this, the rationalistic core of
Milton's politics. A. J. A. Waldock, for example, found the attempt
at a 'Renaissance', as opposed to a Puritan, reading of Milton entirely
untenable. The underlying opposition in *Paradise Lost* cannot be that
between reason and passion, he argues, quite simply because Milton's
own life gives little evidence of a rational 'temperance': 'in his general
outlook it is rarely a question of finding happy compromises,
comfortable and middle ways: it is a question of finding what is right
(or what appeals to him as such) and of pursuing this, even to
extremes'.[131] So all-pervading has been the influence of pragmatic
empiricism on modern English thought that the very meaning of the
term 'reason' has been subverted. The rational man has given way to
the 'reasonable' man, that is, the man whose refusal to draw logical
conclusions, whose willingness to compromise, marks him precisely
as non-rational—as, in the proper sense, non-reasonable. *The Shorter
Oxford Dictionary* entry under 'reasonable' is surely significant: 'adj. 1.
Endowed with reason. Now *rare*.'[132]

Milton's rationalistic epistemology plays a similarly central role in
his *poetics*. The notion that the seventeenth century witnessed a
considerable reassessment of the place of poetry in intellectual life, a
reassessment which involved an extensive downgrading of the status
of poetry, has become something of a commonplace. As Willey
commented, perhaps conceding too much to Eliot's 'dissociation of
sensibility' thesis, 'during the period of such a systematic effort to
displace older world-pictures by "philosophical" conceptions the
position of poetry was likely to be precarious. For in poetry thought is
not pure; it is working in alliance with the feelings and the will.'[133]
The 'dissociation' argument is not in itself particularly germane.
What is significant is that process by which the empiricist conception
of the mind as a passive respondent to external sense-stimuli, and of
truth as that which is revealed in the course of such responses, effected
a progressive trivialisation of the scope of poetry. In Bacon, Hobbes,
Locke, and indeed Dryden, poetry is conceived as trivial, as an art
form which, because it can tell no truths, is essentially concerned only
with 'entertainment'.[134] But Milton's rationalism leads him in an
entirely contrary direction. Precisely because, in Milton's view, the

rational mind can indeed construct its own truths, poetry, and in particular epic poetry, becomes a suitable vehicle for intellectual expression. Milton's conception of poetry is, in fact, as 'high' as Dryden's is 'low'. And as early as 1628, in his initial salute to the English language, Milton had indicated his ultimate poetic intentions:

> Yet I had rather, if I were to choose,
> Thy service in some graver subject use,
> Such as may make thee search thy coffers round,
> Before thou clothe my fancy in fit sound:[135]

In Milton's view, poetry not only can, but should, concern itself with truths, with 'sublime and pure thoughts'.[136] A great poem, he argues, citing as examples the 'songs' of the Old Testament, should be such as can 'imbreed and cherish in a great people the seeds of virtue and public civility'.[137] Thus he dismisses out of hand the 'libidinous and ignorant poetasters, who having scarce ever heard of that which is the main consistence of a true poem, the choice of such persons as they ought to introduce, and what is moral and decent to each one'.[138] Similarly, he is utterly contemptuous of Bishop Hall's satires. A true satire, Milton writes, ought 'to strike high, and adventure dangerously at the most eminent vices among the greatest persons, and not to creep into every blind tap-house, that fears a constable more than a satire'.[139] This 'grand' conception of poetry as concerned with high truths necessarily involves a commitment on Milton's part to didacticism in literature. Describing the contrast between Donne and Milton in terms unfashionably sympathetic to the latter, Tillyard once noted 'the curious stagnancy of some of Donne's poems. His mind goes in circles, turning back upon itself . . . Milton's mind, on the contrary, presses forward to some end.'[140] The end in question is, of course, normally the realisation of the didactic purpose of the poem. And this Miltonic didactic enters into the poetry, not only at the level of content, but also as a formal organising principle. A recent structuralist account of Milton's poetry points to his 'increasing mastery of the ability to make a poem move from one set of ideas (or state of mind) at the beginning of the poem to another at the conclusion; that is, his ability to make use of a functional rather than an inert structure. This functional structure is progressive or dynamic, and carries the poem from initial perturbation to final insight.'[141] This poetic didacticism, which operates at the levels of both form and content, is intimately bound up with Milton's refusal to separate out 'art' from 'life'. For Milton there could be no such thing as 'art for art's sake'. Literature, in his view, necessarily has a purpose, a purpose which is moral and rational.[142] And this is so quite simply because of his high estimation of literature as a rational practice which deals with truths, and not merely with fictions. Donne and the Metaphysicals had only interpreted the world; for Milton, however, the point of poetry was to change it.

We have argued that Milton's aesthetic constitutes an integral part of his over-all rationalist world vision. But, of course, a purely 'rational' poem is an impossibility. As Willey quite rightly observed, poetry is necessarily a product of the feelings and the will as well as of the reason. Milton's poems have an inner 'logic'[143] but there is much more to them than mere logic. Indeed Milton himself when contrasting poetry with rhetoric argues that the former is 'less subtle and fine, but more simple, sensuous, and passionate'.[144] This particular phrase of Milton's has, in fact, been the cause of some regrettable confusion. In an otherwise not unsuccessful critique of Eliot's theory of the seventeenth-century dissociation of sensibility, Frank Kermode seized hold of it in order to demonstrate that Milton 'believed that poetry took precedence over other activities of the soul because it was simple (undissociated by intellect), sensuous and passionate.'[145] Two major objections to Kermode's assessment immediately spring to mind. In the first place, it seems doubtful that a man who really did believe poetry to take precedence over other activities of the soul would have deliberately shelved his major poetic plans for many years in order to polemicise on behalf of the English revolutionary government. And secondly, and rather more seriously, Milton did *not* say that poetry was simple, sensuous and passionate. Rather, he suggested that poetry was *more* simple, sensuous and passionate than rhetoric, which is, to say the least, an extremely non-contentious assertion.[146] For Milton, as for any poet, poetry necessarily operates at the level of the simple, the sensuous, and the passionate, but it is never confined merely to that level. In this sense, Eliot is quite right to suggest that two quite different readings of *Paradise Lost* are possible one for its sound and one for its sense,[147] or rather, one for the senses and one for the mind. But the two readings are by no means as 'dissociated' as Eliot appears to believe.[148] Rather, the one is, at least in intention, always at the service of the other. Milton's poetic method involves an attempt to affect the reader's reason, both directly through the logical structure of the argument, and indirectly through the appeal to the senses. At times, of course, there *is* a discrepancy between the two 'readings'. But in general Milton's poetic method is by no means as unsuccessful as Eliot suggests. Milton's poetry is essentially a poetry of the reason, in which a separate poetry of the senses, and in particular a poetry of sound, is deployed in the service of the rational 'logic' of the poem. In our account of Milton's poetics we have inevitably found ourselves obliged to anticipate the argument a little, and to refer to the modern literary-critical 'Milton controversy', which is, in fact, primarily a controversy over the poetic merits and de-merits of *Paradise Lost*. A fuller discussion of this problem must, however, be deferred until the next chapter when we will turn to a detailed analysis of the three last poems, in each of which Milton attempts to wrestle with the one great problem posed by the shock of the Restoration, that of establishing an adequate response to the triumph of un-reason over reason.

6   A Note on 'Comus'

Thus far, our account of the Miltonic world vision as it developed in the years prior to the Restoration has been primarily focused on the prose writings of the period 1640—60, and has involved only incidental references to the poetry of the pre-revolutionary and revolutionary periods. At the beginning of the chapter, however, we noted the need for some form of check on our hypothesis, and in particular for an analysis of one of the earlier pre-revolutionary poems designed so as to determine the precise extent to which Milton's rationalism can be seen as pre-dating the revolution itself. We designated Milton's *Maske*, to give its original title, or *Comus*, as it came to be known, as a suitable object for such an analysis. *Comus* was originally written during 1634 and was first performed, at Ludlow Castle, in September of that year. A slightly expanded version of the poem was published subsequently in 1637. We shall confine our attention here to the later and better known version of the work, since Milton's moral didacticism is there rather more explicitly formulated than in the earlier version. But it should be emphasised that, since both versions clearly predate the revolution, the later text provides a perfectly adequate test for our hypothesis of a fundamental underlying continuity between the works of the pre-revolutionary and revolutionary periods.

The masque was, of course, an extremely popular literary genre during the early decades of the seventeenth century in both court and aristocratic circles. But the most striking feature of Milton's own masque is precisely its *atypicality*. In general, the masque was spectacular rather than dramatic, 'light' rather than 'serious'. As Bradbrook observes, of Ben Jonson, 'in the masques and plays the tradition of the Elizabethan song was continued, and a number of Jonson's finest lyrics are in the earlier, simpler manner . . . Here Jonson casts his learning aside.'[149] Milton's *Comus*, by contrast, is both genuinely dramatic and, more importantly, profoundly *serious* in intent. The work is thoroughly permeated by its central didactic purpose, which is, in fact, the construction of a sustained eulogy to the merits of Milton's own Protestant-Platonic rationalism. It is this 'message', the celebration of the superiority of a rational 'virtue' over mere sensuality, which is announced in the opening lines of the poem;[150] which structures the central drama of the poem, that is, the conflict between Comus and his revellers, on the one hand, and the Lady and her allies, on the other; and which is reaffirmed in the Attendant Spirit's concluding admonition:

> Mortals that would follow me,
> Love Virtue, she alone is free;[151]

The *dramatic* nature of the work is, of course, intimately related to its moral purpose. We noted earlier Milton's commitment to an essentially activist ethic, his refusal to praise a 'fugitive and cloistered virtue'. And it is precisely this moral insistence on activism which necessitates the drama of Comus's attempted seduction of the Lady. Indeed, at one point, Milton actually permits the character of the Lady's elder brother to affirm his own deeply-felt belief in trial as the precondition for an effective, realised virtue:

> Yea, even that which mischief meant most harm
> Shall in the happy trial prove most glory.[152]

Milton's departure from the prevalent courtly conventions can thus be seen as indicative of the nature of the moral world vision to which he subscribes.

The central philosophical premise upon which the whole poetic edifice of Comus rests is that of individual freedom and individual moral responsibility. Were the Lady's moral fate in any sense predestined, then it would be of no interest to us, the poem would be emptied of its dramatic content, her trial would be merely a 'show trial', a divinely orchestrated Moscow purge. But this is not the case. The Lady is at all times *at risk*; each twist and turn in Comus's attempt to seduce her into drinking from his glass is so arranged as to bring home to the reader the realisation that, though she *will not* succumb to the sorcerer's 'liquorish baits', she nonetheless *could have* done so. Indeed, Comus's last speech, in which he resolves upon a more forceful assault on the Lady's virtue, the speech punctuated by the imperatives 'Come, no more',[153] and 'Be wise, and taste',[154] is so successful in its heightening of the dramatic tension, that the reader is almost tempted to wonder whether or not she might, perhaps, actually be *forced* to submit. Milton's moral individualism demands, not only that the Lady must be faced with real, non-determined choices, but also that she must face up to those choices *alone*. At the point when we first meet her, she has already been stripped of all possible *external* supports: travelling through a wild and (and as we are aware, although she is not) hostile wood, she has been separated from her only companions, her two brothers, she is lost, and, indeed, she has even been deprived of the stars as a possible guide. She is entirely thrown back upon her own *internal* resources,

> The virtuous mind, that ever walks attended
> By a strong siding champion, Conscience.[155]

And she remains alone throughout the whole of her confrontation with Comus. Only when she has proved her ability to withstand his temptations, his 'dear wit and gay rhetoric', do her brothers, and later the Nymph, Sabrina, come to her aid. The moral universe of Comus is thus essentially meritocratic; divine grace, symbolised by Sabrina, is only extended to those who have earned it. The poem's closing lines remind us that

> . . . if Virtue feeble were,
> Heav'n itself would stoop to her.[156]

But that virtue must be evidenced in the first place if Heaven is to be thus forthcoming. As Sabrina herself tells us, it is her office 'To help ensnared chastity',[157] and the implication is surely there that it is chastity, and not merely ensnarement, which elicits such aid.

If *Comus's* central philosophical premise is its moral individualism, then its central organising principle is that of the conflict between reason and passion. The Attendant Spirit's opening address to the audience, with its pointed contrast between the 'frail and feverish being' of this earth and 'the crown that Virtue gives',[158] clearly establishes that structural framework within which the rest of the poem will function. This theoretical opposition between reason and passion is, of course, personified in the opposition between the Lady and Comus. She, on the one hand, is the living embodiment of the Miltonic ideal of rational liberty. Trapped in Comus's palace, and beset by his sorcerish enchantments, she defiantly affirms her belief (and Milton's) in the power of inner freedom to withstand all external oppressions:

> Fool, do not boast,
> Thou canst not touch the freedom of my mind
> With all thy charms, although this corporal rind
> Thou hast immanacled, . . .[159]

Comus, by contrast, is the perfect representation of Milton's un-free man, the man who is the slave of his own sensuality, whose reason is subordinated to his passions. His opening speech, which in the same breath sings the praises of unbridled sensuality and mocks the claims of 'Rigor' and 'Advice', tells us everything there is to know about Comus:

> Meanwhile welcome joy and feast,
> Midnight shout and revelry,
> Tipsy dance and jollity.
> Braid your locks with rosy twine
> Dropping odors, dropping wine.
> Rigor now is gone to bed,
> And Advice with scrupulous head,
> Strict Age, and sour Severity,
> With their grave saws in slumber lie.[160]

This *opposition* between reason (the Lady) and passion (Comus) is heightened to the level of explicit *conflict* only in the 'temptation' scene which takes place in Comus's palace. There, it is most expressly articulated in the actual *content* of the debate which takes place between them and, in particular, in their dispute over the nature of Nature itself. For Comus, Nature is essentially sensuous and carnal, her abundance the occasion only for excess:

> Wherefore did Nature pour her bounties forth
> With such a full and unwithdrawing hand,
> Covering the earth with odors, fruits, and flocks,
> Thronging the seas with spawn innumerable,
> But all to please and sate the curious taste?[161]

In his view, it is precisely that 'pet of temperance' which is unnatural, which turns men from Nature's sons into her bastards.[162] For the Lady, however, it is reason and not passion, temperance and not indulgence, which are natural. The naturalness of Nature consists, not in the abundance of a chaos of sensations, of odours and tastes, but rather in the rational and unchanging laws which impose order and structure on those sensations:

> . . . she, good cateress,
> Means her provision only to the good,
> That live according to her sober laws
> And holy dictate of spare Temperance.[163]

The conflict between reason and passion also shapes the very language with which Comus and the Lady represent their respective positions. Her speeches are characterised by a rational consistency and a moderation of language, which is at times almost prosaic. Her 'lecture' to Comus on social injustice, which is incidentally an almost perfect exposition of the bourgeois world vision as it developed in opposition to the older feudal-cavalier world vision, is prosaic and rational in the extreme. It is shorn of all verbal excess, of all metaphorical superfluities; it reads, indeed, almost as if it were an extract from a revolutionary pamphlet:

> If every just man that now pines with want
> Had but a moderate and beseeming share
> Of that which lewdly pampered luxury
> Now heaps upon some few with vast excess,
> Nature's full blessings would be well dispensed
> In unsuperfluous even proportion,
> And she no whit encumbered with her store;[164]

Comus's speeches, by contrast, are saturated with an ever-present sensuousness and sensuality, and a consistent and persistent reference back to the concrete, which is expressed in an abundance of visual and tactile imagery. His language is the language of odours and tastes, of fruit and flocks, of ore and gems.[165] The chaos of Comus's mind, and the rational purity of the Lady's, inform not only their respective languages, but also their respective modes of argument. Throughout the entire scene, the Lady never once moves from her resolute commitment to the value of a rational temperance. She is rigidly consistent throughout. Indeed, Comus's use of his magic powers to paralyse the Lady actually permits her physical immobility to function as an external visual symbol of this inner consistency, of her determination not to be 'moved' intellectually by his philosophy of intemperance and indulgence. Comus's mind, however, is all change and flux. He moves from a gently seductive persuasiveness at the beginning of the scene,[166] through a sustained panegyric on indulgence,[167] a return to the initial gentle flattery,[168] and a brief moment of self-doubt (not as to purpose, but only as to the likelihood of success),[169] to his final outburst of impatient and threatening anger.[170] He is as inconstant, and as mobile, as she is constant. Thus the entire scene, as it operates at the levels of meaning, of language, and of mentality (i.e. state of mind/mode of argument), is organised around the central structural opposition between unchanging reason and all-too-changeable passion.

The conflict between reason and passion is fought out not only between the good characters and the bad characters, but also within the souls of the good characters. For Milton's ontology articulates a view of each and every man as divided between reason and passion. The Miltonic good man is no empty rational cypher, but rather a real man whose reason must subjugate his own very real passions. Whilst Comus's reason is entirely absent, for he alone of all the characters is entirely wicked, completely in the thrall of his passions, the good human characters are not only rational, but are also beset by their own passions. At the moment when we first encounter the Lady, even she is disturbed by a 'thousand fantasies'.[171] But her resolute moral purity readily permits a decisive internal victory over her doubts and fears, since

These thoughts may startle well, but not astound
The virtuous mind, . . .[172]

If the Lady achieves a quick and decisive conquest of her passions (in this case, of fear), the process is much more protracted in the case of her two brothers. The younger brother is clearly troubled by doubts and anxieties from the very beginning. Indeed, only the presence of his elder brother secures him from blind despair. But the elder brother is himself by no means a paragon of rational virtue. His utter confidence in an ultimately beneficent outcome is, in effect, the smug self-confidence of a 'cloistered virtue', of a reason born out of ease, rather than forged out of trial. His initial response to his brother's alarm suggests an unpleasant complacency which is surely the product of an intemperate sloth rather than of any rational temperance:

> Peace, brother, be not over-exquisite
> To cast the fashion of uncertain evils;
> For grant they be so, while they rest unknown,
> What need a man forestall his date of grief,
> And run to meet what he would most avoid?[173]

As a result of the Attendant Spirit's intervention, disguised as Thyrsius, the two brothers do, of course, eventually surmount their own particular forms of moral paralysis. The younger casts aside his fears, the elder his unimaginative complacencies, and they set out on their mission of rescue. And so their own 'small' internal victories, which lead to the subsequent external victory, function so as to underline the central theme of the poem, which is primarily articulated in the 'greater' struggle between the Lady and Comus. The Spirit's second Song, presenting the Lady and her brothers to their parents, at the end of the masque, clearly stresses the fact that we have witnessed not one, but three, triumphant contests between reason and passion:

> Noble Lord, and Lady bright,
> I have brought ye new delight.
> Here behold so goodly grown
> Three fair branches of your own;
> Heav'n hath timely tried their youth,
> Their faith, their patience, and their truth,
> And sent them here through hard assays
> With a crown of deathless praise,
>   To triumph in victorious dance
> O'er sensual folly and intemperance.[174]

Despite the elder brother's patent moral inadequacies, at the beginning of the poem at least, his speeches do nonetheless often function as a vehicle for Milton's own ideas. Indeed, as we have already noted, it is, paradoxically enough, the elder brother who expresses Milton's belief in trial as the active test of virtue. And this is so because, although both brothers have their own reasons and passions, just as the Lady has hers, the relationship between the two brothers also operates as a type of counterpoint to the main plot (which is embodied in the Lady—Comus opposition) in which the elder brother comes to symbolise reason, and the younger passion. Thus, for example, in the face of his brother's panic-stricken fear, the elder brother resolutely affirms his belief in a very Miltonic, and very Protestant, rationalistic individualism:

> He that has light within his own clear breast
> May sit i' th' center and enjoy bright day,
> But he that hides a dark soul and foul thoughts
> Benighted walks under the mid-day sun;
> Himself is his own dungeon.[175]

And similarly, it is the character of the elder brother who is permitted to explain Milton's own conception of the relationship between the reason/the mind and the passions/the body. Purity of the soul, here exemplified in chastity, he explains, will purify the body and thus:

> . . . cast a beam on th' outward shape,
> The unpolluted temple of the mind,
> And turns it by degrees to the soul's essence,
> Till all be made immortal . . .[176]

The converse process is, of course, that by which the impure lusts of the body come to corrupt the soul:

> . . . when lust,
> By unchaste looks, loose gestures, and foul talk,
> But most by lewd and lavish act of sin,
> Lets in defilement to the inward parts,
> The soul grows clotted by contagion,
> Imbodies and imbrutes, till she quite lose
> The divine property of her first being.[177]

There could be no clearer statement of Milton's own very Protestant, and at the same time very rationalistic, conception of the corrupting power of the body and the purifying power of the mind.

Thus far, we have centred our analysis on the internal structure of *Comus*, and on the problem of determining the extent to which that structure can be seen as dependent on the wider structure of the Protestant rationalist world vision. But this rationalism developed in deliberate *opposition* to an alternative social class world vision, that of the neo-feudal aristocracy and its functionaries who serviced the absolutist state machine. And, in fact, *Comus* itself necessarily partakes of the oppositional character of the world vision as a whole. We have already observed the manner in which, in Milton's prose writings, passion comes not only to stand as an abstract moral category, but also to be explicitly identified with the forces of political reaction. And it needs to be emphasised that in *Comus*, too, reason and passion are not simply universal abstractions, and the Lady and Comus not merely the personifications of such abstractions. On the contrary, they each have very specific and concrete social referents. For *Comus* depicts the clash, not only of abstract principles and of personalities, but also of different social class world visions. We have already pointed to the specifically *bourgeois* nature of the Lady's *temperate* rationalism: her account of the just society is that of the aspirant bourgeois revolutionary. But as surely as she is a Puritan revolutionary, so too Comus is the archetypal cavalier. Milton deliberately and explicitly identifies the character of Comus with the forces of political and social conservatism. He is both wealthy and powerful: his home, after all, is a 'stately palace'. When the Lady, deceived by Comus's disguise as a shepherd, accepts his offer of aid and assistance,

> Shephard, I take thy word,
> And trust thy honest-offered courtesy,
> Which oft is sooner found in lowly sheds
> With smoky rafters, than in tap'stry halls
> And courts of princes, where it first was named,
> And yet is most pretended . . .[178]

she is expressing a traditional pastoral sentiment. And yet, in Milton, it is perhaps not so traditional. For Comus does indeed have a princely palace, and her trust in him is indeed misplaced.

Comus's revelry is, in fact, the revelry of the aristocratic and courtly cavaliers. Indeed, his invocation of the delights of 'joy and feast', 'tipsy dance and jollity', is profoundly reminiscent of the cavalier lyrics of the period. When Comus addresses his followers thus

> What hath night to do with sleep?
> Night hath better sweets to prove,[179]

one is easily reminded of, for example, William Cartwright's 'Drinking Song':

> Now, then the sun is fled
> Down into Tethys' bed,
> Ceasing his solemn course awhile. What then?
> 'Tis not to sleep, but be
> Merry all night, as we:[180]

Comus's sexual libertinism, overtly sensual, yet lacking in all suggestion of emotional commitment, is similarly representative of contemporary cavalier morals.[181] Comus not only sounds like a cavalier, but he also, apparently, looks like one. When the two brothers have learned of their sister's fate, the elder pledges himself either to force Comus to relinquish his victim 'Or drag him by the curls to a foul death'.[182] And who, in the England of the 1630s, but a cavalier, would have 'curls'? It is significant, too, that Milton chooses to associate the character of Comus with the notion of priesthood. At the beginning of the poem, Comus calls to his revellers 'Come, let us our rites begin',[183] and towards its end, he dismisses the Lady's clear superiority in rational debate with the contemptuous retort:

> There is mere moral babble, and direct
> Against the canon laws of our foundation[184]

The Comus who stands for 'rites' and 'canon laws' against 'mere moral babble' speaks the language of Archbishop Laud.[185] And this intentional identification of the cavalier with the cleric should not surprise us; the William Cartwright whose 'Drinking Song' we quoted earlier was both courtier and Anglican priest. The Milton who wrote *Comus* was not yet an apologist for regicide. But the central categories of the Protestant rationalist world vision, categories which would ultimately provide the conceptual 'skeleton' for such an apology, are clearly present in the poem. And, indeed, Milton had already begun to put flesh upon that skeleton; in the person of Comus he had already identified the main characteristics of the future enemy. We have argued that Revolutionary Independency, as a political force, represented the most class-conscious sections of the mid-seventeenth-century English bourgeoisie, that is, those sections which were ultimately prepared to risk a political mobilisation of the masses in order to overthrow the feudal state machine and establish a thorough-going bourgeois republic. In the course of both the political struggles of the 1630s and the revolutionary upheaval of the 1640s and 1650s, this section of the bourgeoisie produced a particular world vision, a specifically English and Protestant version of rationalism. This world vision is structured, as we have seen, around the general rationalist categories of firstly, the discrete rational individual, secondly, freedom from external constraint, and thirdly, freedom from passion. To this is added a specifically Protestant conception of God as present in the world only through the medium of his elect. And this theory of election serves both to provide an 'equality of opportunity' model of how a bourgeois society should function, and as an ideological legitimation for the seizure of power by a small, determined minority. Furthermore, this rationalism gave birth to its own specific epistemological and aesthetic principles. We have pointed to the central importance of this set of categories as constitutive of the structural framework, the realm of discourse, within which developed Milton's own pre-Restoration writings, and in particular his prose works. And we have carried through a detailed examination of the poem *Comus* in order to demonstrate the underlying unity which pertains to the works of the pre-revolutionary and revolutionary periods. This internal philosophical unity is, of course, indicative of an external sociological unity. The philosophical vision of the 1640s emerges logically from that of the 1630s just as the Revolution of the 1640s emerges sociologically from the repression of the 1630s. But, with the collapse of the republic and the Restoration in 1660, this pattern of development, at the levels of both political practice and intellectual practice, was abruptly cut short. The failure of the Commonwealth unleashed the counter-revolution, and brought with it the returning priests and cavaliers. The Good Old Cause lay vanquished, and Comus, restored once more to his stately palace, returned to his revels. A White Terror, relatively restrained, but a terror nonetheless, stalked the land. Harrison, Carew, Cook, Peters, Scot, Clement, Scroope, Jones, Hacker, Axtel, and later Milton's hero, Sir Henry Vane, were executed; the bodies of Cromwell, Ireton and Bradshaw were disinterred and their heads displayed on pikes; Milton himself was forced into hiding and later arrested and imprisoned, and his major political tracts burned by the state authorities; and the Corporation Act of 1661 unleashed a wave of religious persecution, which was to claim amongst its more distinguished victims both John Bunyan and George Fox. The return of the Stuart monarchy in 1660 imposed upon Milton a particular problematic: how to account for the defeat of reason. And it is Milton's wrestling with this problem which gives birth to the later poems. In the next chapter, we will turn to an analysis of the three longer poems, and of the world vision of reason embattled which they each embody.

5 Reason Embattled

In the previous chapter, we outlined the structure of the Miltonic world vision as it developed in the years of struggle and triumph. In this chapter we turn to the problematic of reason embattled, and to a direct analysis of the three longer poems. It should be emphasised, however, that the central structure of the rationalist world vision remained intact even in the face of the Restoration. In each of the three last poems, the notions of the discrete rational individual, and of freedom from both external constraint and passion, recur as central *leitmotifs*. The Restoration effects a transformation, not of the central categories themselves, but rather of their specific conjunctural organisation. In the earlier works, those categories had pointed remorselessly towards an essentially optimistic outcome: the Lady was rescued from Comus, the English people were twice successfully defended and, even at the bitter end, there yet remained a ready and easy way to save the Commonwealth.[1] But that ready and easy way proved elusive. The coffers of the City of London were closed to the revolutionary government, and General Monck sold his second kingdom for filthy lucre.[2] The defeated rationalists were thus faced with the problem of developing an adequate response to the triumph of un-reason over reason. This entailed, for Milton, and for the ex-Independents as a whole, a reorganisation of the central rationalist categories so as to focus their attention upon the specific problem of defeat. As we suggested earlier, two main responses were possible, the one *personal* and individualist, which espouses a stoic resistance to the irrationalities of the world, the other *political* and *historical*, which situates the present defeat of reason within the context of an overall historical schema in which reason is seen as necessarily ultimately triumphant. Each of the last poems has as its central object the problem of defeat, either actual or potential, and each of these responses to defeat are there articulated. We turn now to a general account of the way in which the problem of defeat is posed and resolved in each of the three longer poems.

1   The Problem of Defeat: From Epic to Tragedy

In our earlier discussion of Milton's poetics, we remarked upon both
his commitment to moral didacticism, and his rational and logical
mastery of the organisation of his poetic materials. And nowhere are
these aspects of his work more self-evident than in the longer poems.
Milton's own account of the *moral purpose* of *Paradise Lost*, given in
the opening invocation to the muse, is, of course, well known:

> . . . what in me is dark
> Illumine, what is low raise and support;
> That to the highth of this great argument
> I may assert Eternal Providence,
> And justify the ways of God to men.[3]

But it should be emphasised that this 'introduction' to *Paradise Lost* is
almost equally applicable to *Paradise Regained* and *Samson Agonistes*.
Each of the three longer poems is concerned, admittedly in very
different ways, to justify the ways of God to men. And the high
argument which is broached in the opening lines of *Paradise Lost* only
reaches its final conclusion in the last speech of the Chorus towards the
end of *Samson Agonistes*:

> All is best, though we oft doubt,
> What th'unsearchable dispose
> Of Highest Wisdom brings about,
> And ever best found in the close.[4]

If each of the three poems is directed to the same *purpose*, that of
justifying the ways of God to men, it should be evident that each of
them is also premised upon the existence of the same *problem*, that
of an apparent injustice in the ways of God. The significance of this
problem should not be underestimated. In general, theologies are
accusatory and imperative, rather than justificatory and apologetic, in
tone. In so far as the priest, prophet, or poet mediates between God
and man, his normal function is twofold: in the face of God, he begs
forgiveness for man, and in the face of man, he pronounces sentence
in the name of God. For the religious man, it is normally man, rather
than God, whose ways require justification. But in Milton's last
poems, the polarities have been reversed: man questions and accuses,
and God must justify himself. In a word, religion has become

problematic. And the reasons for this are not difficult to discern. When Milton had sought to prove the existence of God, in the *Treatise on Christian Doctrine*, he had specifically argued, as we have seen, from the evidence of the beauty of the world's order, and from the notion that the ordering principle in question must be morally beneficent.[5] In the years prior to 1660, such a position retained an inherent credibility for the triumphant Independents. Their repeated victories over their political opponents seemed to provide ample evidence of both their own moral rectitude and, more importantly, of the justice of God himself. Thus, for example, Milton could argue with some conviction that 'certainly in a good cause success is a good confirmation'.[6] But with the Restoration, success had apparently gone to the worse cause, to the cause of un-reason and injustice. The ways of God were suddenly thrown into doubt. And, of course, if the order which governs the universe is not morally beneficent, then the very existence itself of God is also thrown into doubt. For Milton it became imperative to seek out a new justification, and to explain the specific problem of the defeat of the godly. It is this concrete social and political problem which poses the general moral problem with which the three longer poems are concerned. Thus, whilst the *general* moral didacticism of *Paradise Lost*, *Paradise Regained* and *Samson Agonistes* follows from Milton's generally rationalist world vision, just as does the moral didacticism of *Comus* and of the prose works, the *specific* moral problem of justification follows from the specific sociopolitical problem of defeat.

In the previous chapter, we suggested the intimate connection between moral didacticism in literature, rationalism as a world vision, and a certain distinctive capacity for *logical and rational organisation* in the practice of literary creativity. Milton's own 'sense of structure', to use Eliot's phrase,[7] has often been remarked upon. Indeed, it is this 'rational' character of Milton's poetry which is its most distinctive feature, and which has marked his work as the object of persistent, and often acrimonious, controversy, even in our own time. For not only is Milton's poetry 'rational', but it is also *uniquely* so. His work is quite unlike any other in the English language. It stands outside the various available 'traditions' in English poetry, and in consequence it tends to defy the aesthetic canons constructed so as to account for those traditions. It is precisely this uniqueness which has provided the fuel for the various 'Milton controversies'. The main features of Milton's poetry, as described by both his champions and detractors, are all, in fact, closely related to this rationalistic 'sense of structure'.

The major modern criticisms, as voiced by Eliot and Leavis, centre on the notion of 'artifice'. Eliot, for example, in his famous, or perhaps infamous, 1936 essay on Milton, argues that Milton's poetic language is merely *artificial* and *conventional*,[8] that his imagery is general, rather than particular, and that his essentially rhetorical style results in a dislocation between the surface 'auditory' meaning of the poem and its inner intellectual meaning. Leavis's critique runs along similar lines. In his view, the major characteristic of Milton's verse is its formalism, a routine stylisation, which exhibits a 'feeling *for* words rather than a capacity for feeling *through* words',[9] and which finds expression, above all, in a latinised English, which is remote from the spoken language, and which is indicative of a deeper, general, sensuous impoverishment.[10] This notion that Milton's poetry is mere 'style', mere form, is, of course, misleading. The intellectual meaning of Milton's poetry is, in fact, extremely explicit, sufficiently so, at least, for both Eliot and Leavis to recognise and reject it.[11] What is true, however, is that there is in Milton's verse no necessary organic unity of form and content, of language and meaning. And indeed, many of Milton's modern apologists, notably Douglas Bush and C. S. Lewis,[12] have recognised that this is so. Lewis, in fact, went so far as to admit that 'Dr. Leavis does not differ from me about the properties of Milton's epic verse . . . He sees and hates the very same that I see and love.'[13] The central feature of Milton's verse, the real object of the 'Milton controversy', is, then, its formalism, its artificiality, its constructedness.

In terms of the organicist aesthetics of Leavis and Eliot, and indeed of Lukács, such artifice is in itself inartistic.[14] Organicist theories of literature do, of course, have a certain appropriateness to the understanding of certain specific literary genres, notably that of the nineteenth-century realist novel, which represents, for both Leavis and Lukács, the epitome of the literary art. But in the case of either the Miltonic epic or, for example, the novels of James Joyce, such theories have little or nothing to say. As Bernard Bergonzi has noted of Leavis's own particular approach: 'This is a perfectly intelligible view of literature, but it leaves out far too much. It quite fails to account for the perennial human desire for the kind of art that asserts itself as art, as something avowedly *other* than the elements of normal human experience.'[15] Bergonzi's precise phrasing should be approached with some caution. For whilst it is certainly true that Milton's epic style is in no sense 'realistic' or 'organic', it is nonetheless no mere example of 'art for art's sake'. Rather, Milton's epic verse is an example of that type of literature which seeks neither to mimic nor to ignore reality, but to comment upon reality through the medium of a specifically literary form of deliberate artifice. Perhaps the point may be clarified by reference to the literature of our own century. In the case of the literary realism of, for example, Thomas Mann and D. H. Lawrence, the paragons of modern literary virtue for Lukács and Leavis respectively, one finds an essentially mimetic notion of the functions of the literary art. In the work of Joyce or Kafka, by contrast, one finds a preoccupation with the problems of literary form and of the psychology of the artist, which might justly be character-ised as art for art's sake. But in the Brechtian epic theatre we find a third type of literature, one which is self-consciously constructed and non-mimetic, but which seeks to establish some kind of statement about the world, a statement which should, ideally, act as a lever on the world, as an instrument for the transformation of reality. And Milton's epic verse is precisely a literary form of this latter type. His is an art which is deliberately artificial, which is non-organic and non-realist, but which nonetheless has as its object the reorganisation of the real world. The coincidence of such a conception of literature in the work of both the seventeenth-century English Puritan, and the twentieth-century German Communist, suggests the possibility, at least, that this particular kind of formalism is, in fact, far more typically 'revolutionary' than the realism which has constituted the main preoccupation of modern Marxist aesthetics. For Milton's formalism is as closely connected to his moral didacticism as Brecht's formalism is to his overtly political didacticism. It is precisely the non-organic nature of Milton's art which permits the explicitness of his moral statement. The intellectual meaning of Milton's verse, a meaning which, in the case of *Paradise Lost*, is so genuinely clear and logical that the poet himself felt able to provide a prose summary of the 'argument', would only be obscured by the kind of poetic organicism which Leavis advocates. In his later essay on Milton, Eliot comes close to recognising this. Commenting upon Milton's versifi-cation, he observes that: 'It is the period, the sentence and still more the paragraph, that is the unit of Milton's verse.'[16] Eliot is, of course, here referring to Milton's famous 'architectonics', his mastery of large structures. But the function of this architectonic quality in Milton's verse is precisely the elucidation of his moral argument. Milton's preference for the abstract statement, rather than the concretely sensuous image, for a poetic effect which is attained through the larger structure rather than through the immediate appeal to the imagination, permits the clear elaboration of what is, in the conventional sense of the term, a complex 'argument'. There is a fine irony here. In general, Milton's critics have subscribed to the view, originally propounded by Eliot, that, in contrast to Donne, Milton is a 'reflective' rather than an 'intellectual' poet.[17] But, of course, as Eliot came later to realise, Donne's much vaunted unified sensibility is a product rather of confusion than of thought.[18] And it is, in fact, Milton who is the more truly 'intellectual' poet of the two, in the specific sense that in his poetry the so-called 'dissociation' between thought and sense is utilised so as to yield primacy to the former.

Generally, Milton's modern apologists have sought to reject the strictures of organicist aesthetics by pointing to the demands of the epic and tragic literary genres within which Milton chose to work, and in particular to those of the former, since it has tended to be *Paradise Lost*, rather than either *Paradise Regained* or *Samson Agonistes*, which has been the major object of the various literary critical controversies. So far as it goes, such a 'defence' is unobjectionable. But the problem nonetheless remains of determining *why* Milton chose to adopt these particular classical models. If Milton's latinised English and rhetorical style derive from the nature of the epic form itself, as Lewis, Bush, and Tillyard[19] argue, then it might still be objected that that form itself is inappropriate to the English language. Bush's response to Leavisite criticisms of Milton's poetry that all such criticisms are equally applicable to the classical Greek and Roman poets[20] seems singularly inappropriate. For, of course, it is Leavis's contention that the English language, *as distinct from* both Latin and Greek, demands a verse form in which 'words seem to do what they say'.[21] Furthermore, the very fact that Milton's *Paradise Lost* is the *only* major epic poem written in the English language suggests the necessity for some sort of explanation of Milton's choice of genre. It might prove valuable here to consider briefly the young Lukács's suggestive remarks on the nature of the epic form, in the earlier chapters of *The Theory of the Novel*. The classical epic, argues Lukács, 'gives form to the extensive totality of life',[22] and as such is essentially the product of 'integrated civilisations'. In the classical civilisations, in which man is essentially one with his word, an extensive totality is directly given in *reality* and therefore the artistic representation of that totality remains possible. By contrast, the novel is, in Lukács's view, the epic of a detotalised age in which the only conceivable totality is a postulated aim, rather than a self-evident given. Significantly, however, Lukács finds in Dante's verse a notable exception to this over-all schema.

Dante's epic, he argues, is 'architectural' rather than 'organic', and it has as its organising principle a hierarchy of fulfilled postulates, attained through a present, actually experienced transcendence of reality, which stands in marked contrast to both the postulate-free organic nature of the Homeric epic, and the world of unfulfilled postulates which structures the modern novel.[23] Dante's epic is, then, 'a historico-philosophical transition from the pure epic to the novel'.[24] Now much of Lukács's account of Dante's verse is, in fact, equally applicable to Milton's own epic. Indeed, a number of literary critics have pointed to the various affinities which exist between Dante and Milton.[25] *Paradise Lost* does itself postulate an achieved, realised, transcendence of the rift between life and meaning. Such a transcendence was possible, even in seventeenth-century England, quite simply because the detotalisation which gave birth to the novel form was a product, not of the modern world as such, but, as Lukács later came to recognise, of capitalism itself. For the revolutionary-bourgeois 'idea' is not that of the thoroughly detotalised capitalist social order which eventually emerged, but rather of a new integrated society, albeit a society integrated by a series of 'invisible hands'. But nonetheless, Milton's epic is not that fully realised synthesis of the classical epic and the novel into the *epopoeia* which Lukács recognised in Dante. The Miltonic transcendence is only achieved with diffi-culty, and then only partly so; it has to be strained for, it has to be constantly asserted and reasserted. Hence Milton's repeated in-terventions in his own argument to point out to the reader the real message of the poem. This 'strain' which runs through the whole of *Paradise Lost* is, of course, a function of Milton's place in history. Unlike Dante, whose social point of reference was a still essentially feudal system, Milton's own social point of reference is the *precise* moment in history at which the feudal system collapses and the new bourgeois social order comes into being. The postulated transcen-dence is thus immanent in the new social forms, but is nonetheless not an idealisation of any existing social forms. Furthermore, the specific conjuncture of the Restoration colours the entire epic adventure. The transcendence which is postulated is strained for against all the odds, against the immediate background of colossal defeat. The achieve-ment is astonishing; it is barely surprising that it is flawed.

Milton's choice of the epic form thus follows from his central moral project, that is the need to reassert, in the face of defeat, the immediate possibility of a transcendence of reality. And the architec-tural qualities of his verse derive from the sheer effort imposed upon him by the near-impossibility of realising that project. In this respect, *Paradise Lost* stands at the furthest remove from the Homeric epic that any poem can, whilst still actually remaining a genuine epic. In fact, Lukács's schema of classical epic/Dantesque *epopoeia*/modern novel is almost certainly over-simplified. Lukács himself noted the 'utopian stylisation' of Virgil's epic verse,[26] an epic whose heroes lead a 'shadow-existence' by comparison with their Homeric models. And C. S. Lewis, in his account of the epic form, has postulated a distinction between the 'primary epic' (the *Iliad*, the *Odyssey*, *Beowulf*), which is premised upon the assumption, or rather the reality, of an unchanging human environment, and the 'secondary epic' (the *Aeneid*, *Paradise Lost*), which is organised around the principle of movement and transition.[27] Perhaps one might usefully substitute for these schema the notion of an epic continuum running between the completely organic nature of the Homeric epic, at the one extreme, and the completely constructed nature of the Miltonic epic, at the other. The epic is, as Lukács argued, the literary form which expresses a given totality rather than a to-be-achieved totality. But the 'givenness' of the epic totality can be more or less organic, more or less constructed, and the precise location of a particular epic on that epic continuum is dependent upon the nature of the surrounding social formation. The integrated civilisations of classical Greece permit the organic epic of Homer; the relatively more constructed epic verse of Virgil is a product of a Roman civilisation in which the gap between life and meaning had opened up, but in which that gap still appeared as bridgeable; Dante's epic is a product of the new medieval synthesis which conceived of the Church as a new *polis* and which postulated an immediate transcendental totality; and Milton's *Paradise Lost*, as artificial and constructed, as non-organic, as an epic poem can be, becomes possible, briefly possible, at the precise moment in history when the bourgeois revolution, temporarily overcome by the feudal counter-revolution, finds it necessary, indeed urgently essential, to postulate an immediately attainable transcendence of the chasm, not between meaning and bourgeois reality, but between bourgeois ideal and feudal reality. The ultimate triumph of the bourgeois revolution (in England in 1688) permits a fully developed capitalism to emerge, and ensures that detotalisation of social life which precludes even a transcendental totality, and which guarantees only the problematic totality-as-aim of the modern novel. Thus, despite Dryden's strictures on *Paradise Lost*, Milton's work remained nonetheless 'the nearest realization of the epic ideal that

England would have'.[28] We have, then, attempted a sociological account of the reasons both for Milton's choice of the epic form, and for the architectonic and artificial qualities of his own particular epic. Only the epic form would suit the purposes of Milton's moral project, and only an extremely artificial style would enable such a project to be realised. Milton's formalism is a product not of any simple-minded or single-minded determination to do damage to the English language, but rather of the very nature of his deepest moral, political and aesthetic preoccupations, and of the social context in which they came to be articulated. We have demonstrated that Milton could only have dealt with the fundamental problems which concerned both himself and the social group to which he belonged through the medium of the epic form, and that that epic would be of necessity a self-consciously constructed, and non-organic, epic. But of course, such an explanation does not, and indeed cannot, answer Leavis's charges. Leavis's dogmatic aesthetic allows of only one kind of literature, and if a particular poet can only write poetry of a different kind, then he nonetheless stands condemned. Milton's achievement, his epic forged, against all the odds, out of the bitter agony of defeat, remains worthless quite simply because he should never have embarked upon the undertaking in the first place. Leavis's organicist aesthetic, like that of Lukács, seeks to censor rather than to comprehend, it erects a particular ideal into a universal ideal, and it is as unanswerable as the barrel of a gun. One can only reflect upon the good fortune that Leavis's aesthetic, unlike that of Lukács, never became the accepted dogma of the *apparatchiki* of a totalitarian state.

We have pointed to the transient nature of the opportunity which Milton seized upon, that is, the opportunity to write a major epic poem in the English language. That Milton himself came near to recognising the uniqueness of his achievement is suggested both by his own very high estimate of *Paradise Lost*,

> . . . my advent'rous song
> That with no middle flight intends to soar
> Above th'Aonian mount, while it pursues
> Things unattempted yet in prose or rhyme.[29]

and by his own subsequent poetic work. For Milton never again attempted that actually experienced, present transcendence of the break between life and meaning which is articulated in *Paradise Lost*. In *Paradise Lost* the fall of man, and all the future falls to come, including, of course, the Restoration itself, is overcome by the synthesis of a realisable individual moral purity with an over-arching, morally beneficent, and divinely ordered, historical process. But in neither *Paradise Regained* nor *Samson Agonistes* is such a transcendence either attained or even attempted. In *Paradise Regained*, this epic synthesis collapses into a one-sided emphasis on individual salvation, on the internal development of the human soul, which is devoid of all epic significance. Despite its nominally epic status, *Paradise Regained* is, in fact, more of an anti-epic than an epic; its style is bare and sparse, its plot is static, it lacks the drama and the glory of *Paradise Lost*. In *Paradise Regained*, Milton concentrates his attention on the ideal of the isolated, discrete rational individual, an ideal which is certainly integral to *Paradise Lost*, but which is here, in the later poem, extracted from the previous transcendental synthesis, and pushed towards its own, dreadfully sterile, logical conclusion. As the full extent of the catastrophe of the Restoration was brought home to Milton, the postulated but fulfilled transcendence became no longer tenable. Thus, a purely private and personal stoicism in the face of an irrational world remained as the only alternative possibility. Milton was, of course, by no means alone in this turn towards quietism. Indeed, the modern Quaker movement still stands as the petrified fossil of this particular moment in the history of the English bourgeoisie. But history will not stand still, not even for George Fox, and this moment eventually passed. By the time *Paradise Regained* was published along with *Samson Agonistes*, in 1671, the failure of the counter-revolution to turn back the clock to 1640 must have become apparent. Clarendon's impeachment in 1667 had been a portent of things to come; and in the years that followed, the Restoration monarchy was to be rocked by a series of major political crises, the Exclusion Crisis of 1678–81, the Rye House Plot in 1683, Monmouth's rebellion in 1685, and, of course, the final act in the drama of a failed restoration, the Glorious Revolution itself. It is impossible to determine the precise point at which Milton himself came to the conclusion that all was not lost. But in his last great poem, *Samson Agonistes*, the old revolutionary returned to his former overtly political preoccupations.

Just as *Paradise Lost* is a genuine epic, so too *Samson Agonistes* is a genuine tragedy. Indeed, Milton deliberately excludes all mention of an explicitly Christian theology from the poem so as to ensure that the Christian doctrine of the after-life in no way militates against the work's tragic effect. In *Samson Agonistes* the earlier dual concern with both personal morality and historical destiny reappears but, in the process, it is radically transformed. Lukács's account of the development of classical Greek thought from epic to tragedy is here relevant. The epic, he argues, had posed the question 'how can life become essential?', but as essence becomes divorced from life and becomes located at a level of being beyond life, so tragedy poses the new question 'how can essence come alive?'.[30] The epic unity of life and meaning achieved in *Paradise Lost*, albeit through the non-classical means of a posited transcendence, is no longer possible. Rather, *Samson Agonistes* is premised upon the assumption of a rift between meaning and life, but a rift which is nonetheless bridgeable. Samson's problem is the classically tragic problem of restoring meaning to life, of actualising essence. Milton's change in form is thus determined by the shift in his overall conception of the world. The significance of his adoption of the new tragic form should not be underrated. For in a very real sense, the dramatic medium was essentially alien to the blind poet. The theatres had, of course, been closed by the revolutionary regime, and Milton no doubt shared in this common Puritan prejudice against the dramatic form. Indeed, he is extremely careful to assure the reader that 'this work never was intended'[31] for the stage. The sheer weight of the Puritan antipathy towards drama suggests the corresponding power of the force which compelled Milton towards the dramatic form. Clearly, Milton's experiment in tragedy is the product, not of any mere whim or of simple intellectual curiosity, but rather of the demands of his own deepest felt convictions. This historico-philosophical difference between epic and tragic preoccupations gives rise to the difference between the epic and the tragedy. Whereas the classical epic represents, in Hegelian terminology, a 'totality of objects', drama, which is necessarily stripped of all descriptive detail, becomes a 'totality of movement'.[32] It is thus necessarily centred around the fact of *collision* extracted from that total context of human experience which can only be fully rendered in a more extensive literary form. As Lukács has pointed out, the central problem in classical drama is the fusion of the individuality of the dramatic hero with the surrounding collision of concrete socio-historical forces.[33] The tragic hero is thus a ' "world-historical individual", who is portrayed in such a way that he not only finds an immediate and complete expression for his personality in the deed evoked by the collision, but also draws the general social, historical and human inferences of the collision'.[34] And this is precisely what we find in *Samson Agonistes*. Samson is, indeed, a 'world-historical individual' whose own personality is only fully expressed in the great deed performed at the temple, and who, at the same time, articulates the full significance of the collision between God and Dagon, Israel and the Philistines, reason and passion, freedom and tyranny. This 'public' character of the content of drama is, as Lukács observes, closely linked to the public effect of drama, as expressed in the relationship between the play and its audience.[35] The three classical unities of action, time, and place, to which Milton conforms in *Samson Agonistes*, clearly spring from the public nature of drama itself, as does the classical chorus, a device which, once again, Milton himself adopts. The compression demanded by the dramatic form is thus a necessary correlate of that fusion of the world-historical individual with the world-historical collision which is the dramatic theme. We can see, then, that the strict formal classicism of Milton's tragedy derives from the strictly dramatic nature of his concerns. Thus the transcendental epic synthesis of the particular and the universal attained in *Paradise Lost* is finally superseded by the new dramatic synthesis which is embodied in *Samson Agonistes*.

In *Paradise Lost* the problem of defeat is overcome by a postulated metaphysical transcendence; in *Paradise Regained* it is swept aside in favour of a purely internal, private stoicism; but in *Samson Agonistes* it is both posed and resolved in concretely human and dramatic terms. If *Paradise Regained* is the literary embodiment of Quakerism, then *Samson Agonistes* is a clear anticipation of the Rye House Plot. This inner movement from epic transcendence to dramatic confrontation, via that abortive half-epic which is *Paradise Regained*, is, of course, paralleled in the progressive *humanisation* of Milton's literary themes. We noted earlier that Milton's theology is, in a strong sense, logically atheistic. But in the wake of the Restoration and the disintegration of the Commonwealth which had immediately preceded it, Milton was obliged to posit that explicitly metaphysical transcendence which is expressed in his great epic, an epic of angels and devils, of God and Satan, and of a Son of God who is divine rather than human. In *Paradise Regained*, however, we are confronted with a Christ who is very recognisably human, a perfect man but a man nonetheless. And in *Samson Agonistes*, the drama concerns real, frail, imperfect—but perfectable—human beings who are involved in a real historical collision between concrete social forces. Milton's God is here quite simply the god of classical Greek tragedy. The later synthesis between the particular and the universal, the personal and the historical, is incapable of any epic transcendence of the divorce between life and meaning. Rather, it recognises the immediate reality of that divorce, and concretely poses the new problem of bringing meaning to life, the solution to which is, of course, contained in Samson's 'great deed', a deed which is, in fact, the perfect embodiment of that active virtue which is central to the world vision of revolutionary rationalism. The journey from *Paradise Lost* to *Samson Agonistes* had no doubt been tortuous. But in his last great work Milton was able to reassert many of the central canons of his earlier political faith. As Tillyard observes: 'During Milton's life his various props had failed him in varying degrees: human love, human goodness, human progress. But in the end he regains a potential faith in them and in the earthly order of things. He holds himself ready to act as if he might believe in them.'[36] Milton's earlier conception of history as a simple process of transition from tyranny to the free kingdom of the saints is superseded by a much more complex conception, which incorporates within it the possibilities of defeats and setbacks, the notion of the interrelatedness of triumph and tragedy, but which nonetheless retains at its core both the major rationalist categories themselves and a conception of historical progress. In his last speech, Samson's father, Manoa, reassures the Chorus thus:

> Come, come, no time for lamentation now
> Nor much more cause; Samson hath quit himself
> Like Samson, and heroicly hath finished
> A life heroic, . . .[37]

So, too, Milton had quit himself like Milton. He died in November, 1674, three years after the publication of *Samson Agonistes* and only four years before Titus Oates's denunciation of the Popish Plot. Barred from Westminister Abbey by his republicanism, he was buried in Cripplegate in the heart of old revolutionary London. Fourteen years later, almost to the day, the Stuart monarchy came crashing down, and the 'untidy interruption' which was the attempted restoration came to a suitably ignoble end.

2   The Protestant Epic and the Spirit of Capitalism

We turn now to an analysis of the internal structures of each of the three major poems, beginning with Milton's epic, *Paradise Lost*. In general, nineteenth-century literary criticism focused its attention on the 'music', rather than the meaning, of Milton's epic, and this particular preoccupation has been carried over into the twentieth-century literary criticism which has been developed in England itself. Both Milton's modern English critics and his modern English apologists have subscribed to this nineteenth-century notion of *Paradise Lost* as an essentially unproblematic poem which requires little explication. The supposed paucity of Milton's ideas, his simple 'Puritanism', and the common assumption that these ideas were in themselves of little or no interest, led to an exclusive concern with matters of style. This might reasonably be expected of critics as hostile as Leavis and, of course, Eliot, who frankly admitted to 'an antipathy towards Milton the man'.[38] But it is surprising to note the extent to which, for example, C. S. Lewis's intentionally sympathetic account of *Paradise Lost* comes to provide indirect confirmation of Raleigh's well-known description of the work as 'a monument to dead ideas'. Indeed, Lewis's admission that 'for the student of Milton my Christianity is an advantage. What would you not give to have a real, live Epicurean at your elbow while reading Lucretius?'[39] is tantamount to an endorsement of Raleigh's judgement. For Lewis, as also for the American Douglas Bush,[40] *Paradise Lost* is only a restatement in verse of a grimly ebionitic Christianity whose central message is 'obey!'; it is a monument to the dead idea, no longer of Puritanism *per se*, but of Christianity in general. The fact that Lewis and Bush happen to believe in that dead idea permits their enjoyment of the poem. But they have little to offer to the non-Christian reader other than conversion, or, as a poor second, the appreciation of its merely formal 'beauty'. Hence the sermonising quality of Lewis's criticism, which Waldock pointed to in his discussion of Milton's Hell.[41] The only major modern English critic who has attempted a sympathetic account of the meaning of *Paradise Lost* which manages to avoid the tone of the Sunday morning sermon, is, of course, Tillyard. But Tillyard's own astonishing conclusion that 'Milton's importance is simply that of his own personality',[42] and that *Paradise Lost* provides a way into the mind of the man, is not only simplistically psychologistic in its account of the relationship between the writer and his work, but is also extremely cavalier in its denial of the objectivity of the literary text itself. The only genuinely successful attempts to provide a literary, rather than a theological or psychological, account of *Paradise Lost* have been made by Americans, such as Hanford,[43] and, in particular, by the Frenchman, Denis Saurat.[44] And significantly, both Hanford and Saurat point to the essentially rationalist premises upon which the poem rests. The fact that it has been American and French, rather than English, literary critics who have been able to embark upon such an undertaking, is not without wider sociological significance. For perhaps the central feature of modern English bourgeois thought, in contradistinction to both its French and American counterparts, it is denial of its own historical origins. It is no accident that, whereas the fourth and fourteenth of July are public holidays in the United States and France respectively, the thirtieth of January, the date of Charles Stuart's execution, goes unmarked in England. In so far as English bourgeois thought recognises that anything at all of significance occurred in the seventeenth century, it fixes its attention upon the 'Glorious Revolution', rather than the 'Great Rebellion'.[45] This historio- graphical substitution of the 1688 Settlement for the Revolution clearly correlates with the ideological substitution of gradualist empiricism for rationalism. Thus the Revolution itself, its rational- istic world vision, and its great poet are all rendered fundamentally inaccessible to the modern English bourgeois mind. The class compromise of 1688, which has no enduring counterpart in either France or America, casts a surprisingly long shadow.

What, then, is the meaning of *Paradise Lost*? The poem's obvious theme is, of course, that of the Fall. In the poem itself there is a twofold fall, the fall of the angels and the fall of man. But these two specific falls are only, as it were, 'case studies' of a wider problem, the problem of the fall-in-general, and it is to an analysis of the general structural characteristics of this latter problem that we now turn. As a starting point for our analysis, let us consider the nature of the beings who inhabit Milton's epic universe. Let us note, in the first place, that there are no radical discontinuities in Milton's chain of being. All of his creatures, both men and angels, both fallen and unfallen, essentially partake of the same nature. As Raphael tells Adam, men and angels differ 'but in degree, of kind the same'.[46] And the highest common factor in this underlying affinity is, in fact, individuality. This strong sense of the *individuality of personality* is indeed one of the most striking features of the Miltonic epic. The organic nature of the classical epic, and in particular the Homeric epic, is such that, as Lukács observes, the dependence of the parts upon each other, and upon the whole of which they are parts, prevents the appearance of 'interiority' and, hence, also of personality.[47] But in Milton's constructed epic there is a very real development of character and of individual personality. The most obvious example is Satan. Waldock's criticisms to the contrary,[48] there can, in fact, be no doubt of the very real continuity in the development of Satan's persona. He is at all times a concrete individual, and, even admitting John Peter's suggestion that he is progressively and necessarily simplified,[49] one still retains the strong impression of a distinct personality. The famous soliloquy at the beginning of Book IX is, of course, entirely non-epic in its deliberate revelation of the mind of Satan; it is reminiscent of Shakespeare, rather than of Homer.[50] But if Satan is the most striking example of individualised and interiorised personality, he is by no means the only one. Adam and Eve are both well developed, and also eminently sympathetic, characters. To a lesser extent, so too is the Son of God. And both angels and devils are permitted a surprising degree of individualised experience. The Council in Hell in Book II is a real debate between real individuals; Moloch, Belial, Mammon and Beelzebub are living personalities, rather than mere cardboard spokesmen for particular strategies. On God's side, both Raphael and Michael are similarly individualised, the former as a rather stuffy, but nonetheless essentially affable, schoolteacher, the latter a type of friendly policeman, who sympathises with the offenders but yet has no doubts as to the propriety of his duties. And in the two confrontations with Satan, at the end of Book V and at the beginning of Book VI, the angel Abdiel appears fully equipped with the psychology of one of the soldiers in Cromwell's army of the saints. This latter *motif* of individual resistance to external power recurs throughout the poem. For, just as Abdiel resists Satan and his hordes, so Satan resists God, and so, too, Adam and Eve heroically bear the burden of their punishment. Milton's epic cosmos is, then, one which is constituted out of, and premised upon the existence of, real *individuals*.

If both angels and men possess a common individuality, they are both equally honoured with the gift of rationality: men, angels, and devils are all 'creatures rational'.[51] For in Milton's system, the notion of individuality necessarily implies the notion of a corresponding rationality and free will. These central Miltonic conceptions are first introduced into the poem at the beginning of Book III, in the first of God's speeches. Referring, in the first place to man and thence to the fallen angels, God explains to the Son that:

> . . . I made him just and right,
> Sufficient to have stood, though free to fall.
> Such I created all th'ethereal Powers
> And spirits, both them who stood and them who failed;
> Freely they stood who stood, and fell who fell.[52]

All rational creatures are, then, in possession of free will and this is necessarily so because, as God says, 'reason also is choice'.[53] And yet there is an irony here. For God's earnest assertion of human free will is actually inserted into the argument at the specific point at which God demonstrates his divine omniscience by predicting, in advance, the successful outcome of Satan's mission of temptation. Moreover, it fulfills a peculiarly defensive function. Having predicted man's fall, God himself poses the inevitable question, 'Whose fault?', and returns the rather less inevitable answer, 'Whose but his own?'[54] God's exposition of the Miltonic theory of free will thus appears in a distinctly self-justificatory and apologetic context. That contradiction between the notion of divine determinism implicit in the conception of an omniscient and omnipotent God and the voluntarism of Milton's own rationalist philosophy is thus apparent at the very moment at which God, the person, enters into the action of the poem. And it can be no accident that Milton broached the problem so immediately. *Paradise Lost* was intended to justify the ways of God to men, and God's first speech in the poem is, in fact, a speech in self-justification. And in *Paradise Lost*, as in the *Treatise on Christian Doctrine*, the ultimate justification consists in a postulated radical distinction between divine foreknowledge, on the one hand, and divine predetermination, on the other:

> . . . they themselves decreed
> Their own revolt, not I. If I foreknew,
> Foreknowledge had no influence on their fault,
> Which had no less proved certain unforeknown.[55]

Thus the moral destinies of the poem's protagonists are the outcome of processes which are essentially internal and volitional, rather than external and deterministic. The moral responsibility for the fall itself, and for all the future falls, rests upon man himself, rather than upon God. And these linked notions of individual rationality, free will, and individual moral responsibility, are repeatedly reasserted in the course of the poem's development, as, for example, in Raphael's warning to

Adam at the end of Book VIII,[56] or in Michael's account of the human condition in Book XII. At the level of its formal theology, then, *Paradise Lost* reiterates Milton's earlier belief in human action as the ultimate determinant of human destiny. But, as we shall see, this Miltonic rationalism is persistently belied by the Biblical materials with which the poet is working.

At first sight, this moral individualism might appear to stand in sharp contrast to the hierarchical nature of Milton's epic cosmos. For, of course, this world of angels and devils, of men and women, is subject to a process of very clear 'social stratification'. But, as we have already noted in our discussion of Milton's prose writings, Miltonic individualism results in a meritocratic, rather than an egalitarian, conception of social order. Bourgeois individualism challenges not the inegalitarianism *per se* of feudalism, but rather its non-meritocratic basis. And Milton's Heaven and Hell are both organised according to thoroughly bourgeois principles. In fact, Milton goes to some lengths to reject the traditional notion that the superior status of the Son of God derives from the principle of hereditary right. God himself tells us that the Son is

> By merit more than birthright Son of God,
> Found worthiest to be so by being good,
> Far more than great or high; . . .[57]

This claim is repeated by Abdiel in his disputation with Satan at the end of Book V.[58] And in Milton's view, even Satan, the prince of darkness, is

> . . . by merit raised
> To that bad eminence; . . .[59]

Apparently, that meritocratic principle which the Stuart monarchy resisted with such tenacity found a readier acceptance in the constitution of both heavenly and infernal social structures. Of course, Milton's belief in the meritocratic principle runs counter to the strict sense of much of the original Biblical story. Indeed, the notion that Sonship is an achieved, rather than an ascribed, status appears somewhat implausible, to say the least. But nonetheless, Milton repeatedly attempts to recast the original myth in this new meritocratic mould. At one point, he even permits the angel Raphael to suggest to Adam that if only men persist in the path of virtuous obedience, they may themselves achieve angelic status.[60] Thus, C. S. Lewis's suggestion that the central principles upon which *Paradise Lost* is based are those of obedience and hierarchy,[61] represents an essentially partial, and hence distorting, account of the poem. Of course, Milton does believe in 'hierarchy', but then so, too, do absolute monarchs, feudal landlords, liberal parliamentarians, and revolutionary Marxists. The point, however, is that they all believe in different types of hierarchy. And the problem which faces us, in reading *Paradise Lost*, is that of understanding *what sort* of hierarchy Milton believed in. The answer is, as we have already suggested, a meritocratic hierarchy of achieved, rather than ascribed, statuses. And that particular conception of hierarchy is as alien to the sense of the original Biblical myth as it undoubtedly is to C. S. Lewis.

The world of *Paradise Lost* is, then, a world of discrete rational individuals, each in possession of free will, which is hierarchically ordered according to the principle of promotion according to merit. The only exception to this rule is to be found in the character of God. For Milton's God is not so much a particular personage who stands by merit at the top of the cosmological hierarchy, as an abstract principle which transcends that hierarchy altogether. And here we come to what is widely recognised as the central weakness of *Paradise Lost*: its characterisation of the personality of God himself. Even Milton's most charitable critics have found his anthropomorphic rendering of the deity profoundly unsatisfactory. We have already noted the self-justificatory and defensive tone of God's first speech in the poem. And this pattern is repeated throughout the work. For in general, God's appearances are necessitated by the demand for some authoritative exposition of the poem's theology. The only obvious exception to this observation is located in Book VIII, where God appears briefly as a genuinely paternal, and even quite good-humoured, father to Adam.[62] But even here this apparent divine jocularity is overshadowed by the earlier grim warning to shun the tree of knowledge:

> The day thou eat'st thereof, my sole command
> Transgressed, inevitably thou shalt die,[63]

Since the main purpose of the poem is precisely the justification of the ways of God to men, Milton's decision to turn God into the major mouthpiece for the poem's theology has the unfortunate consequence of rendering him as obsessively preoccupied with his own defence. And, of course, this impulse towards self-justification is a somewhat less than divine attribute. As John Peter observes, 'in representing God anthropomorphically, and then obliging him to speak his own defence at some length, Milton has conveyed a most unfortunate impression of uneasiness'.[64] Many literary critics have, in fact, suggested that Milton could have avoided the pitfalls of his characterisation of God by approaching the deity indirectly, rather than directly, somewhat in the manner of Dante. But this Dantesque 'tact' was surely unavailable to Milton quite simply because his God was a quite different God to that of Dante. A genuinely mysterious God, such as that of medieval Catholicism, can only be represented obliquely. But Milton's whole habit of mind, his rationalising mode of thought, demanded precision and definition. Milton's God is a God of reason, rather than of mystery, and such a God can hardly be merely hinted at. Nor, however, can he be presented anthropomorphically. For the God in which Milton actually believed is, as we have already demonstrated, not so much a person as an abstract principle. He is law, he is reason, he is the first cause. And in all these respects he is necessarily *impersonal*. Consider the lines, which we quoted earlier, in which God forbids Adam to eat from the tree of knowledge. There, God warns that if Adam does eat, he will 'inevitably' die. In the mouth of a personal God, these lines appear the product of an arbitrary tyranny of the most brutal and unsympathetic kind. For if God is a person, and a person moreover in possession of absolute power, then the inevitability of this death follows only as a consequence of his own arbitrary decision. But, in fact, Milton *intends* by these lines to imply quite the contrary. The inevitability of Adam's death follows precisely from the impersonality of the laws of reason and of nature, rather than from any merely personal whim. The generally unsympathetic nature of God's character derives from the same source. Milton attempts to represent a thoroughly impersonal God, not so much a God of reason even, as a God who *is* reason, in personal terms. And lines which would seem perfectly acceptable as a summary of the workings of an abstract law, become dreadfully unacceptable as the spoken words of a particular omnipotent person. Why, then, did Milton so personalise his own impersonal God? The answer to that question is, of course, to be found in the nature of the original Biblical myth itself. For whatever rationalised theology Milton himself may have subscribed to, the God of the Old Testament stubbornly remains a person rather than a principle, a king rather than a law. Milton could neither portray a Dantesque God of mystery obliquely, nor could he represent the fully rationalised God of his own theology without bursting assunder the constraints imposed upon him by the Book of Genesis. In consequence, the God of *Paradise Lost* appears as an unfortunate hybrid, a Biblical personage mouthing sentiments which do justice to Milton's theology—that is, his conception of the ways of God—but which nonetheless fail to justify the person of God to men. As Waldock observed, in a slightly different context, Milton believed in his myth much less than he thought he did.[65]

We have given an account of the nature of the various beings which inhabit Milton's epic universe, of both those who stand and those who fall. But in what exactly does the fall itself consist? In the Biblical myth the fall is twofold: it is, firstly, disobedience *per se*, and secondly, and more specifically, the search for forbidden knowledge. Milton's rationalism leads him necessarily to reject this latter conception out of hand. For the one thing that Milton's tree of knowledge does not yield is, in fact, knowledge. As Willey quite rightly observes, in Milton's view, 'Adam *learnt* nothing from the tree, he merely fell into the fate of "knowing good by evil", that is, of experiencing sin and misery and contrasting them with past innocence.'[66] In the whole of *Paradise Lost* the only person who suggests that the tree does confer knowledge is, significantly enough, Satan,[67] and he, it is made clear, is lying.[68] And when Adam and Eve eventually eat of the fruit, the effect is not revelation but intoxication. As Adam tells Eve:

> . . . We know
> Both good and evil, good lost and evil got,
> Bad fruit of knowledge, if this be to know,[69]

In rejecting the notion that the tree conferred forbidden knowledge, Milton finds himself obliged to place the whole weight of the argument upon the alternative notion that the fall consists solely in the very fact of disobedience. Indeed, Milton is insistent that the divine decree forbidding the tree of knowledge to Adam and Eve is simply a test of obedience. That decree is, as God himself affirms,

> . . . the sole command,
> Sole pledge of his obedience; . . .[70]

And Adam, too, describes God's injunction, in very similar terms, as:

The only sign of our obedience left
Among so many signs of power and rule
Conferred upon us, . . .[71]

Baldly stated, the thesis that the fall consists simply in disobedience to God represents not so much a modification, as a partial rendering, of the Genesis myth. But, as we have already suggested, Milton's God is not the God of Genesis. Rather, he is abstract reason itself. And so Milton attempts to reconstruct the original Biblical story in such a way that its central theme becomes, not that of obedience and disobedience, but rather that of the conflict between reason and passion. As Saurat ably demonstrated in his pioneering study,[72] Milton's *Paradise Lost*, in fact, redefines the nature of the fall of man. It is no longer either disobedience *per se* or, still less, the search for forbidden knowledge, which characterises that fall. Rather, the fall consists essentially in the triumph of passion over reason. Raphael's final warning to Adam at the end of Book VIII contains within itself, by implication, a complete summary of this new Miltonic theory of the fall:

. . . take heed lest passion sway
Thy judgement to do aught which else free will
Would not admit;[73]

Free will properly exercised will result in a necessary obedience to the dictates of reason. But if passion should gain sway over reason, then the fall of man, the defeat of his true rational nature, becomes certain. This, then, is the central core of Milton's own rationalist theory of the fall, a theory which stands in marked contrast to the meaning of the original Biblical myth which Milton attempted to employ in its service.

We have outlined the general contours of Milton's own particular theory of the fall. But before turning to a more detailed consideration of some of the possible objections to Milton's rendering of the fall of man, let us consider briefly his account of the earlier fall of the angels, an account which operates, much in the manner of a dramatic sub-plot, so as to reinforce our understanding of the meaning of the main theme. The rationalistic nature of Milton's new reading of the earlier Biblical myth is, in fact, most clearly exemplified in the case of this first fall. The exchange between Abdiel and Satan at the beginning of Book VI is here extremely significant. In response to Satan's claim that his side stands for liberty as opposed to servility, the angel Abdiel replies thus:

Unjustly thou deprav'st it with the name
Of servitude to serve whom God ordains,
Or nature; God and Nature bid the same,
When he who rules is worthiest, and excels
Them whom he governs. This is servitude,
To serve th'unwise, or him who hath rebelled
Against his worthier, as thine now serve thee,
Thyself not free, but to thyself entralled;[74]

In Abdiel's speech is contained almost the whole of the Miltonic theory of politics. Abdiel asserts, in truly Miltonic fashion, the doctrine that God and Nature are essentially one, that the divine dictates are in no sense arbitrary, but are rather in conformity to the laws of nature, and hence also those of reason. He maintains, too, Milton's own meritocratic theory of government, in which just government is seen as the government of the worthy over the unworthy. Servitude, by contrast, is obedience to the tyranny of the unworthy. And finally, and most significantly, he recognises that Satan, the grand tyrant, is himself un-free, is himself enthralled to his own passions. One cannot help but recall Milton's own judgement on Charles Stuart. The precise nature of the passion which rules over Satan's mind has, in fact, already been explained to us; at the end of Book IV, the angel Gabriel denounces Satan's pretensions to libertarianism, and identifies his purpose as the usurpation of the divine monarchy itself.[75] Satan's ruling passion is, then, that of pride. John Peter has objected to Milton's presentation of the motive forces behind the revolt of the angels on two main counts. He suggests, firstly, that Satan's jealousy of God has the unfortunate consequence of identifying the person of God with the role of arbitrary ruler, and secondly, that Satan's own personal pride provides no adequate explanation for the defection to his side of the other rebellious angels.[76] This latter objection seems thoroughly misconceived. For it is, of course, precisely Milton's point that the angelic rebellion is irrational, that there cannot possibly be any genuinely legitimate grounds for its occurrence. Peter's own preference for Vondel's account,[77] which identifies a wide-spread resentment at acting as servants to man as the real source of the rebellion, seems inexplicable. If the angels did, indeed, have just cause for their act of rebellion, then that rebellion would be justified, or, at least, justifiable. It is hardly remarkable that a poet whose intention it is to justify the ways of God, rather than those of Satan, should choose to avoid such an alternative. Peter's first objection has, however, much more point to it. Indeed, the God of *Paradise Lost* is almost permanently exposed to the danger of becoming transformed into an arbitrary tyrant. But this risk derives, not so much from any particular error of Milton's—as, for example, in his account of Satan's motivation—as from his singularly unsuccessful attempt to personalise an essentially impersonal God. Satan's rebellion against the God in whom Milton actually believes, that is the God who is reason, law, and truth, would redound entirely to his own discredit. It is only the abortive attempt to transform that God into a *dramatis persona* that affords Satan any residual moral credibility. Those few problems which do arise out of Milton's account of the fall of the angels are, then, not so much a product of his handling of this particular part of the myth as of the general failure of his attempted characterisation of the personality of God.[78]

The second fall, the fall of man, which constitutes the primary subject of the poem, follows as a direct consequence of the first. For the defeated Satan determines to revenge himself upon God by seducing man into evil. In his attempt to recast this second fall into the form of a triumph of passion over reason, Milton found himself confronted with rather more serious obstacles than had arisen in the case of the fall of the angels. For, of course, the Biblical myth is here much more specific, and Milton is therefore necessarily obliged to remain within the confines of, at least, the general outline provided by the Book of Genesis. Milton's own account of the fall as a triumph of passion over reason is clearly asserted both in Raphael's earlier warnings, and in Michael's subsequent commentary, which perform the functions of, as it were, a prescript and a postscript, respectively, to the main body of the action. The action itself, however, remains problematic. Saurat's suggestion that the fall is essentially a product of sensuality[79] undoubtedly captures the substance of Milton's intention, the form of the myth which the poet would have preferred to have found in Genesis. But the Biblical account contains not the slightest hint that this is the case.[80] Milton does indeed clothe the episode of the fall in an aura of pervasive sensuality, just as Saurat suggests. Eve greedily 'engorges' the fruit and is intoxicated by it 'as with wine',[81] Adam is 'fondly overcome with female charm',[82] and the immediate outcome of their actions is, firstly, carnal lust,[83] and subsequently, anger, hate, mistrust, suspicion and discord.[84] But, as even Saurat himself admits, all of this is a consequence, rather than a cause, of the fall. Various attempts have been made to define the precise cause of the fall: Tillyard sees it as 'mental levity' in both Adam and Eve, compounded by gregariousness in the former,[85] Lewis as pride, in Eve's case, and uxoriousness in Adam's,[86] Waldock as disobedience in Eve, and an all too attractive and sympathetic human love in Adam,[87] and Peter merely concludes, in despair, that 'God alone knows why they've fallen'.[88] But all of this is surely disingenuous. Milton tells us over and over again that they have fallen because they have allowed their passions to subordinate their reasons. This overall theoretical conception is, perhaps, inadequately realised in Book IX. But nonetheless this is the meaning of the fall of man. The failure to embody this notion directly in the dramatic action of Book IX derives from the stubborn intractability of the Biblical material itself. For, of course, un-fallen man, even, indeed especially, if in possession of free will, cannot be depicted as driven by essentially post-lapsarian passions. Milton's repeated reminders to the reader that the fall is, in fact, determined by the triumph of passion over reason, and his sustained attempt to shroud the immediate aftermath of the fall in an atmosphere of irrational sensuality, thus appear, not as symptoms of a belated realisation that things are not quite working out as they should, but rather as the product of a conscious realisation of the difficulties inherent in his theme, and of an equally conscious resolved to overcome those difficulties. Moreover, Milton's retention of our underlying sympathy for Adam and Eve, in the course of the fall itself, is by no means as inappropriate as Waldock, for example, appears to believe.[89] On the contrary, if we are to care about their ultimate fate, and if we are to be adequately prepared for the poem's eventual optimistic outcome, then Milton cannot afford to consign Adam and Eve too readily to the devil's party. Eliot's belated recognition that the poetic effectiveness of *Paradise Lost* resides in its general design[90] is here extremely apposite. A 'close reading' of Book IX in isolation from the rest of the poem may well highlight its particular inadequacies. But the general impression of the poem gained from a 'total' reading only affords an impressive confirmation of Milton's success in the realisation of his project. Against the whole weight of the initial Biblical story Milton actually manages to sustain the notion that the fall of man is indeed the product of the subordination of reason to passion.

We have suggested that the fall of man is, in *Paradise Lost*, not only a specific act, but also a general moral category. The subsidiary theme of the fall of the angels is, in fact, specifically intended to highlight this wider general applicability. But this generalisation of the specific instance into a universally applicable ethical and political category is even more explicitly articulated in the angel Michael's account to Adam of the future course of human history. At the beginning of Book XII, Michael reveals to Adam the occasion of the world's first tyranny, that of Nimrod, architect of the tower of Babel. Michael's explanation of the origins of Nimrod's rule is clearly intended as an account, not only of this particular tyranny, but also, and more especially, of tyranny in general:

> . . . yet know withal,
> Since thy original lapse, true liberty
> Is lost, which always with right reason dwells
> Twinned, and from her hath no dividual being;
> Reason in man obscured, or not obeyed,
> Immediately inordinate desires
> And upstart passions catch the government
> From reason, and to servitude reduce
> Man till then free. Therefore since he permits
> Within himself unworthy powers to reign
> Over free reason, God in judgement just
> Subjects him from without to violent lords;
> Who oft as undeservedly enthrall
> His outward freedom: tyranny must be,
> Though to the tyrant thereby no excuse.
> Yet sometimes nations will decline so low
> From virtue, which is reason, that no wrong,
> But justice, and some fatal curse annexed,
> Deprives them of their outward liberty,
> Their inward lost: . . .[91]

We have quoted this particular passage at some length because it is almost certainly one of the most important in the poem. Here Milton deliberately poses the problem of the fall as a general problem, and one which has, moreover, overtly political implications. For Milton, freedom is first and foremost freedom over one's lower self, the self of the passions. However, once that internal freedom has been lost, a parallel loss of external freedom will follow as a necessary consequence. Those who fail in the government of themselves will, then, necessarily fall prey to a tyrannical government imposed from without. Milton is, of course, careful to add that the necessity of tyranny in no sense justifies the role of the tyrant. But, nonetheless, the central conclusion is clear: the defeat of the godly, the triumph of unreason over reason, whether acted out in the Garden of Eden or in the England of 1660, is always determined ultimately by the moral failure of the godly themselves. Adam and Eve's fall was thus their own fault, and not that of either the angels who failed to guard them securely or Satan who tempted them. And similarly, the responsibility for the Restoration rests neither with the Stuarts nor with those Independents who had failed to provide adequate political guarantees against the possibility of a restoration, but rather with that English nation which had declined so low from virtue that it no longer deserved any fate other than that of tyranny. This, then, is Milton's initial explanation of the problem of defeat. But, nonetheless, there is yet more to be said. For even if the imposition of an external tyranny derives its political opportunity from a prior moral failure on the part of those who become subject to that tyranny, the two processes, the one external, the other internal, are nonetheless distinguishable. In the previous chapter, we pointed to the significance in Milton's system of the typically rationalist categories of, firstly, freedom from external constraint, and secondly, freedom from passion. Here, in Michael's speech in Book XII of *Paradise Lost*, the former category is seen as essentially dependent on the latter. This relationship of dependence does not, however, necessarily imply a relationship of identity. At the beginning of Book III, in his first speech, Milton's God had, in fact, deliberately sought to distinguish between the two. Comparing the fallen angels with man, God observes that:

> . . . they themselves ordained their fall.
> The first sort by their own suggestion fell,
> Self-tempted, self-depraved; man falls deceived
> By the other first; man therefore shall find grace,
> The other none.[92]

Now this distinction is of some considerable significance. For Satan or Charles II to succeed in their intentions, their 'victims' must first have experienced an internal moral collapse. But the moral statuses of predator and victim yet remain quite different. The one, self-tempted, is doomed, but the other, the deceived, may yet find grace. As Michael had said, for the tyrant there is 'no excuse'; but for the victims of his tyranny there yet remains hope. And in the last two Books of *Paradise Lost* Milton attempts to explain in what that hope might consist.

In so far as we are concerned with *Paradise Lost*'s meaning, as opposed to the merely formal properties of its poetic texture, there can be no real doubt that the often much maligned last two books, in fact, perform an essential function within the work.[93] It is only here that Milton offers a solution to the problems initially posed in the course of the earlier books. And that solution is necessary for both theoretical and specifically 'literary' reasons. For, as a recent American writer has noted, Milton's work generally achieves its poetic effect through the movement from one, normally perturbed, state of affairs to another which is essentially harmonious.[94] Without the last two books, we would be left only with the fall itself, with the experience of defeat, and the poem would be merely that tragedy which Kermode believes it to be.[95] But *Paradise Lost* is *not* a tragedy. On the contrary, it succeeds not only in posing the problem of defeat, the problem of the fall of man, and not only in explaining that problem in terms which are, as we have seen, essentially psychologistic, but also in proposing a solution to that problem. If the first ten books of *Paradise Lost* posit a particular question, then, in the last two books, and in particular in Book XII itself, that question finally elicits an appropriate answer. For in Book XII Adam receives from the angel Michael a double pledge, the promise of, firstly, an ultimate external victory of the godly over the ungodly, and secondly, an immediate internal happiness. The outlines of this pledge clearly conform to the contours of Milton's own solution to the problem of defeat. Michael explains to Adam the eventual outcome of Christ's incarnation, the dissolution of the world and the judgement of both the quick and the dead. Then, Michael predicts,

> . . . the earth
> Shall all be Paradise, far happier place
> Than this of Eden, and far happier days.[96]

In the long run, then, there can be no doubt of the ultimate victory of reason and justice over unreason and injustice. And even in the immediate present there yet remains the possibility of a purely private personal salvation. Michael explains to Adam the role of the Holy Spirit, which will write the law of faith upon the hearts of believers, and which will guide them in the truth.[97] And when Adam himself acknowledges Christ as Redeemer, thus incidentally, becoming, perhaps somewhat prematurely, the first Christian, Michael replies:

> . . . then wilt thou not be loth
> To leave this Paradise, but shalt possess
> A paradise within thee, happier far.[98]

The double promise, of a future time when the earth will be a 'far happier place' than Paradise, and of a 'paradise within thee, happier far' permanently and perennially available to the truly good man, thus reveals Milton's own initial reaction to the problem of defeat. In Milton's view, the solution to the problem of the triumph of unreason is twofold: it is, firstly, a *personal*, stoic defence of reason against unreason, and secondly, a conviction that ultimately *history* will secure the triumph of reason. The poem's formal conclusion is thus essentially optimistic. And yet this optimism is only possible as a consequence of a tremendous effort of both the will and the imagination on Milton's part. This fusion of meaning and reality can only be achieved, as we suggested earlier, at the level of a posited transcendence of reality. Hence the 'constructed' nature of the entire epic, and of its last two books in particular. And hence, too, the residual ambiguity of the poem's closing lines:

> The world was all before them, where to choose
> Their place of rest, and Providence their guide:
> They hand in hand, with wand'ring steps and slow,
> Through Eden took their solitary way.[99]

The mournful tone of the last two lines stands in sharp contradiction to the proclaimed optimism of the poem's conclusion, as, indeed, does the pessimism of Michael's earlier account of the origins of tyranny. For despite the heroic magnificence of Milton's attempted transcendence of the rift between meaning and life, his solution to the problem of defeat still remains essentially formal. In the early 1640s, Milton had believed in the imminent establishment of the kingdom of the saints; in the early 1660s that prospect had been relegated to the distant future.

3 'Paradise Regained'

We have argued that in *Paradise Lost* Milton's solution to problem of the triumph of unreason is, at one and the same time, both personal and historical, and that this fusion of the particular and the universal, which is effected at the level of a posited over-arching transcendental synthesis, permits the creation of a poetic work which is, despite its self-evidently constructed nature, nonetheless genuinely epic in character. But, as we suggested earlier, the sheer reality of the Stuart restoration necessarily came to undermine the imaginative basis upon which that transcendence had been erected. And with the collapse of the intellectual credibility of Milton's posited transcendence—that is, of the poet's epic *theme*—so the epic *form* itself is rendered similarly inaccessible. Thus we find in *Paradise Regained* a poetic theme which is *simply* that of personal redemption, and a poetic form which is anti-epic rather than epic. *Paradise Regained* is, of course, generally much less admired than *Paradise Lost*. And the reason for this is not too difficult to discern: the quietism of its subject matter demands a literary form which is almost everything that *Paradise Lost* is not. *Paradise Lost* contains within itself all of those elements which one might reasonably expect to find in an epic poem. In truly Virgilian fashion, it begins *in media res*, and is thus obliged to recapitulate the immediate prehistory of the poem's action, and ends with a prediction of the future outcome of that action, which seeks to invest it with a wider, universal significance. And in the course of the poem's movement from its opening lines to its conclusion, Milton utilises both typically epic devices, such as those of suspense and dramatic conflict, and specifically epic incidents. There is, for example, the battle in heaven in Book VI, which, despite its many weaknesses, nonetheless manages at times to attain genuinely epic heights, in particular in the course of the dramatic confrontations between Abdiel and Satan, and Michael and Satan, and in the Son's triumphant entry into the fray which finally determines its outcome. There is Satan's epic voyage from Hell to Eden in Books II, III, and IV. And there is the romantic theme centred on the love affair between Adam and Eve. Of course, even in *Paradise Lost*, Milton's own sense of his relationship to the classical epic remained problematic. The quietism inherent in the theme of Adam and Eve's fortitude in the face of adversity demanded a rejection of classical epic subjects. Thus, for example, Milton's invocation to the muse at the beginning of Book

IX explicitly advocates the substitution of this 'higher argument' for the martial themes of earlier epics.[100] But in *Paradise Lost*, Milton's double concern with both universal history and individual redemption still permitted the incorporation into the work of these earlier classical *motifs*. In *Paradise Regained* this is no longer the case. The poem's subject is simply that of Christ's personal resistance to Satan's temptations. And its central formal organising principle is a purely internal movement from one state of mind to another; it is quite literally devoid of almost any action at all. Saurat suggests that the general mood of the poem is one of fatigue.[101] In specifically literary terms, this is almost certainly not the case. Milton displays a degree of mastery over his material which is far in excess of that evidenced even in *Paradise Lost*, and which surely contradicts the suggestion of any individual fatigue on his part.[102] But in a wider, sociological sense, Saurat is indeed correct. For the theme which Milton masters so perfectly, the theme of quietism, is itself an indication of a general fatigue in the revolutionary movement. The collapse of the Commonwealth and the subsequent persecutions of both political and religious radicals, had drained English radicalism of its capacity for resistance. And in the face of this general, social 'fatigue', quietism appeared the only remaining viable political option.

We have emphasised the marked discontinuity between *Paradise Lost* and *Paradise Regained*. But, nonetheless, the elements of continuity are equally significant. Milton's world is still, for example, a world of discrete rational individuals. But here the interplay between individuals is reduced to a minimum. The minor characters—God, Andrew and Simeon, Mary, and Belial—are all entirely marginal. The poem is, in effect, a sustained dialogue between Christ and Satan, and even Satan's significance derives from his role as the external occasion of Christ's internal development. But Milton does achieve a very real characterisation of the personality of Christ, and, moreover, the specific outlines of this personality are distinctly human. In *Paradise Regained*, the Son of God is no longer the cosmic hero of *Paradise Lost*. On the contrary, it is re-emphasised again and again that he is a *man* living in history. The opening lines of the poem inform us that its subject is:

> . . . one man's firm obedience fully tried
> Through all temptation, and the Tempter foiled.[103]

And even Satan recognises Christ

> . . . as a center firm,
> To the utmost of mere man both wise and good.[104]

Milton's decision to allow Christ to recall his untypical, perhaps, but nonetheless human childhood,[105] is clearly dictated by his concern to establish Christ as a *human personality*. So, too, are the repeated references to the particular historical time in which the action occurs, as, for example, in Christ's own concern to see Israel freed from the Roman yoke,[106] and in Satan's very detailed accounts of the present political situation, which range from an analysis of the balance of power between Rome and Parthia,[107] to a description of the foibles of the ageing Emperor Tiberius.[108] Milton's concern with individual personality persists from *Paradise Lost* to *Paradise Regained*, but in the latter work the quietistic theme demands that the poem should be devoted to the characterisation of only one individual, rather than of a plurality of particular, separate individuals. A second element of continuity is contained in Milton's continuing adherence to the notion of meritocracy. Indeed, there is a sense in which *Paradise Regained* is, in fact, designed to demonstrate that meritocratic entitlement to the Sonship of God which had only been asserted in *Paradise Lost*. The only speech actually assigned in *Paradise Regained* to God, who is, of course, as in *Paradise Lost*, the mouthpiece for authoritative doctrinal statement, carefully explains that Christ has been exposed to Satan,

> That all the angels and ethereal powers,
> They now, and men hereafter, may discern
> From what consummate virtue I have chose
> This perfect man, by merit called my Son,
> To earn salvation for the sons of men.[109]

And Christ's ultimate revelation of his Sonship, to both himself and Satan, comes only as the culminating point of his successful resistance to Satan's temptations. A third element of continuity is located around Milton's preoccupation with the dualism between reason and passion. Saurat suggests that *Paradise Regained* can, in fact, be read as an allegorical account of the conflict between these two principles, in which Christ embodies reason, and Satan passion. But there are a number of problems with such a reading. In the first place, Milton's detailed characterisation of the personality of Christ militates against an allegorical interpretation. And secondly, it is by no means clear that Satan stands merely for passion; indeed, simple sensuality is remarkably absent from the poem. Whilst it is certainly true that Milton intends that Satan should, in part, represent passion as opposed to reason, he also develops, in the course of his treatment of the various temptations of Christ, a distinctly new poetic theme which might better be characterised in terms of the polarisation between quietism, on the one hand, and activism, on the other.

Let us consider Milton's handling of the temptation motif in a little more detail. Milton's model for the temptation sequence is, presumably, the Gospel according to St. Luke.[110] In Luke's version three particular temptations are outlined—the temptation to turn stone into bread, the temptation of 'the kingdoms of the world', and the temptation to jump from the pinnacle of the Temple. The relative weight given to the three temptations is interesting: the first takes up two verses,[111] the second four verses,[112] and the third, again, four verses.[113] But in *Paradise Regained* these relative weights are significantly altered. There, the first temptation proper occupies less than 50 lines of verse in Book I.[114] The food *motif* is, however, repeated at greater length in Book II, where it takes up over 150 lines of the poem.[115] But the second temptation, the temptation of the kingdoms of the world, is so greatly expanded that it provides the subject matter for the last 8 or so lines of Book II,[116] the whole of Book III,[117] and well over a half of Book IV.[118] The third and culminating temptation, by contrast, occupies only the last 140 lines of the poem.[119] Thus, although the final temptation actually constitutes the poem's climax, it is the second temptation, the specifically political temptation, which provides the main subject matter of *Paradise Regained*. Let us consider each of the temptations in turn. The first temptation is indeed clearly based on the opposition between the demands of reason and those of the senses, in this case those of hunger. But Satan's first attempt, in which he suggests, in strict conformity to the account given in St.Luke, that Christ should turn stone into bread, is hurriedly passed over. The Son of God immediately recognises Satan for what he is,[120] and asserts the simple anti-materialist doctrine that:

> Man lives not by bread only, but each word
> Proceeding from the mouth of God, . . .[121]

Milton's lack of interest in this particular incident is evident, and the action hurriedly moves on to a dispute between Christ and Satan as to the nature of the latter's role in the divine order. In Book II the theme of sensuality is taken up once again, in the first place in Belial's recommendation to 'Set women in his eyes and in his walk',[122] which Satan himself rejects as clearly doomed to failure, and secondly, in Satan's own proffered gift of

A table richly spread, in regal mode,
With dishes piled, and meats of noblest sort
And savor, beasts of chase, OR FOWL OF GAME,
In pastry built, or from the spit, or boiled,
Gris-amber-steamed; . . .[123]

The banquet scene, in fact, represents one of the very few points in the poem at which the theme of sensuality genuinely comes to life. The poetic texture of this particular passage,[124] with its fragrant smells, tall stripling youths, Nymphs and Naiades, chiming strings and charming pipes, is peculiarly and distinctly sensual. But Milton hurriedly moves on from this incident too, and indeed it appears as little more than a brief introduction to the second, and, in the poem, by far the most important temptation, that of the kingdoms of the world. There are obvious doctrinal reasons for Milton's lack of interest in the first temptation. Having established, in God's speech at the beginning of Book I, that Christ is the perfect man, it remains extremely unlikely that he will be tempted by the offer, no matter how lavishly presented, of mere food; Satan's banquet is only a little less ridiculous than Belial's women. But the main reason for Milton's apparent indifference to the subject of the first temptation surely resides elsewhere: Milton himself is eminently preoccupied, not with the rival claims of reason and passion, but rather with the problematic nature of political action.

Whilst the first temptation is premised upon the simple opposition between reason and passion, the set of oppositions which underlies the second temptation, that is, the temptation which is the poem's major concern, is much more complex. In part, of course, Satan does venture an appeal to Christ's passions: wealth, power, and glory, if desired for their own sake, would indeed be the objects of a passionate, rather than a rational striving. But Satan offers these gifts not only, and not even primarily, as valuable in themselves, but rather as means to the attainment of desirable political ends. Thus his offer of wealth is justified on the grounds that 'Great acts require great means of enterprise'.[125] So, too, he argues that Christ should accept the gift of political power out of

> Zeal of thy father's house, duty to free
> Thy country from her heathen servitude;[126]

The throne of Parthia is depicted by Satan as a means to those same ends.[127] And his spectacular offer of the imperial Roman throne itself is vindicated on the grounds that Christ may

> . . . expel this monster from his throne
> Now made a sty, and in his place ascending
> A victor people free from servile yoke.[128]

The issue at stake in the case of the second temptation is, then, no longer that of the simple opposition between reason and passion. This underlying structural opposition is, in fact, here augmented by a sustained dialogue between Christ and Satan as to the relative merits and demerits of political action. Milton is not, of course, an opponent of political activism *per se*. Indeed, he is extremely careful to establish the legitimate nature of political concerns. Well before Satan actually raises the question of politics, Christ himself recalls his own youthful political aspirations:

> . . . Victorious deeds
> Flamed in my heart, heroic acts: one while
> To rescue Israel from the Roman yoke,
> Then to subdue and quell o'er all the earth
> Brute violence and proud tyrannic pow'r,
> Till truth were freed, and equity restored;[129]

And these aspirations, it is made clear, are shared by both Andrew and Simeon.[130] How, then, does Milton's Christ respond to Satan's own explicitly political temptations? Satan's first offer is not that of political power, but rather that of riches as a means to political power. Christ's reaction to the offer is by no means a simple one. Initially, he argues that, without virtue, valour, and wisdom, wealth in itself can provide no adequate guarantee of political success, and he cites as examples those leaders of the old Roman republic whose political achievements were based, not upon the possession of wealth, but rather upon simple political integrity.[131] But then he proceeds, in a quite different vein, to question the very desirability itself of political power:

Yet he who reigns within himself, and rules
Passions, desires, and fears, is more a king;
Which every wise and virtuous man attains:
And who attains not, ill aspires to rule
Cities of men, or headstrong multitudes,
Subject himself to anarchy within,
Or lawless passions in him which he serves.
But to guide nations in the way of truth
By saving doctrine, and from error lead
To know, and knowing worship God aright,
Is yet more kingly; . . .[132]

The moral ambivalency of this particular speech should be self-evident: on the one hand, Milton's Chirst condemns those who would seek to govern others whilst being themselves subject 'to anarchy within', thus surely reasserting, by implication, the Miltonic doctrine that only good men are fit for the exercise of political power; but on the other, he turns back from this political conclusion and argues for the moral superiority of the role of the philosopher/teacher over that of the political leader. And Milton's earlier eulogy to Quintius, Fabricius, Curius, and Regulus only serves as to heighten the reader's impression of the decidedly ambivalent character of Milton's own attitude towards political activism.

Having failed to tempt Christ with the offer of wealth, Satan then offers glory, and again Christ dismisses the proferred gift as in itself of no value.[133] But then Satan shifts his ground somewhat. Christ, he observes, is the real heir to the throne of King David, and the present usurpers of that throne are, moreover, essentially bad rulers. Why, then, should Christ not accept Satan's assistance in pursuit of his own perfectly legitimate title to the government of Israel? Christ's reply is extremely significant. The outcome of such matters, he argues, rests in God's hands, rather than in men's:

What if he hath decreed that I shall first
Be tried in humble state, and things adverse,
By tribulations, injuries, insults,
Contempts, and scorns, and snares, and violence,
Suffering, abstaining, quietly expecting

> Without distrust or doubt, that he may know
> What I can suffer, how obey? Who best
> Can suffer best can do;[134]

Here Milton's Christ perfectly captures the tone of patient stoicism which informed the Quaker–quietist response to the Restoration. But there is still an ambivalency, for, unlike the Quakers, Milton himself refuses to abandon politics altogether. For the present, of course, there is only suffering and abstaining, but this moral fortitude in the face of adversity, which Milton here advocates, is also, in addition to being in itself virtuous, a preparation for that future time when 'doing', rather than 'suffering', will become the order of the day. Milton's own rejection of the kingdoms of the world is much more conditional, much less absolute, than that sustained by the followers of George Fox. For Milton, quietism is evidently a tactic rather than a strategy, an expedient rather than a principle. But a tactical quietism such as that to which Milton here adheres is always exposed to the objection that the political iniquity to which it counterposes itself, and which it promises, ultimately, to oppose by activism, is so immediately pressing that it demands an immediate, rather than an ultimate, political response. And none could have been more susceptible of the power of such an objection than the former revolutionary who had once declared reformation to be 'no point of controversy to be argued without end, but a thing of clear moral necessity to be forthwith done'.[135] The objection is raised, and raised forcefully, by Satan, who offers Christ, in turn, the throne of Parthia as a means to free both the Israelites and the lost tribes from their oppressors, and the imperial Roman throne as a means to the political liberation, not only of Israel, but also of the Roman people themselves. In each case, Satan is particularly insistent as to the dire state of the oppressed peoples.[136] Milton's solution to this problem, posed in the voice of Satan, but answered in the voice of Christ, consists, on each occasion, in a discrete shift in emphasis from the political realm of discourse to the psychological and the ethical. The captive tribes, he argues, are not worth the saving for they are themselves responsible for their plight, they have themselves foresaken the ways of God and embraced strange and heathen deities:

> Should I of these the liberty regard,
> Who freed, as to their ancient patrimony,
> Unhumbled, unrepentant, unreformed,

Headlong would follow, and to their gods perhaps
Of Bethal and of Dan? . . .[137]

And the Romans, too, are equally unworthy of rescue:

What wise and valiant man would seek to free
These thus degenerate, by themselves enslaved,
Or could of inward slaves make outward free?[138]

Political activism can be postponed, then, quite simply because the
political problem is not in itself primary. Rather, it is derivative, it
is a secondary factor, a consequence of the primary problem, the
problem of internal moral collapse. A nation that has sunk so low
from virtue requires a teacher rather than a liberator: the ethical
preconditions for political liberation must first be established before
political activism can be considered a legitimate enterprise. Political
quietism is thus justified whenever these preconditions are absent.
And there can, surely, be little doubt that Milton diagnosed such an
absence, not only in the body politic of the first-century Roman
Empire, but also in that of Restoration England.

In his account of the second temptation, Milton is dealing with a
theme which clearly embodies his own most profound political and
ethical preoccupations. The political defeat inflicted upon the Puritan
revolutionaries at the Restoration had necessitated a searching re-
examination of the efficacy of political action, and in *Paradise
Regained* Milton himself attempted an assessment of the relative
merits of both quietistic and activistic responses to political oppression. It is, of course, significant that Milton never even touches
upon the possibility that political activism is always, and in itself,
immoral, that the Christ of the Gospels rejected the kingdoms of the
world quite simply because those kingdoms are necessarily tainted by
the sins of the world. Milton's account is concerned with the
appropriateness, rather than the morality, of political action. And he
presents Christ's rejection of Satan's various offers as conditioned by
the *inappropriateness* of political solutions to the *particular* problems
which Satan poses. The possibility that political involvement may
indeed be appropriate to other circumstances is always actually kept
open. Hence the ambivalency of many of Christ's responses, which
we noted earlier. Milton does, in fact, suggest explanations of
Christ's resistance to Satan's temptations other than that of simple inappropriateness. Undoubtedly, Christ's insistence that the desirability

of a gift, in this case food, cannot be divorced from the nature of the giver, that is, Satan,[139] is intended as a comment, not merely on the first temptation, but on the whole series of temptations. And Satan's ultimate revelation of the terms upon which his various offers are made is similarly presented as a contributory factor in determining Christ's refusal.[140] But at no point does Milton ever suggest that the exercise of political power is itself immoral. Rather, it is, like food, a thing morally indifferent of itself. And exactly the same considerations apply to Satan's final offer, the offer of knowledge. There is, of course, no mention of such a temptation in any of the Gospels, and Milton presumably intends it as the final stage of the second temptation, rather than as an entirely new fourth temptation. Christ's strident denunciation .of classical Greek wisdom[141] has horrified countless readers of *Paradise Regained*, and it is indeed very far removed from the spirit of the *Areopagatica*. But this rejection, too, has to be seen as conditional, rather than absolute. Milton is here concerned to establish the paramount significance of internal moral strength as the only truly reliable foundation for any human endeavour. And neither classical knowledge nor political power can provide an effective substitute for such strength:

> . . . who reads
> Incessantly, and to his reading brings not
> A spirit and judgement equal or superior . . .

> . . . Uncertain and unsettled still remains,
> Deep versed in books and shallow in himself,[142]

The needs of the moment, the needs of the early Restoration period, demanded, above all, in Milton's view, the virtues of fortitude and resilience, of faith and hope. And in the myth of the second temptation Milton discerned a literary theme which would permit this ritual exorcism of his earlier political and intellectual concerns in favour of a new preoccupation with the politics of quietism. But, it must be insisted, Milton never actually effects a complete renunciation of the beliefs of his youth. Just as Christ's rejection of political activism is qualified by his endorsement of the behaviour of the old Roman republican leaders, so too, his condemnation of classical Greek culture is tempered by the recognition that even in pagan literature

> . . . moral virtue is expressed
> By light of nature not in all quite lost.[143]

After the sustained intellectual intensity of the debate between Chirst and Satan occasioned by the second temptation, the third and final temptation appears somewhat anti-climactic. And the very brevity of Milton's treatment indicates something of his own lack of interest in the intellectual substance of the matter. This is not to suggest that the poetry itself is in any sense uninteresting. On the contrary, the third temptation represents one of the few truly dramatic moments in the poem, and the verse moves vigorously and boldly towards its conclusion. Milton here achieves a moment of high drama, which does indeed represent the poem's *dramatic* climax, but only at the expense of emptying the incident of any real doctrinal content, and thus in a sense rendering it into an intellectual anti-climax. The drama of this last scene is, in fact, deliberately contrived. Throughout the poem, Milton is careful to sustain the impression that both Satan and Christ himself are only partially aware of the true nature of Christ's Sonship. Thus, for example, Milton repeatedly permits Christ to express ignorance as to the true nature of his divinely ordained mission.[144] And indeed, the poem is only compelled towards its dramatic climax, the third temptation itself, by Satan's nagging doubts as to the true identity of Christ.[145] This uncertainty is, of course, at first sight extremely implausible, since both Christ and Satan actually hear God the Father pronounce the former his beloved Son at the very beginning of the poem. But Milton goes to great lengths to suggest that neither is necessarily cognisant with the full meaning of that pronunciation. Their confusion is explicable, in Milton's account, according to the doctrine, here asserted by Satan— who, for once, is apparently speaking the truth—that all angels and men are in reality sons of God. As Satan says,

> The Son of God I also am, or was,
> And if I was, I am; relation stands;
> All men are sons of God; . . .[146]

The dramatic function of this carefully contrived uncertainty only finally becomes apparent at the pinnacle of the Temple, where both Satan and Christ simultaneously realise the awesome and dreadful truth that this Son is *the* Son, the man born of woman's seed who will bruise the head of the serpent:

> To whom thus Jesus: 'Also it is written,
> "Tempt not the Lord thy God." ' He said, and stood.
> But Satan smitten with amazement fell . . . .[147]

Thus the poem achieves its dramatic climax in this moment of discovery and self-discovery, a climax which is only rendered plausible on the basis of the assumption of a prior lack of, respectively, knowledge and self-knowledge. But Milton's treatment of the third temptation is determined, not only by the purely 'literary' necessity for such a moment of climax, but also, surely, by his own lack of interest in the intellectual meaning of the episode. In *Paradise Regained*, the third temptation is not a temptation at all. Rather, it is merely the dramatic *dénouement* of all that has gone before, that is, of the first temptation, built around the opposition between reason and passion, and the second temptation, built around that of quietism and activism. And, as we have already noted, Milton's treatment of the first temptation is peremptory in the extreme. *Paradise Regained* is, then, little more than a sustained dialogue as to the extents and limitations of political action. That dialogue is circumscribed by both a doctrinal prescript and a dramatic postscript. But it remains, nonetheless, the central theme of the poem. And we misread the poem if we believe otherwise.

The central intellectual meaning of *Paradise Regained*, the poem's thematic *content*, is contained in the doctrine of quietism. And the work's *formal* properties, which have generally proved so unpopular, derive from the nature of that content. Its language is as bare and as sparse as its doctrine, and its pronouncedly non-dramatic character derives from the non-dramatic nature of that same doctrine. If the poem's message is that of a hymn in praise of patience, fortitude, and a purely internal resistance to the world, a doctrine, as it were, of passivity rather than of activity, then it is barely remarkable that its poetic texture should partake of that same passive, and essentially static, quality. The aridity of the verse follows surely from the aridity of the doctrine. The style of *Paradise Regained* denies the glory and the brilliance of the epic style, just as its moral and political quietism denies the doctrinal content of the earlier epic theology. Christ's denunciation of classical Greek culture thus appears as no mere incidental element in the poem. On the contrary, Milton's new and decidedly non-classical doctrinal stance demands a renunciation of the forms of classical literature, a renunciation which is effected, at its most obvious, in the content of this particular speech, and, more generally, and more importantly, in the very form itself of the entire poem. Condee's suggestion that *Paradise Regained* represents some form of 'transcendence over the epic'[148] is, in fact, nonsensical. The term 'transcendence' clearly implies the notion of the reformulation of a particular problematic such that its component elements are qualitatively transformed by being raised to a higher, and more inclusive, level of discourse. In this sense *Paradise Lost* does, perhaps, represent a transcendence of the classical epic tradition. But in *Paradise Regained* no such transcendence is possible. Rather, the work is characterised by the process of renunciation: renunciation of the world, of political action, of both the forms and the content of classical literature—renunciation, in fact, of the poet's own past. But, of course, that renunciation is never total. The bareness and restraint of the poem's verse is intermittently qualified by, for example, the naked sensuality of the banquet scene, Satan's epic account of the battles in Parthia, and the high drama of the third temptation. And, as we noted earlier, Milton's renunciation of both activistic politics and classical literature is tempered by a repeated insistence on the conditional nature of this renunciation. The full significance of these repeated insertions, interruptions, and qualifications only becomes apparent, however, when we turn to Milton's last work, *Samson Agonistes*, a tragedy on the classical Greek model which takes as its theme precisely the related problems of political action and political liberation.

4 'Samson Agonistes'

In *Samson Agonistes*, just as in the earlier *Paradise Lost*, Milton is once again able to attain a synthesis of the particular with the universal, and the personal with the historical. That rift between the individual and history, and between life and meaning, which had necessitated both the formal and the doctrinal 'restraint' of *Paradise Regained*, does indeed reappear in *Samson Agonistes*, and an epic transcendence is thus no longer possible. But here that rift is no longer irreparable, the chasm is yet bridgeable. And Milton is able, therefore, to reformulate the central question of classical Greek tragedy, 'how can essence come alive?' This classical tragic theme demands, of course, an appropriately classical tragic form. And hence we arrive at a work, which is, in the proper sense of the term, a genuine classical tragedy, written in the English language, but nonetheless more akin to Sophocles than to Shakespeare. Thus Milton becomes the author, not only of the last, and in a real sense the only, major epic poem in the English language, but also of the last, and only, major classical tragedy born out of the modern, rather than the ancient, world.[149] *Samson Agonistes*'s strict formal classicism is indeed remarkable. The work conforms faithfully to the three classical unities of action, time and place; its use of the Chorus is archetypically classical; the texture of its verse has precisely the stiffness of Greek tragedy; and both the world-historical predominance of the personality of Samson over the poem's action, and the all-prevailing presence of a divine irony at the fate of men, clearly attest to Milton's resolute fidelity to both the form, and the spirit, of the earlier Greek models. Perhaps the most striking evidence of Milton's classicism is discernible in his determined abstention from any doctrinal pronouncement which could possibly be characterised as specifically Christian. As Saurat points out, Milton's omission of any mention of the doctrines of original sin and of salvation through Christ, and of any precision in the idea of God, is somewhat striking, to say the least.[150] And the absence of any mention of the notion of the after-life, a notion which would inevitably militate against the force of Samson's tragedy, is surely equally significant. The God of *Samson Agonistes* is the God of classical Greek tragedy, rather than that of Christian theology; he is, indeed, little more than destiny itself. This exclusion of any detailed elaboration of Christian doctrine clearly correlates with the poem's intensely human focus of attention: *Samson Agonistes* takes as its theme the destinies of particular men in a particular human situation. In both these respects, in both its relative indifference to the doctrinal content of an abstract theology, and its marked humanisation of Milton's poetic concerns, *Samson Agonistes* represents the culmination of a process of development which had been readily discernible in the movement from *Paradise Lost* to *Paradise Regained*. For in comparison to Milton's earlier epic, *Paradise Regained* too had appeared as a particular moment in the linked processes of a progressive humanisatioñ of thematic concerns and a progressive elimination of explicitly doctrinal content. *Paradise Regained* is devoid of the detailed elaboration of specifically Christian theological notions which characterises *Paradise Lost*, and its Christ is, as we noted earlier, a man rather than a cosmic hero. But in *Paradise Regained*, this movement away from the universality of theology and towards the specificity of the concretely human gives rise only to a preoccupation with the psychology of the abstract individual divorced from any over-arching context, whether metaphysical and religious or historical and social. In *Samson Agonistes*, however, Milton attempts once again to link the particular with the universal, to reconnect the isolated individual to the total chain of being. And the result is his political and literary testament, his ultimate solution to the problem of the triumph of unreason, his final justification of the ways of God.

The precise dating of *Samson Agonistes* has, of course, been a matter of some contention. It was published along with *Paradise Regained* in 1671, but whereas the opening lines of the latter work clearly indicate its status as a 'sequel' to *Paradise Lost*, there is no such obvious internal evidence for the date of composition of Milton's tragedy. We have assumed throughout that the later, and more generally accepted dating is, in fact, correct. But let us consider briefly a recent argument in favour of the view that *Samson Agonistes* is actually a much earlier work than either *Paradise Lost* or *Paradise Regained*. R. W. Condee argues, firstly, that whereas the two 'epic' poems exemplify an essentially 'instrumental' approach towards the epic tradition—that is, an approach which creatively utilises, rather than simply imitates, that tradition in order to achieve a distinctly new poetic effect— *Samson Agonistes* is merely imitative in its relation to the classical Greek tragedy. And he argues, secondly, that whereas the movement from *Paradise Lost* to *Paradise Regained* represents a movement from martial heroism towards spiritualised heroism, *Samson Agonistes* exemplifies a degree of commitment to the former conception which must predate that moment of transition between the two embodied in *Paradise Lost*.[151] Condee's first, purely 'literary', point is itself open to objection, however, since, as we argued above, *Paradise Regained* represents not so much a transcendence of the classical epic as its negation, and, in this respect, it is *Samson Agonistes*, rather than *Paradise Regained*, which most closely resembles *Paradise Lost* precisely because of its relative fidelity to the earlier classical models. But Condee's second point is by no means as purely 'literary' as he appears to believe. It presupposes an account of Milton's entire system of thought, his view of the world rather than merely of literature, which represents his intellectual development as proceeding along a purely linear course from one state of mind to another. Now it is, of course, perfectly possible that any particular individual's thought should conform to this particular pattern. But such a pattern is certainly neither inevitable nor universal. Its existence has to be demonstrated, rather than merely asserted. However, despite, for example, Woodhouse's earnest conviction that an understanding of Milton's state of mind provides the key to the problem of dating *Samson Agonistes*,[152] it remains unfortunately the case that the mind of a long-dead individual is a somewhat intractable object of study. The state of mind of an entire social group, by contrast, is necessarily much more readily accessible to our enquiries. And here, of course, we find the solution to our problem. For in the period of the Stuart Restoration, the period between the two revolutions, English radical thought follows a fairly clear pattern. In the face of the immediate impact of the Restoration, it became predominantly quietistic in character. But, as the endemic instability of the restored monarchy became increasingly discernible, English radicalism turned once again towards the possibilities of political action. Only seven years after the publication of *Samson Agonistes*, England was to be plunged into a political and constitutional crisis which would once again take the country to the very brink of civil war. Once again Parliament was to attempt to impeach the King's chief minister, once again a Stuart prince was to be obliged to go into exile, once again the House of Commons was to use its control over government finance as a lever on monarchical policy, and once again parliaments were to be dissolved and prorogued. Only the combination of a reign of legal terror directed against Whigs and dissenters, a timely remodelling of the borough charters in the Crown's interest, and the discovery of an undoubtedly politically premature plot to seize the King, would secure Charles II's crown from the fate of that of his father.[153] And his successor was, of course, to prove rather less fortunate. Social and political crises of this order rarely, if ever, emerge from out of nothingness, and it is surely inconceivable that the ideological preconditions for the Exclusion Crisis had not already been established, at least in part, well before 1678. The movement from quietism to activism in English radical thought as a whole clearly suggests a parallel movement in Milton's own thought, and we are thus led to the conclusion that the composition of *Samson Agonistes* must postdate that of both *Paradise Lost* and *Paradise Regained*.[154]

How, then, does Milton's tragedy articulate that new, and later, synthesis between the particular and the universal to which we have already, in outline, briefly referred? Those elements of continuity in Milton's thought, located around the central structural categories of the Protestant—rationalist world vision, which we identified in our earlier analysis of *Paradise Regained*, necessarily persist into *Samson Agonistes*. Once again, Milton is pre-eminently concerned with characterisation of *individual personality*: Samson's own inner development provides the central focus of interest for *Samson Agonistes*, just as that of Christ did for *Paradise Regained*. But in the later work, the poem's protagonist is a world-historical individual, a concretely human embodiment of a wider socio-historical collision, rather than a merely abstract individual, extracted out of any wider, social context. Whilst the ultimate development of Samson's individuality is, in a sense, immanent within his own previously defined identity, that immanence is only actualised as a consequence of a series of interactions with other human personalities. In *Samson Agonistes*, the minor characters—Manoa, Dálila, Harapha, and even the Chorus— are essential to the poem's inner movement in a manner in which those of *Paradise Regained* were not. The poem's action thus proceeds on two levels, that of, firstly, Samson's own internal regeneration, and secondly, Samson's series of encounters with other, external, agencies. And these two levels are, in fact, inextricably interconnected: Samson's inner moral strength both determines, and is determined by, the outcome of each of the major incidents in the poem. Like *Paradise Regained*, *Samson Agonistes* also attests to Milton's persistent attachment to the notion of meritocracy. Whilst the Miltonic Chorus does not normally represent, as the classical Greek chorus did, the 'voice' of the poem, and hence, too, that of the poet, there can be little doubt that it is the blind poet himself, rather than any mere character of his creation, who affirms that:

> For him I reckon not in high estate
> Whom long descent of birth
> Or the sphere of fortune raises;
> But thee whose strength, while virtue was her mate,
> Might have subdued the earth,
> Universally crowned with highest praises.[155]

Indeed, Milton's tragedy is, surely, the meritocratic tragedy *par excellence*. For Samson *earns* both his previous defeat at the hands of the Philistines, and his subsequent victory over them. And the entire action of the poem is centred on its hero's struggle to prepare himself, to fit himself, for that great deed which will represent the culminating point, at one and same time, of both his own moral career and his nation's resistance to oppression. The third, and final, element of continuity between the three poems is located around Milton's concern with the ethical and political implications of the ontological dichotomy between reason and passion. For, of course, that ethical and political collapse on Samson's part which occasions the events with which the tragedy is concerned is directly attributable to the untoward influence of passion, and specifically of sexual passion, over

Samson's reason. In the course of the poem's development, Samson will thus be obliged to demonstrate—to himself, to his God, to the poem's other characters, and so, too, to the reader—a new imperviousness to the claims of passion. And this repudiation of the passions enters into the poem, not only at the level of its content, but also at the level of its form. Milton's prose introduction to the work clearly indicates his commitment to a cathartic, rather than a catastrophic, definition of the nature of tragedy.[156] The work's intended function is that of a purgation of the passions. And the poem's closing lines proclaim a 'calm of mind',[157] a rational control over the passions, which is the property of its author and of its audience as much as of its protagonists.

Of the three longer poems, *Samson Agonistes* offers most clearly and concretely a politico-historical solution to the problem of the triumph of unreason. Of course, the theme of the personal solution does not disappear; any rationalistic individualism must necessarily pose political problems in personal terms. But in Milton's tragedy the personal solution, that of Samson's own individual redemption, is indissolubly linked to the political solution, that of the overthrow of the Philistines, and, moreover, the effective operation of this dual solution is, as we noted earlier, firmly situated within the context of a concrete historical situation. Samson is not only a man, as was the Christ of *Paradise Regained*, but also an ordinary man; the triumph over passion is not here a half-allegory, but rather an actual political triumph situated in historical time. *Samson Agonistes* is, as it were, an account of the fall *made specific*. The poem opens with Samson defeated, personally by his betrayal of the secret of his strength to Dálila, and politically by the Philistines. Once more, the source of the fall lies in the triumph of passion over reason, and once more the decision to succumb to passion is freely made. Thus Samson cries:

> Whom have I to complain of but myself?
> Who this high gift of strength committed to me,
> In what part lodged, how easily bereft me,
> Under the seal of silence could not keep,
> But weakly to a woman must reveal it,
> O'ercome with importunity and tears.
> O impotence of mind in body strong!
> But what is strength without a double share
> Of wisdom?[158]

When Samson's father, Manoa, attempts to question the justice of the divine order, and to indulge in special pleading on behalf of his son, Samson himself remains insistent that the fault is his own, and not that of God.[159] Samson appears, then, at the very beginning of the poem, in precisely that pose of repentant obedience and patient quietism which had previously, in *Paradise Regained*, appeared to Milton as the only possible response to the defeat of reason. But if Samson's own voice is the voice of self-rebuke, if Samson himself is capable of an immediate justification of the ways of God, the voice of the Chorus, by contrast, is much less certain. From the very beginning, the Chorus is concerned to emphasise the extent of Samson's past virtue and to bewail his present fate, thus, implicitly at least, casting doubt on the justice of his present situation. Indeed, Milton even permits the Chorus to raise the possibility, but only, of course, in order to reject it, of atheism.[160] In the course of the brief interlude between Samson's exchanges with his father and with Dálila, the Chorus comes to express a sense of the apparent injustice of God's ways which had surely, at some point, been close to Milton's own. The Chorus's commentary on Samson's plight here undoubtedly provides an echo of Milton's own perplexity at the course of events which had overtaken revolutionary England:

> God of our fathers, what is man!
> That thou towards him with hand so various –
> Or might I say contrarious? –
> Temper'st thy providence through his short course, . . .[161]

The directly political implications of this speech are made explicit as the Chorus proceeds to emphasise its interest, not in men of 'the common rout',[162] but in those who are elected

> To some great work, thy glory,
> And people's safety, which in part they effect;[163]

And in the lines that follow, the Chorus's description of the possible fates of such men[164] clearly invokes the full tragedy of the persecution of the former Independents. This reference to the old republican regicides is, of course, too obviously intentional to be ignored. Milton permits the Chorus to question Samson's belief in the essentially beneficent nature of the divine order in lines deliberately resonant with the memories of recent events in England, lines which derive much of their emotional power and strength from his own deeply felt perplexities. There is, then, an apparent contradiction here between the voice of Samson, on the one hand, which reiterates the earlier Miltonic arguments in favour of moral self-responsibility and fortitude in the face of adversity, and the voice of the Chorus, on the other, which naggingly questions those older certainties. And it is by no means clear which of these voices can, as yet, be considered as truly and properly that of the poet himself.

If one were to assess the relative merits of Samson's declared stance against those of that of the Chorus in terms of the moral universe of *Paradise Regained*, one would, of course, be obliged to conclude that Samson's moral posture is by far the superior of the two. Now this is, in fact, extremely significant: Samson has attained, at the very *beginning* of the poem, that stoic heroism which the *whole* of *Paradise Regained* is designed to exhibit as constitutive of Christ's special virtues, which, indeed, provides the earlier poem with its essential *telos*. But in *Samson Agonistes* this quietistic virtue is itself exposed to criticism. The Chorus's doubts are not the doubts of mere waverers situated within the poem; rather, they are here the doubts of the poem itself. Their problem is Milton's problem, and the poem's development is designed so as to provide a solution to that problem. That solution is, in fact, located in the movement, on Samson's part, away from quietism and towards activism. In *Paradise Regained* political quietism is presented as the height of moral virtue, as the product of an inner strength which can resist all the temptations of the world. But there are, nonetheless, other possible alternative characterisations of the nature of quietism. In his diary entry for 7 August 1664, Samuel Pepys recalls a brief encounter with the Quakers thus:'While we were talking, came by several poor creatures carried by Constables for being at a conventicle. They go like lambs, without any resistance. I would to God they would either conform, or be more wise and not be ketched.'[165] Here quietism appears, not so much as heroism, although it does indeed partake of something of that character, even in Pepys view, but rather as a form of fatalism. Pepys is clearly appalled at the sheer submissiveness of it all; they 'go like lambs, without any resistance', and to the slaughter, he might well have added. And in *Samson Agonistes*, Milton too is apprehensible of the weaknesses of such a fatalism. Samson, at the beginning of the poem, is not yet truly heroic; rather, he is merely submissive to the blind decrees of fate. Samson has, indeed, recognised his fault, but in so doing he has also abandoned all hope. As he tells his father:

Nor am I in the list of them that hope;
Hopeless are all my evils, all remediless;[166]

And it is, significantly enough, at precisely this point in the poem that the Chorus intervenes in order to question the efficacy of 'patience as the truest fortitude'.[167] Samson's quietism is as indicative, or even more so, of the 'sense of Heav'n's desertion',[168] as is the Chorus's transparent perplexity at his fate. For the Milton of *Samson Agonistes*, quietism and patient fortitude are no longer in themselves sufficient. In the process of development from *Paradise Regained* to *Samson Agonistes*, the figure of the quietistic hero had, as it were, been rotated in the light of Milton's vision, and in the later work it displays a different, and far less attractive, face, the face of fatalism, the face of those who 'go like lambs, without any resistance'.

How, then, does Milton effect this transition from quietism to activism? Dr Johnson's view that *Samson Agonistes* had a beginning and an end, but no middle, is, of course, well known. And if Samson's state of mind at the beginning of the poem, his admission of blame and his acknowledgement of divine justice, were in themselves sufficient psychological preconditions for the attainment of his ultimate act of heroism, then Johnson would indeed be correct. But, in fact, that earlier fortitude is insufficient. As Condee rightly observes, the 'middle' of *Samson Agonistes* consists in Samson's reconstruction of his own personality so as to prepare himself for his final encounter with the Philistines.[169] But Condee's account is inadequate as an explanation of the nature of that process of reconstruction. That which is reconstructed is, above all, Samson's *martial vigour*. And, in this respect, it is the encounter with Harapha, the Philistine warrior, rather than that with Dálila, which provides the poem with the key 'structural linkage' between its beginning and its end. The dramatic function of Samson's exchange with Dálila is, to say the least, somewhat self-evident. Having betrayed his secret to her, and having thus subordinated his reason to the demands of sexual passion, it is necessary that Samson should now provide some firm proof of his future imperviousness to the claims of passion. Dálila is clearly intended by Milton as a symbol of passion as opposed to reason, and of indulgence as opposed to duty. She quite literally *tempts* him:

> . . . Though sight be lost,
> Life yet hath many solaces, enjoyed

Where other senses want not their delights
At home in leisure and domestic ease,[170]

But Samson is already a new man, a man who has overcome his
weaker passions, a man who refuses to be deceived a second time, and
who is able to dismiss her thus:

. . . I know thy trains,
Though dearly to my cost, thy gins, and toils;
Thy fair enchanted cup and warbling charms
No more on me have power, their force is nulled;[171]

As Christ resisted Satan, so Samson resists Dálila. Samson's own
personal triumph over the 'enchanted cup and warbling charms' of
sexual passion is not, however, the final stage in the reconstruction of
his personality; it is no longer a sufficient answer to the problem of
unreason triumphant. It still remains for him to re-attain his own
previous martial courage. And this is, of course, the significance of the
subsequent confrontation between Samson and Harapha, the only
major incident in Milton's tragedy which is entirely the poet's own
invention.[172] In the face of Harapha, the blind champion of the
Israelites reveals himself as prepared once more for military conflict.
The Christ of *Paradise Regained* could suffer and obey. But Samson
must do more: Samson must act. Harapha, in fact, declines to accept
the challenge which Samson throws down. And he does so, not only
on the grounds that the blind warrior is no worthy opponent, but
also, and perhaps more importantly, on the grounds that he is a
'murtherer, a revolter, and a robber'.[173] Israel, Harapha observes, is
subject to the Philistine lords, and that subjection is, moreover,
perfectly legal, since the Israelite magistrates themselves have acquiesced in its imposition. Samson's previous resistance was, therefore, an
act of rebellion against duly constituted authority. In 1660, English
magistrates, too, had sold their nation into bondage. In *Paradise
Regained*, Christ had rejected the possibility of political action on the
grounds that an internally unfree people deserve only an external
tyranny. But in *Samson Agonistes*, Samson proclaims the right and
duty of the elect to resist such tyranny, whatever the moral state of the
people at large:

I was no private but a person raised
With strength sufficient and command from Heav'n

To free my country; if their servile minds
Me their deliverer sent would not receive,
But to their masters gave me up for naught,
Th' unworthier they, whence to this day they serve.
I was to do my part from Heav'n assigned,[174]

In the late 1660s and the early 1670s, the ghosts of the Interregnum were beginning once more to walk the land.

Samson's confrontation with Harapha marks the introduction into the work of a new mood of political hope, a mood which, in fact, persists right through until the poem's closing lines. This shift in tone is initially inaugurated by Samson himself, who, for the first time, now anticipates the possibility of the overthrow of the Philistines.[175] But it is quickly taken up by the Chorus which perfectly expresses the dual emphasis of the poem, on both personal and political regeneration, in the lines that follow:

Oh how comely it is and how reviving
To the spirits of just men long oppressed
When God into the hands of their deliverer
Puts invincible might
To quell the mighty of the earth, th'oppressor,
The brute and boist'rous force of violent men,[176]

and:

But patience is more oft the exercise
Of saints, the trial of their fortitude,
Making them each his own deliverer,
And victor overall
That tyranny or fortune can inflict;[177]

Milton retains that belief in the importance of inner moral strength which had characterised the entire corpus of his work, but here in *Samson Agonistes*, unlike *Paradise Regained*, he is also able to reaffirm his belief in another, active virtue, the virtue that challenges tyranny. And it is this second, active virtue, the virtue of the warrior and of the revolutionary, which provides *Samson Agonistes* with its real thematic focus. The Chorus's suggestion that Samson's blindness marks him out as destined, probably, to a quietistic, rather than an active, virtue,[178] is, of course, intentionally ironic. But this irony serves also

to emphasise precisely those possibilities for activism, even in the face
of an apparent inappropriateness, which *Paradise Regained* had been
concerned to deny. So, too, does the subsequent encounter between
Samson and the Philistine Officer. It is important to note that
Samson's declared reasons for obeying the Philistine commands, his
recognition of a 'resistless' power which is owed 'absolute subjection',[179] are not, in fact, his real reasons. Rather, they are
deliberately intended by Samson so as to mislead the Officer. Samson
has, indeed, already demonstrated his typically Miltonic disdain for
the constraints which external tyranny attempts to impose:

> Where outward force constrains, the sentence holds;
> But who constrains me to the temple of Dagon,
> Not dragging? The Philistines lords command.
> Commands are no constraints. If I obey them,
> I do it freely, venturing to displease
> God for the fear of man, . . .[180]

On precisely such grounds did both Milton himself, and the dissenters
generally, refuse to obey the commands of the Restoration
monarchy's attempted ecclesiastical dictatorship. For the truly
rationalist thinker, a command is in itself no constraint; only that
which either physically constrains the body or successfully persuades
the mind can be properly afforded the title of a 'constraint' upon
action. It is, of course, interesting to note the element of continuity
which runs between this early manifestation of bourgeois rationalism
and the existentialist theories of our own time. But even in the face of
adversity, the earlier theoretical formation remains much more
essentially optimistic in its implications. Certainly, the relationship
between meaning and life has already become problematic; but the
break between the two has not yet become a yawning chasm, and
despair has not yet substituted itself for tragedy. For Milton, bad faith
can so readily be overcome, and *angst* so readily be transcended into
activism, that the moment of doubt barely registers on the conscious
mind. Samson senses the possibility of action, and, grasping at the
proffered opportunity, determines to go with the Philistine
Officer.[181] His victory, and with it his death, thus become inevitable.
    The poem's tragic *dénouement* hurriedly follows. Samson is led
away to provide the Philistines with sport in their festivities. And
shortly after we learn from the Messenger of Samson's great deed, his
act of self-sacrifice which achieved the destruction of the Philistines.

In the commentary which follows, the Chorus pointedly contrasts the Philistines, slaves to their own passions, 'only set on sport and play',[182] with Samson, the Israelite hero, physically blind, but nonetheless with 'inward eyes illuminated'.[183] Samson, the embodiment of reason, and of an active virtue which knows no external tyranny, destroys the Philistine lords, whose presence here clearly symbolises that fusion of political despotism with psychological subservience to the passions which had provided perhaps the single most powerful and persistent image in the whole of Milton's political thought. Thus the ageing revolutionary reasserted the possibility of political activism and, indeed, of political victory. It might be objected that this solution is not genuinely political, that it is merely a personal solution writ large, since Samson acts alone, both triumphs and perishes alone. But Milton's individualism had always led him, as do all individualistic philosophical systems, into a reduction of the political to the personal, and the social to the individual. Within the terms of the parameters set by an individualistic world vision, the final outcome of *Samson Agonistes* remains genuinely political. And it is surely precisely the function of Manoa's closing remarks to underline the specifically political aspects of Samson's tragedy. Samson's heroism, his father emphasises, has brought honour and freedom to Israel,[184] and the monument which will be erected over his tomb will serve as an inspiration to future generations of Israelite youth.[185] Tillyard is surely right to point to the importance of these overtly political and self-evidently this-worldly ramifications of the poem's ultimate resolution.[186] Paradoxically, Milton's great tragedy is, in a sense, much less genuinely tragic than is *Paradise Lost*, for whereas Adam merely receives the formal promise of personal and political redemption, Samson concretely attains them both. Hence, the paradox of *Samson Agonistes*'s markedly optimistic conclusion, which stands in sharp contrast to the mournful tone of the last two lines of *Paradise Lost*. Manoa's judgement on the action that:

Nothing is here for tears, nothing to wail
Or knock the breast, no weakness, no contempt,
Dispraise, or blame; nothing but well and fair,
And what may quiet us in a death so noble.[187]

has a certain solidity, a certain inner conviction, which makes Adam's closing optimism ring distinctly hollow. And the poem's last lines have that same air of inner certainty. Each of the three longer poems

ends, of course, on an essentially 'quiet' note which is characteristically Miltonic, and this 'quietness' is, in each case, a manifestation in
form of Milton's own conviction that the poem's central thematic
problem has indeed been resolved. But, despite this common
'quietness', the three conclusions are nonetheless radically distinct.
Paradise Lost ends, as we noted above, with a residual ambiguity
which finds expression in the contradiction between the poem's
formally optimistic conclusion and the mournful tone of its last two
lines. *Paradise Regained* has the quietest ending of the three. The
poem, which has been characterised throughout by an indifference to
physical action, as opposed to inner moral development, ends with a
simple and unadorned description of Christ's return to his mother's
house, his own, though not the poem's, initial physical starting
point.[188] And this return from the privacy of the wilderness to the
privacy of domesticity provides an appropriate enough symbol of the
poem's quietistic theme. But the closing lines of *Samson Agonistes* are
neither ambiguous, in the manner of *Paradise Lost*, nor 'passive', in
that of *Paradise Regained*. In the last lines of poetry which Milton
wrote, there is an underlying note of certainty, a certainty born out of
the active test of an uncloistered virtue, which indicates, surely, that
the old revolutionary had, at last, found the answer to that problem
which had beset him, which had worried, and troubled, and inspired
him, for the ten years or more that had followed on the failure of the
republic:

> His servant he, with new acquist,
> Of true experience from this great event,
> With peace and consolation hath dismissed,
> And calm of mind, all passion spent.[189]

We have pointed to the profoundly optimistic nature of Milton's
last great poem. The Milton of *Samson Agonistes* had regained his
earlier conviction in the potentialities for both individual and political
regeneration. And it is, of course, precisely this optimism which has
led to doubts as to the genuinely 'tragic' nature of Milton's tragedy.
That Milton himself had no doubts as to its tragic status is apparent
from his own introduction to the poem. Woodhouse, however,
argues that Milton intended to follow the model of Greek tragedy
only in respect of structure and convention, and not in that of spirit
and effect.[190] Certainly, that effect of consolation and reassurance,
which Woodhouse rightly characterises as marking the poem's end, is

alien to the tradition of classical Greek tragedy. For Milton located the essence of tragedy, as we have already observed, not in the fact of unmitigated catastrophe, but rather in the process of catharsis. As he himself says, quoting Aristotle, tragedy is 'of power, by raising pity and fear, or terror, to purge the mind of those and suchlike passions, that is, to temper and reduce them to just measure with a kind of delight, stirred up by reading or seeing those passions well imitated'.[191] But Woodhouse is, however, surely mistaken to suggest that Milton's attempt at a mitigation of catastrophe derives from the specifically Christian nature of the theology to which he adheres. Indeed, the entire problem which Woodhouse poses—that is, the problem of reconciling the un-tragic nature of Christianity with the demands of the tragic form—is, in a sense, unreal. For there is little or nothing of Christian doctrine to be found in *Samson Agonistes*. On the contrary, it is precisely the absence of certain obviously relevant Christian notions, and in particular that of the notion of the after-life, which constitutes one of the most distinctive features of the poem. Furthermore, Christianity is not in itself inherently un-tragic; Goldmann's studies of Jansenism attest sufficiently to the tragic possibilities of the Christian religion. Woodhouse himself argues that Milton manages to attain a specifically Christian tragic effect through, firstly, the introduction into the poem of a strong element of irony, and secondly, the presentation of Samson's responses to his situation in purely human terms. Tragic irony is, indeed, a constitutive element in the poetic texture of the entire work. It is particularly evident in the exchange between Manoa and the Chorus immediately prior to the news of Samson's death. But it is present, too, in many of Samson's own speeches. Thus, for example, when Samson determines to accompany the Philistine Officer, he predicts that:

If there be aught of presage in the mind,
This day will be remarkable in my life
By some great act, or of my days the last.[192]

It will, in fact, be both his last day and the day which marks the greatest act of his life. But it is difficult to see this irony as the product of anything specifically Christian. Is it not, rather, a typically tragic device, that device by which the protagonists are driven, as a consequence of their own actions, towards an ultimate outcome which is far removed from their initial intentions? Samson's fate is surely no more ironical than that of Oedipus. As to Woodhouse's second point, that Samson's situation is posed in entirely human terms, that is undoubtedly the case. But Woodhouse is here suggesting that Milton attains a truly tragic effect by, as it were, bracketing out the prospect of Samson's ultimate reconciliation with God from the preceding action. This observation would only be of any real significance if the final processes of mitigation and re-assurance were represented, by Milton, as essentially spiritual affairs. In reality, they are not. The tragedy of Samson's death is mitigated, not by the prospect of an after-life, which would be the one obviously mitigating factor in orthodoxly Christian theology, but rather by the concretely human facts of victory over the Philistines, of the liberation of Israel, and of the future fame which will accrue to both Samson himself and his father's house. The tragedy of *Samson Agonistes* is indeed, as Woodhouse suggests, and as Milton himself explicitly affirms, cathartic rather than catastrophic. But the final mitigation of the poem's tragedy is in no sense specifically Christian. Rather, it derives from the underlying optimism of the rationalist world vision itself. *Samson Agonistes* is the product, not of a tragic vision, whether Christian or non-Christian, but of an optimistic rationalism. And it is here an optimism made concrete, an optimism almost entirely shorn of transcendental notions, an optimism which stands on the very brink of an explicitly atheistic rationalism. This optimism is, of course, very different from that of the revolutionary period itself. It is an optimism grounded, not on a belief in imminent victory, but rather on a conception of progress which incorporates into itself an understanding of the possibilities for defeat. And the mediating agency between present defeat and ultimate victory, clearly embodied in the symbol of Samson's 'great deed', is, of course, moral and political activism. Thus did Milton succeed in bringing meaning once more to life; and thus did English rationalism attain its highest form of literary and philosophic truth.

6 A Note on Christopher Hill's *Milton*

The interim period between the completion of the manuscript for the above work and its final publication witnessed the appearance of Christopher Hill's *Milton and the English Revolution*.[1] Dr Hill's book is much more than a conventional work in literary criticism or history; indeed, in its general outline, though not in its substantive content, his intellectual project appears remarkably similar to my own. I therefore feel obliged to attempt some sort of appraisal of Dr Hill's book. I had considered the possibility of integrating a critical assessment of Hill's *Milton* into the main body of my own book. But, on consideration, it seemed to me that Dr Hill's approach is deserving of a more detailed treatment than could possibly be carried through in that fashion. I therefore offer the following account of the main differences which exist between Dr Hill and myself, and of the main ways in which, in my opinion, my own approach is theoretically the superior of the two. I make no claim to a familiarity with the empirical details of seventeenth-century English history which could possibly equal, let alone surpass, that of Dr Hill. He brings to his work an immense erudition, acquired in the course of a lifetime's commitment to the study of the English Revolution, which I could not conceivably hope to match. However, I would maintain that the theoretical apparatus which I have made use of in my work is clearly superior to that deployed by Dr Hill and that this superiority gives to my work an analytical cutting edge which is lacking in Hill's. I leave it to the reader to pass final judgement.

By the standards of previous Milton criticism, Hill's *Milton* is boldly adventurous. It restores the poet to that social context from which he has been wrenched by the ahistorical idealism of mainstream literary criticism. Its emphasis on the radicalism both of that context and of the poet himself serves as a valuable corrective to those who have sought to subsume Milton under the mantle of conservative orthodoxy. Milton the dour Puritan is superseded by

Milton the libertarian revolutionary, and much that has previously appeared obscure becomes clarified. The central argument of Hill's *Milton* can be summarised thus: the English Revolution arose initially out of a conflict between two cultures, that of the court and that of the respectable Puritan 'country';[2] behind the backs of these two propertied cultures there existed, however, a third, popular heretical culture which found expression in the various outbursts of lower class heresy from the fifteenth century onwards;[3] once the Revolution got underway, this third culture emerged from its previously submerged state and came to constitute the extreme radical wing of the Parliamentarian camp;[4] Milton himself was neither a Puritan proper, nor a radical proper, but rather occupied a position, in some sense, mid-way between the second and third cultures,[5] accepting much of the radical position, but always drawing back whenever that position appeared to threaten the continued existence of propertied society.[6] Hill proceeds to analyse Milton's work in terms of this underlying conflict between the demands of the second and third cultures. Thus, summarising his own account of Milton's Interregnum prose writings (and also of the *Treatise on Christian Doctrine*), Hill concludes that there exists a fundamental 'uncertainty at the heart of Milton's personality', an uncertainty characteristic of all 'perplexed middle-of-the-road radicals'.[7] He detects a similar uncertainty at the core of the three great longer poems. Each of the three poems is concerned, in part at least, with the need to make sense of the political defeat which the revolutionaries suffered at the hands of the Restoration in 1660.[8] And each offers a solution to the problem of defeat: in *Paradise Lost* that solution consists in a purely internal happiness, in *Paradise Regained* in divine Sonship, in *Samson Agonistes* in political activism in the service of God.[9] But nonetheless, despite the apparently definitive nature of their respective solutions, each work retains this Miltonic uncertainty. In Hill's view, all Milton's great poems 'have ambiguities at the centre', ambiguities which arise out of Milton's peculiarly 'eclectic position between the second and third cultures'.[10] Hill offers us, then, a powerful new reading, not only of Milton's life, but also of his work, and the key to the understanding of each is this notion of the poet as straddled uneasily between two cultures.

1   *An Absent Presence: the Independents and the English Revolution*

An account of Milton such as Hill's, or indeed my own, necessarily stands and falls on the basis of the validity of the corresponding account of the Revolution. An assessment of Hill's *Milton* therefore demands an assessment of Hill's Revolution. Hill's version of the English Revolution derives from a number of sources. As one might reasonably expect of a writer with Hill's background, it owes something to Marx: the Revolution is a 'middle-class' revolution;[11] and the conflict between second and third cultures is essentially a class conflict between, on the one hand, the propertied Puritans, and, on the other, the lower class heretics. But Hill's debt to Marx coexists alongside that owed to those historians, such as Hugh Trevor-Roper, who have sought to explain the Civil War as the consequence of a rupture between the court and the country. In Hill's account, the court/country opposition is crucial to the explanation of the initial conflict between Royalists and Puritans, whereas the Marxian emphasis on class conflict is primarily relevant to that of the subsequent divisions within the Parliamentarian camp. Clearly, this represents a considerable revision of the classical Marxist account of the Revolution to which Hill once subscribed.[12] In itself, such 'revisionism' is, of course, no crime. Quite the contrary; theoretical innovation is often a necessary precondition for the production of new knowledge. But this particular revision has certain rather unfortunate consequences. Let us consider the matter in a little more detail.

Trevor-Roper's original version of the court/country thesis was developed in deliberate opposition to that type of Marxism which seeks to explain political phenomena as simple consequences of other, economic phenomena. Clearly, Hill shares little of Trevor-Roper's hostility to 'economic' explanations *per se*. And yet he is strangely silent on the class nature of both the court and the country. We learn merely that: 'Under the pressures of expanding population, economic crisis and ideological rivalry, the consensus which had held Elizabethan society together was breaking down.'[13] Yet the class alignments of the Civil War are not too difficult to discern: as we attempted to demonstrate in Chapter 3, the court drew its support from the titular nobility and their retainers, the great merchant and financial monopolists, and the traditional northern gentry, Parliament its support from the smaller merchants, the 'progressive' southern gentry, and the tradesmen, shop-keepers, artisans, and apprentices of urban England. And these alignments are by no means random; rather, they are structured around the central contradiction between the economic and political restrictiveness of the absolutist state, on the one hand, and the demands of the expanding capitalist mode of production on the other. Hill barely touches on any of this: a 'middle-class' revolution this may be; a bourgeois revolution, in the classical Marxist sense, it is not. This is not to suggest, however, that Hill merely incorporates the earlier court/country thesis wholescale into his own account. On the contrary, there are, in fact, very clear differences between his and earlier versions. Despite whatever criticisms may be made of the court/country thesis, the variant propounded by Trevor-Roper did at least have the great merit of its insistence on the institutions of the state as the central locus of conflict. Now Hill's version, by comparison with the Trevor-Roper account, is surprisingly *depoliticised*. The conflict between court and country as it appears in Hill's *Milton* is neither 'economic' nor even especially 'political' in its origins. Rather, it is essentially a conflict of cultures. Indeed, if there is any one term which is crucial to the structure of Hill's argument it is this word 'culture'. In the theoretical terrain inhabited by Hill's *Milton*, 'cultural' variables occupy all the commanding heights; in this strange land, 'cultures' come into conflict with each other and nations are torn apart by 'cultural crises'. Hill's account of the actual *politics* of the revolutionary period is as cursory as his discussion of its material preconditions.

   This indifference to the political is discernible, not merely in Hill's recasting of the court/country thesis but even at that point at which a more orthodoxly Marxian element enters most readily into his analysis—that is, that point at which he discusses the splits which occurred within the Parliamentarian camp. Most accounts of these divisions including, previously, Hill's own,[14] point to three main political groupings which formed on the Parliamentarian side, the Presbyterians, the Independents, and the Levellers. But Hill's *Milton* pays scant attention to these specifically political formations; rather, its focus of attention remains the two main Parliamentarian 'cultures', the Puritan and the radical. This substitution of two cultures for three parties has certain interesting consequences. In very general terms, Hill does postulate a relationship between culture and politics: the binary opposition between Puritan and radical cultures is seen as in some sense analogous to that between Presbyterian and radical politics.[15] But what, then, becomes of the Independents? The answer is that they simply disappear from view, or rather that Hill fails to draw any clear distinction between them and their more radical allies. Now this is very unfortunate indeed. The absence from the scene of the Independents as a distinct political force renders much of

Interregnum history quite simply unintelligible. A two-party model, based on the opposition between Presbyterians and radicals, will suffice to explain the conflict between Parliament and Army and its final resolution at Pride's Purge. But it provides us with no way of analysing the divisions *within* the Army which finally came to a head with the Leveller revolt and its suppression.

Hill's failure to distinguish with any real clarity between Independents and radicals is a direct consequence of his insistence on 'cultural', as opposed to 'political', explanations. For, of course, there is a sense in which Independents and radicals do share some elements of a common 'culture'. The various radical heresies which Hill points to as constitutive of the third culture[16] exercised a considerable attraction, not only for lower-class heretics, but also for many of the Independent grandees, including, indeed, even Oliver Cromwell. But once we move from the 'cultural' level of analysis to the more explicitly 'political', this common culture collapses into two opposed political groupings, the two groupings which opposed each other at Putney and later at Burford. And clearly, these political differences are actually far more significant than any 'cultural' affinities. They are so in the first place because revolution is essentially a political matter, and secondly because it is precisely in the process of *conflict* that social groups become effective social actors. As Marx understood very well, social classes only become actors, rather than mere categories, at that point at which they become conscious of their own collective interests as *opposed* to the interests of others. The same might be said of any social group, including the Interregnum political parties. If one is to understand the radical milieu in which Milton moved it becomes necessary, then, to analyse these political differences, between Independents and Levellers, in a way that Hill simply does not do. (Hill's key term is, of course, 'radical' rather than 'Leveller'. And there were indeed cultural radicals who were not political Levellers. But the Leveller party remains the only effective political voice of the lower classes, and as such it must remain the focus of attention. In terms of political efficacy, lower-class radicalism *is* Levelling.)

Once we dispense with Hill's notion of a unitary third culture and substitute for it the notion of a class conflict between bourgeois Independents and petty bourgeois Levellers, Milton's own precise social and political location becomes much easier to situate. He is, in fact, an Independent pure and simple. Certainly, his own social position is that of a bourgeois Independent rather than a petty bourgeois Leveller. His family background was, as Hill himself states,

'Protestant, bourgeois and cultured'.[17] His father was a successful and ruthless businessman[18]—and so apparently was Milton himself.[19] And his political beliefs are similarly Independent, rather than Leveller, in character. On each of the four major points at issue between the two parties, which we discussed in Chapter 3 above, Milton unequivocally supported the Independent position. On the question of the franchise, Milton remained consistently anti-democratic throughout his political career.[20] He fully supported the invasion of Ireland[21] and, indeed, even went so far as to provide his party with a coherent rationale for English imperialism *in general*.[22] Nowhere does Milton actually discuss the rival schemes for the internal organisation of the Army, but his broad political outlook would suggest that he can have had little sympathy for the rank-and-file democracy proposed by the Levellers. Moreover, Milton expressed unreserved admiration for the Army leadership on more than one occasion.[23] And, as we demonstrated above, the limits of Milton's tolerationism were almost identical to those actually imposed by the Independent revolutionary governments: it did not extend to the point of tolerating Papism. Milton's politics were, then, those of the Independent party. And if there is any residual doubt as to the matter, then surely Milton's panegyric to Cromwell[24] provides the final, decisive, article of evidence, the last piece which completes the jigsaw puzzle. In this context, Hill's observation that 'Milton never attacked the Levellers, but he never associated himself with their political tradition'[25] appears a little disingenuous. Milton may not have actually explicitly attacked the Levellers by name. But he was busily committed to propagandising on behalf of a political position to which the Levellers were opposed.

2   *The Writer and Society*

We have argued in Chapters 4 and 5 that Milton was not only socially and politically an Independent, but that he was also, in a sense, culturally an 'Independent' writer. This brings us to a more general problem, a problem which we discussed at length in Chapter 1, that of, to pose it rather abstractly, the relationship between the writer and society. It is a problem which has figured prominently in the debates of both academic sociology and western Marxism, and which has attracted much attention of late in a whole series of English-language publications. English-speaking audiences are today familiar, in a way that they once were not, with the views on such matters of writers as diverse as Sartre, Brecht and Benjamin, Lukács and Goldmann, Althusser and Gramsci. But if Hill himself is familiar with those debates, then he determinedly conceals that fact from his reader. That characteristically 'English' contempt for theory, which Hill's work has often exhibited in the past, surfaces once again in his *Milton*. But, of course, theory is never absent; it is only ever concealed. And even if Hill does refrain from any explicit theorisation, an implicit theory of the relationship between writer and society nonetheless informs and orders the whole of his argument. Let us examine the nature of that theory.

Hill views Milton, in the first place, as straddled uneasily between the second and third cultures and as, in a very real sense, *marginal* to both. Thus: 'If we think of two eccentric circles, one representing the ideas of traditional Puritanism, the other those of the radical milieu, Milton's ideas form a third circle, concentric to neither of these but overlapping both.'[26] Now there is a whole tradition in sociological writing about literature which would tend to regard this notion of the great writer as marginal as inherently improbable. Lukács and Goldmann certainly see the great writer as normally necessarily *representative* of a social class or group. But such a position does seem too abstractly categorical to remain universally tenable (and both Lukács and Goldmann do, at times, attest to the marginality of certain writers, and, in particular, certain modern writers). However, if there is any point at all in a sociology of literature (and Hill's own project clearly suggests that he believes there to be such a point), then such cultural marginality needs to be related to the social marginality of the writer's position. This is perfectly possible in the case of modern writers such as Kafka and Joyce. But it is not possible in the case of Milton. Hill himself establishes the poet's class position as solidly bourgeois; Milton was, moreover, an active participant, rather than a marginal observer, in both the revolutionary movement and, later, in Cromwell's revolutionary government; and, as Hill's own work clearly demonstrates, Milton was, in fact, an eminently sociable man, firmly rooted in, and enjoying the pleasures of, a distinct and particular social milieu.[27] He simply *cannot* be the uneasy occupant of a culturally marginal position which Hill's account makes of him.

Closely related to this notion of Milton as marginal is Hill's peculiar insistence on the poet's *unoriginality* as a prose writer. Hill consistently argues that 'Milton was not an original thinker'.[28] What Hill means by this is that many of Milton's ideas were shared by many of his contemporaries, some by 'radicals' and others by 'Puritans' (although this latter point is not fully developed, since Hill is mainly concerned to establish, against the views of literary-critical orthodoxy, the full extent of Milton's radicalism). The method of exposition adopted in Hill's account of Milton's prose writing is often remarkably simple: a particular heresy of Milton's (radical Arminianism, millennarianism, anti-Trinitarianism, belief in the sonship of believers, antinomianism, mortalism, materialism) is defined, and then we are subjected to long lists of individuals or groups who shared each of those beliefs, thus finally demonstrating both Milton's partial affinity with the radicals and his apparent unoriginality as a political and theological thinker. But this will not do at all. Original thought never comes into the world by way of virgin birth; it *always* draws on the raw materials to hand in its immediate context. Hill argues that Milton 'is unique only in the way he combined their [i.e. his radical contemporaries'] ideas'[29] and that in other respects he is unoriginal. But it surely is of the very essence of originality that it consists in a reconstitution, at an in some sense 'higher' level, of an existing body of thought. We have repeatedly referred to Lucien Goldmann's view that the originality of great philosophical and artistic works consists precisely in their nature as particular, exceptional expressions of notions present, either explicitly or implicitly, in pre-existing collective world visions. In this sense, Milton is an original thinker, and his originality can be located around his ability to combine these various disparate, heretical notions into a structured intellectual system. Hill's failure to acknowledge Milton's originality derives, in part, from his insistence on the poet's marginality. Because Hill views Milton as torn between two cultures, he fails to detect any underlying intellectual coherence to the various Miltonic prose writings. Rather, he sees in them merely an 'eclectic' admixture of various notions taken from various sources. But this distinctly uncharitable assessment also derives from a second source, that is, from the very fashion in which Hill reads, from the very nature of his *literary-critical method*.

How, then, does Hill read? In essence, it is a very simple, and not entirely unfamiliar, procedure. Hill breaks down each of Milton's works into a series of component elements, then seeks to establish a set of comparisons between each of those elements and, in the case of the prose writings, similar views expressed elsewhere, and, in the case of the poetry, to which we shall return later, real historical events. In both cases, the internal coherence of the work under analysis is necessarily destroyed. Now this is quite simply the technique of vulgar empiricist sociology (and also of vulgar Marxism), in which partial aspects of the content of a literary work are compared with partial aspects of the content of other, external, realities. The central weakness of such an approach is obvious: it detotalises the literary work, thus denying the integrity of the literary text and rendering the text's underlying structure fundamentally inaccessible. But the literariness of literature (and the thoughtfulness of thought) consists in its nature, not as a reflection of reality, but rather as a distinct mode of practice. Poets create poetry, not 'reflections' of reality, and if a poem is to be comprehended, then its own internal structure must be fully analysed in the course of the attempt to establish any relationship between it and external social reality. Hill does not do this, and it is because he does not do it that he is so readily able to detect such incoherences in Milton's work. But the incoherence is Hill's, rather than Milton's. After some 470 pages of *Milton and the English Revolution*, Hill comes to admit that 'It is disconcerting to try to depict a man who has strong moral principles, for which he would die, without being able to state clearly what these principles are, and so being unable to submit them to precise rational analysis.'[30] It is a stunning indictment of his literary-critical method.

My own literary-critical method derives substantially from that of Lucien Goldmann. I argued that the 'third circle' of Milton's views is, in fact, homologous to the rationalist world vision of the revolutionary section of the English bourgeoisie. This approach permitted us to reinterpret Milton's originality in terms of the way in which he is able to provide a coherent and articulate expression of that world vision. And it made it possible to reconstitute Milton's political and theological works as a theoretical totality, and his great poems as a set of literary totalities. We were thus able to analyse Milton's prose writings in terms of the fundamental structural categories of the rationalist world vision: the discrete rational individual, freedom from external constraint, freedom from passion and, finally, the notion of God as agent only via the medium of the elect. Hill's approach permits no such general theoretical conception; for him, Milton's work remains an aggregate of parts, uninformed by any total structure. This weakness in Dr Hill's overall theoretical position gives rise to a whole series of particular misreadings. Thus, for example, Hill clearly misinterprets Milton on the question of scriptural authority. He sees the poet as torn between the radical rejection of Biblical authority, on the one hand, and the Puritan insistence on the Bible, on the other.[31] But, as we have seen in Chapter 4, Milton did, in fact, decisively opt in the last instance for conscience over scripture. Here Hill's 'two-culture' model clearly leads him to a misunderstanding of the poet's own position. Hill is, of course, quite right to emphasise Milton's commitment to private property and class distinction, his character as, specifically, a *bourgeois*. But this does not find expression in any ambivalence over the question of Biblical authority, as Hill argues.[32] Rather, it finds expression in Milton's peculiarly meritocratic theory of election, and in his correspondingly elitist theory of politics. And there is nothing half-hearted or 'middle-of-the-road' about this theoretical position. Far from representing a mid-way, eclectic, stance between Puritanism and radicalism, as Hill would have it, it actually represents a third perfectly coherent theoretical approach. As against both the half-feudal notions of the Presbyterians and the utopianism of the Levellers, this third 'Independent' position provides, as we argued above, both a clear theoretical rationale for early bourgeois society and a specific rationale for the Independents' own seizure of power. Unless one sees Milton as specifically a bourgeois revolutionary, this theoretical structure must remain unintelligible. And so it remains for Dr Hill. For him, Milton's politics are merely a more 'realistic' version of Levelling,[33] and this realism derives merely from the fact that none of the Levellers were actually 'practical politicians'.[34] It is a surprising judgement, not only on Milton, but also on the men who organised the Leveller party, who gave it a national structure and a regular dues-paying system, who published its regular newspaper; but if one insists on seeing Milton as a 'half-hearted', but 'realistic', fellow-traveller with the radicals, then such distortions become virtually unavoidable. Similarly, Hill misinterprets the significance of the opposition between reason and passion in Milton's writings. He assumes, quite wrongly, that Milton experienced this opposition as a *tension*, that he was, at least in part, a proto-romantic, that reason and passion enter into Milton's work each as an expression of one or the other of the two cultures to which the poet was attracted, reason as an expression of Puritanism, passion of radicalism.[35] And this leads to Hill's misreading of the three great poems.

3   From 'Paradise Lost' to 'Samson Agonistes'

Dr Hill's account of the three longer poems is perhaps the single most

unsatisfactory element in *Milton and the English Revolution*. And yet
its beginnings are promising. In contradistinction to the determined
idealism of much orthodox literary criticism, Hill quite rightly
situates the poems within the context of the political defeat suffered at
the Restoration. He is aware, as few commentators are, that each of
the last poems has as its central object the problem of defeat, and that
this problem was posed for Milton by the defeat of the political cause
to which he had dedicated much of his life. But, from this insight, Hill
proceeds to an attempt to establish a series of direct parallels between
'events' in the poems and 'events' in real life which appears the more
forced the more it continues. There are quite literally pages and pages
of such comparisons. To take one example, in his discussion of the
war in heaven in *Paradise Lost*, Hill suggests direct parallels between:
Satan and Charles I both raising their standards in the north; a third of
the angels supporting Satan and a third of the MPs supporting
Charles; the inconclusiveness of the first battle in heaven and that of
the battle of Edgehill; the offer of truce negotiations by the Satanic
angels and that by the Royalists in 1643; the angelic resort to hurling
mountains and the Parliamentary resort to the *levée en masse*; the
intervention of the Son and that of the New Model Army.[36] Hill
even suggests that the first two days of the battle are analogous to the
years 1642–4, and the third to the year 1644–5.[37] Now an approach
such as this can only be appropriate to the analysis of literary works in
which such parallels are intentionally constructed, for example
Swift's *Gulliver's Travels*. But, in the case of Milton, there is
absolutely no evidence of such intentionality. The comparisons add
nothing to our understanding of *Paradise Lost*; they merely serve to
distract attention from the poem's own internal structure. And it is
that structure which remains the central object of inquiry for any
literary-critical method worthy of the name, no matter how
'sociologically' aware that method may become. As we suggested
earlier, comparisons between literary artifact and social reality are of
immense value, but only if such comparisons operate at the level of
structure, rather than that of content. The unanswered questions,
which Hill fails to ask, are these: given that the problem of the fall is
posed for Milton by the Restoration, what, then, are the general
structural characteristics of that problem, how does that structure
function within each of the poems, and how, in turn, is it solved in
each of the poems?

These questions can only be answered if we situate the three poems
in relation to that structure of the rationalist world vision which we

outlined above. The central problem in the three great poems is the problem of defeat, the problem of the fall, and in each case the fall consists simply in the triumph of reason over passion. Thus the fallen angels succumb to the passion of pride, Adam, Eve, and Samson to that of sensuality, whilst, by contrast, Christ resists the claims of passion and triumphs over his Satanic adversary. In each case the capitulation to passion renders the fallen being subject to the rule of an external tyranny, the fallen Angels and fallen mankind to that of Satan, Samson to that of the Philistine lords. Hill does not see the fall in these terms. In fact, he is unclear as to in what exactly the fall consists. And this uncertainty clearly derives from his view of Milton himself as uncertainly torn between the rival claims of reason and passion. Thus Hill gives much more credence than it deserves to the notion of Milton as a proto-romantic poet, if not a covert supporter of the devil's party, then at least, a supporter of both parties.[38] But this is perverse. Each of the three great poems is equipped with explicit accounts of the poem's theology (often, in *Paradise Lost*, placed in the mouth of God so as to emphasise their full import). It is simply pointless to suggest that Milton did not really mean what he said. Certainly, he gave the devil a good run for his money. But, equally certainly, he had no doubts as to his own position; Milton was of the godly party, and he knew it. We might note in passing that Hill's misreading of Milton's intentions is closely related to his fairly conventional unease in the face of Milton's God.[39] As we have seen, Milton's characterisation of the personality of God is widely recognised as one of *Paradise Lost*'s central weaknessess. And it is often interpreted as evidence of Milton's covert sympathy for the devil's party. But our analysis permitted an alternative interpretation: that Milton's anthropomorphism fails because the God in which he actually believes is not so much a person as an abstract principle. Milton's poetic treatment of his God is, then, a function of the nature of that God. It is, as Hill argues, somewhat unconvincing. But that lack of conviction is a product, not of any uncertainty on Milton's part as to the rival claims of reason and passion, but rather of the inherent difficulties imposed by the attempt to situate his own rationalistic theology within the confines of a pre-existing Biblical mythology.

We have discussed Hill's account of the nature of Milton's problem, the problem of defeat. But what of his approach to the solution (or rather, solutions)? We argued in Chapter 5 that each of the three poems is built around a different variant of the dual solution, the personal and the politico-historical, to the problem of unreason triumphant. We argued too that the shifts in emphasis between the three poems can clearly be related to the changing fortunes of the revolutionary opposition: *Paradise Lost* is forged out of the experience of the very moment of defeat, *Paradise Regained* out of the awful, delayed, recognition of the full extent of the catastrophe of the Restoration, and *Samson Agonistes* out of a renewal of hope inspired by the progressive destabilisation of the Restoration Monarchy after 1667. Hill's own account of the three poems does, indeed, discuss these differences. But it remains insufficently aware of the full extent of the *discontinuities* which pertain between each of the poems. Hill represents the movement from *Paradise Lost* to *Samson Agonistes* as one of progressive evolution. Thus, for example, he writes that: 'Men can be regenerate on earth: that is the theme of *Paradise Regained.* Then God will show ways in which political problems which now seem insoluble can solve themselves: that is the theme of *Samson Agonistes.*'[40] This interpretation leads Hill into a distinctly un-satisfactory reading of *Samson Agonistes* in particular. Hill's Samson is merely the Christ of *Paradise Regained* relocated fortuitously in a particular situation which happens to offer opportunities for political activism: 'Samson got his chance only after abandoning his illusions of heroism . . . Samson failed utterly so long as he relied only on his heroic qualities . . . But gradually he came to reject his aspirations to heroism, to accept the role of God's fool.'[41] Now this interpretation seems to me to be radically mistaken. In fact, the central theme of *Samson Agonistes* is the reconstruction of precisely Samson's *heroism.* In this respect, it is, as we argued above, the encounter with Harapha, the Philistine warrior, rather than that with Dálila, which provides the poem with its key 'structural linkage'. Hill completely ignores the significance of the fact that Harapha, alone of the poem's leading characters, is entirely Milton's own creation. But such an innovation cannot be merely accidental; it must serve a vital purpose within the overall plan of the work. And yet, on Hill's account, the exchange between Samson and Harapha is extraneous to the poem's central theme. Clearly, something is sadly amiss with an interpretation which fails to attach any real significance to the one major modification of the Biblical account which Milton actually effects. We have argued that the absence of a notion of structure from Hill's theoretical framework leads to a series of analytical misinterpretations. But finally, we should note one other important consequence of this absence: an indifference to the problem of literary form. Hill makes no attempt whatsoever to explain Milton's choice of a particular set of classical literary models upon which to base his own great poems. It is possible, of course, that our own attempt to explain sociologically Milton's choice of literary form, in Chapter 5, is inadequate. But Dr Hill's failure to pay any real attention at all to the problem of literary form is a very serious weakness indeed in a work which sets out to deal with poetry, perhaps the most truly 'formal' of all literary forms.

4   Conclusion: Politics Lost

One of his more hostile, conservative, critics has recently described Dr Hill's intellectual evolution as one in which 'the hard-nosed young Stalinist and vulgar Marxist of 1940' developed into 'a less young, warmly emotional New Leftist of the 1970s'.[42] The account has a certain appropriateness (although Hexter's actual critique of Hill's work does not; Hexter belongs to that school of historians whose main intellectual project is that of dissolving historical reality into meaningless flux). But we must be careful with our terms: recent British history has witnessed more than one 'New Left'. Hill's own intellectual affinities lie very clearly with that particular intellectual grouping which might best be described as, in David Widgery's phrase, the 'Old New Left'.[43] This 'Old New Left' exhibited certain characteristic habits of thought: a commitment to 'culture' at the expense of politics ('Socio-Culture', as Widgery terms it); a residual political practice which combined together the twin elements of romantic utopianism and reformist *realpolitik*; and, to put it bluntly, a distinct lack of theoretical rigour. Hill's *Milton* exhibits much of both the characteristic strengths and the characteristic weaknesses of the Old New Left. That grouping's central achievement, exemplified *par excellence* in Raymond Williams's earlier work, was its commitment to theoretical totalisation, its insistence on the interconnectedness of social, political, and cultural phenomena. In marked contrast to the drab formalism of much mainstream literary criticism, Hill's work actually succeeds in forcing these connections to the fore. Hill's *Milton* lives in the combined space of literature and politics, religion and philosophy, history and sociology. But, as we have seen, the work exhibits the characteristic weaknesses too: the overemphasis on cultural variables, the relative indifference to politico-economic problems, the unrigorous nature of much of the theorisation.

As a distinct *political* formation the Old New Left effectively ceased to exist during the early 1960s, but, as an *intellectual* current, it received a surprising second lease of life, albeit in a much vulgarised form, from the 'counter-culture' of the late 1960s.[44] This peculiar recasting of the Old New Left's cultural obsessions into an updated 'hippy' form, appears to have had some influence on Dr Hill. It is most readily apparent at that point at which he seeks to establish the poet's 'contemporary relevance'. The conclusion is significant: 'Milton's political experience led him to attach more importance to changes in people's modes of thought and conduct, less to political manipulation and institutional change. This would seem to give him a certain modern relevance.'[45] It is a conclusion which might possibly have won Milton readers amongst the 'student left' of the late 1960s. But, more than ten years later, Hill's judgement sounds surprisingly dated. The British Left today displays rather more interest in institutional change, and rather less in the politics of experience, than it did during the last golden days of the post-war boom. It is just possible that John Milton, the critical-rationalist thinker, the regicide revolutionary, might have proven of more genuine modern relevance than either John Milton, the seventeenth-century hippy, or John Milton, the perplexed middle-of-the-road liberal.

Notes

CHAPTER ONE

1. L. Goldmann, *Immanuel Kant*, London, 1971, p. 31.
2. L. Goldmann, *The Hidden God*, London, 1964.
3. 'My whole effort was to work in terms of concrete judgements and particular analyses: "This—doesn't it?—bears such a relation to that; this kind of thing—don't you find it so?—wears better than that?" '—F. R. Leavis, *The Common Pursuit*, London, 1952, p. 215. Cf. R. Wellek, 'Literary Criticism and Philosophy', *Scrutiny*, vol. v, no. 4, pp. 375—83.
4. 'Literature/Society: Mapping the Field', *Working Papers in Cultural Studies*, no. 4, pp. 24—5.
5. Cf. J. Fekete, 'The New Criticism: Ideological Evolution of the Right Opposition', *Telos*, no. 20, Summer 1974, pp. 2—51.
6. Cf. M. Lifshitz, *The Philosophy of Art of Karl Marx*, London, 1973, pp. 32—9.
7. Goldmann, *The Hidden God*, p. 7.
8. K. Marx, *Grundrisse*, London, 1973, p. 100.
9. Ibid.
10. Ibid., p. 101.
11. K. Marx and F. Engels, *The Holy Family or Critique of Critical Critique*, Moscow, 1956—cf. especially the comments on Szeliga (p. 82) and Eugene Sue (p. 242).
12. K. Marx and F. Engels, *The German Ideology*, Part I, London, 1970, p. 47.
13. K. Marx, *A Contribution to the Critique of Political Economy*, London, 1971, pp. 20—1.
14. Ibid., p. 21.
15. C. Caudwell, *Illusion and Reality*, London, 1946, p. 55.
16. P. Anderson, 'Components of the National Culture' in A. Cockburn and R. Blackburn (ed.), *Student Power*, Harmondsworth, 1970, p. 221.
17. F. Engels, 'Letter to Heinz Starkenburg, January 25, 1894', in K. Marx and F. Engels, *Literature and Art*, New York, 1947, p. 9.
18. R. Williams, 'Base and Superstructure in Marxist Cultural Theory', in *New Left Review*, no. 82, Nov/Dec 1973, p. 6.
19. I. Birchall, 'The Total Marx and the Marxist Theory of Literature', in P. Walton and S. Hall (ed.), *Situating Marx*, London, 1972, pp. 118—43.
20. Cf. K. Marx, *Capital*, vol. 1, London, 1970, p. 132.
21. K. Marx, *Economic and Philosophic Manuscripts of 1844*, London, 1959, pp. 136—41.
22. Caudwell, op. cit., p. 76.
23. C. Sparks, 'Shakespeare and Society' (unpublished paper).
24. E. Burns and T. Burns, *Sociology of Literature and Drama*, Harmondsworth, 1973, p. 18.

25. Cf., for example, P. L. Berger and T. Luckmann, *The Social Construction of Reality*, Harmondsworth, 1971.
26. In the wake of the reaction against subjectivism in Marxism, Goldmann's prestige has suffered somewhat in recent years. This has occurred primarily on the basis of a glib identification of Goldmann's position with that of Lukács. But, as we shall see below, the comparison between Lukács and Goldmann is striking in so far as it points to dissimilarities rather than similarities. For a recent, unfashionably charitable assessment of Goldmann, cf. F. Mulhern, 'Introduction to Goldmann', in *New Left Review*, no. 92, July/August 1975, pp. 34–8.
27. 'If in the nineteenth century phenomenology made the idea of significant structure *explicit*, it was already *implicit* in classical philosophy'—L. Goldmann, 'The Aesthetics of the Young Lukács', in *New Hungarian Quarterly*, vol. XIII, no. 47, Autumn 1972, p. 130.
28. L. Goldmann, 'The sociology of literature: status and problems of method', in *International Social Science Journal*, vol. XIX, no. 4, 1967, p. 495.
29. Ibid., p. 500.
30. T. Todorov, 'The Structural Analysis of Literature: The Tales of Henry James', in D. Robey (ed.), *Structuralism: An Introduction*, Oxford, 1973, p. 74.
31. L. Goldmann, 'Structure: Human Reality and Methodological Concept', in R. Macksey and E. Donato (ed.), *The Languages of Criticism and the Sciences of Man*, Baltimore, 1970, p. 99.
32. Trotsky maintained a very similar position to that of Goldmann in his polemic against the early Russian Formalists, who were in many respects the immediate forerunners of modern structuralism. Cf. L. Trotsky, *Literature and Revolution*, Michigan, 1971, ch. v. On the formalists cf. V. Shklovsky, *Mayakovsky and His Circle*, London, 1974, and J. Tynianov and R. Jakobson, 'Problems in the Study of Language and Literature', in R. T. de George and F. M. de George, *The Structuralists: From Marx to Levi-Strauss*, New York, 1972. Structuralism is, of course, an extremely heterogeneous theoretical current. The French structuralist writer, Roland Barthes, accepts the need for both historical and formal analyses, and thus concedes much to the Trotsky/Goldmann position. But even he insists on the need for a separation out of these two levels of analysis. Cf. R. Barthes, *Mythologies*, London, 1973, p. 137, and R. Barthes, 'The Structuralist Activity' in de George and de George, op. cit., p. 150. A Marxist theory of literature aims at the *integration* of formal and historical analysis. It can accept neither the total exclusion of the latter which is evident in much of Russian Formalism, nor the mechanical juxtaposition of the two which we find in Barthes.
33. Goldmann, *The Hidden God*, p. 8.
34. Cf. Goldmann, "The Aesthetics of the Young Lukács".
35. G. Lukács, *History and Class Consciousness*, London, 1971.
36. Goldmann, *The Hidden God*, p. 17.
37. L. Goldmann, *The Human Sciences and Philosophy*, London, 1970, p. 130.
38. Goldmann, *The Hidden God*, p. 19.
39. Goldmann, *The Human Sciences and Philosophy*, p. 103.
40. M. Weber, *The Methodology of the Social Sciences*, New York, 1949, p. 90.
41. Ibid., p. 93.
42. Ibid.

43. Ibid., p. 172.
44. Ibid., pp. 95–6.
45. G. Lukács, The Theory of the Novel, London, 1971, p. 97.
46. Ibid., pp. 97–111.
47. Ibid., pp. 112–31.
48. Ibid., pp. 132–43.
49. Lukács, History and Class Consciousness, p. 51.
50. Ibid.
51. Ibid., p. 79.
52. K. Marx, The Civil War in France, Peking, 1966, p. 171.
53. V. I. Lenin, The State and Revolution, Peking, 1965, p. 48.
54. Goldmann, The Hidden God, p. 15.
55. Goldmann, The Human Sciences and Philosophy, p. 103.
56. 'It would be difficult to name a major representative of this philosophy [i.e.
    dialectical materialism] today, since it is still in the process of formation;
    however, much ground has been covered in the works of Kant, Hegel, Marx,
    and in our time, Georg Lukács.' (Goldmann, Immanuel Kant, p. 53) Later,
    Goldmann came to interpret Jansenism in terms of those self-same tragic
    categories which he had initially developed in his study of Kantianism. The
    implication is surely there, then, that Pascal, too, should be added to the list.
57. Goldmann, The Hidden God, p. 69.
58. Ibid., p. 90. Cf. also L. Goldmann, 'Is There a Marxist Sociology?', in
    International Socialism, no. 34.
59. Goldmann, The Human Sciences and Philosophy, p. 129.
60. Goldmann, The Hidden God, p. 98.
61. Ibid., p. 99.
62. Goldmann, 'The sociology of literature: status and problems of method',
    p. 496.
63. Ibid.
64. Barthes, 'The Structuralist Activity', p. 152.
65. As Trotsky wrote, 'A work of art should, in the first place be judged by its own
    law, that is by the law of art' (Trotsky, op. cit., p. 178).
66. Marx, The Holy Family, p. 82.
67. A. J. Ayer, Language, Truth and Logic, London, 1967, pp. 102–14.
68. According to Durkheim, social facts 'are ways of acting, thinking, and feeling
    that present the noteworthy property of existing outside the individual
    consciousness' (E. Durkheim, The Rules of Sociological Method, Chicago, 1962,
    p. 2).
69. T. S. Eliot, Selected Essays, London, 1963, p. 15.
70. Ibid., p. 16.
71. 'A man cannot become a child again, or he becomes childish. But does he not
    find joy in the child's naivety, and must he himself not strive to reproduce its
    truth at a higher stage? . . . Why should not the historic childhood of
    humanity, its most beautiful unfolding, as a stage never to return, exercise an
    eternal charm?' (Grundrisse, p. 111.) Marx's analogy between childhood and
    antiquity rests on the premise that modernity negates (in the Hegelian sense of
    transcendence rather than abolition) antiquity, just as adulthood negates
    childhood. It follows then, that the aesthetic sensibility of the later age will be
    susceptible to the earlier artistic forms.

72. T. S. Eliot, *Milton: Two Studies*, London, 1968, pp. 9–21.
73. Cf. Eliot, 'The Metaphysical Poets', *Selected Essays*, pp. 281–91.
74. F. Kermode, 'Dissociation of Sensibility', in *The Kenyon Review*, vol. XIX, no. 2, Spring 1957, pp. 191–4.
75. Eliot, *Milton: Two Studies*, pp. 22–48.
76. Leavis, however, made the mistake of taking Eliot's initial assessment at its face value, and thus found himself obliged to return repeatedly to the defence of that assessment. .
77. K. Marx, 'Ueber die neueste Preussische Zensurinstruktion', in Marx and Engels, *Literature and Art*, p. 60.
78. L. Goldmann, *Towards a Sociology of the Novel*. London, 1977. Here Goldmann argues for a relationship, not between the novel form and the world vision of any particular social class, but rather between the novel form and market society as a whole. The conclusions which he reaches in many ways represent a radical rupture with his earlier work. Indeed, his final assertion that the *nouveau roman* of Robbe-Grillet is a valid literary form is in direct contradiction to his earlier aesthetic principles. Previously, he had argued that only progressive world visions could give rise to great works of art. Now, quite clearly, Robbe-Grillet's novels express a partial and distorted—that is, in Goldmann's terminology, an 'ideological'—view of reality and, equally clearly, they in no way express the only possible progressive world vision, which on Goldmann's own terms must be, in the contemporary world, that of socialism. Goldmann subsequently retracted much of his argument (cf. L. Goldmann, 'Criticism and Dogmatism in Literature' in D. Cooper (ed.), *The Dialectics of Liberation*, Harmondsworth, 1971), arguing that the position he adopted in *Towards a Sociology of the Novel* arose from the dogmatic emphasis on the criterion of coherence in 'Lukácsian' sociology. But this is not in itself sufficient to explain the weakness of the work. Its central weakness in fact consists in the elimination of the theory of mediation from Goldmann's conceptual apparatus.
79. Lukács, 1967 'Preface' to *History and Class Consciousness*, p. xxxviii.
80. H. Gallas, 'The Part Played by Georg Lukács in Working Out a Marxist Theory of Literature in the League of Revolutionary Proletarian Writers', in *Alternative*, no. 4, October 1969, translated in part in *Working Papers in Cultural Studies*, no. 4.
81. In the early 1920s, the Proletcult (organisation for proletarian culture) writers of the *Kuznitsa* and *Na Postu* groups proclaimed the slogan 'style is class' and argued the supremacy of all 'proletarian culture' over 'bourgeois culture'.
82. G. Lukács, *The Meaning of Contemporary Realism*, London, 1972, pp. 115–35.
83. Ibid., p. 115.
84. Swingewood is mistaken to suggest that, in *The Theory of the Novel*, Lukács analyses literary structures 'as "atemporal essences" which transcended social structure'. (D. T. Laurenson and A. Swingewood, *The Sociology of Literature*, London, 1972, p. 64.) On the contrary, Lukács explains the differences between classical and modern literary forms precisely in terms of the changed nature of social reality. Lukács does not, of course, discuss the classical mode of production, but he *does* discuss the nature of the Greek social 'world'.
85. C. Sparks, 'Georg Lukács', in *Working Papers in Cultural Studies*, no. 4, pp. 83–4.

86. B. Brecht to W. Benjamin, 25 July 1938, in W. Benjamin, *Understanding Brecht*, London, 1973, p. 118.
87. Or, as Trotsky termed it, the 'concentration camp of artistic literature' (L. Trotsky, *The Revolution Betrayed*, London, 1937, p. 175).
88. F. Engels, 'Letter to Margaret Harkness, April 1888', in Marx and Engels, *Literature and Art*, p. 41.
89. Ibid.
90. F. Engels, 'Letter to Ferdinand Lassalle, May 18 1859', in Marx and Engels, *Literature and Art*, p. 52.
91. B. Brecht, 'Über den formalistischen Charakter der Realismustheorie', in 'Against George Lukács' in *New Left Review*, no. 84, March/April 1974, p. 45.
92. G. Lukács, *Solzhenitsyn*, London, 1970, p. 34.
93. G. Lukács, *Writer and Critic*, London, 1970, pp. 42—3.
94. G. Lukács, *Studies in European Realism*, London, 1972, p. 8.
95. Ibid., p. 6.
96. Ibid., p. 9.
97. Lukács, *Writer and Critic*, pp. 246—7.
98. Ibid., p. 34.
99. Ibid., p. 234.
100. Ibid., p. 86.
101. Ibid., p. 83.
102. Ibid., p. 85.
103. Lukács, *The Meaning of Contemporary Realism*, p. 60.
104. Ibid., p. 115.
105. Ibid., p. 63.
106. Lukács, *Studies in European Realism*, p. 6.
107. Ibid.
108. Ibid., p. 91.
109. Ibid., p. 93.
110. Ibid., p. 8.
111. Lukács, *The Meaning of Contemporary Realism*, pp. 51—2.
112. Ibid., p. 50.
113. Ibid., p. 77.
114. Ibid., p. 79.
115. Ibid., p. 80.
116. B. Brecht, 'Die Essays von Georg Lukács,' in 'Against George Lukács', p. 40.
117. Ibid.
118. Cf. B. Brecht, 'Volkstümlichkeit und Realismus', in 'Against Georg Lukács', p. 51.
119. Ibid., p. 50.
120. J.-P. Sartre, contribution to 'Symposium on the Question of Decadence', in L. Baxandall (ed.), *Radical Perspectives in the Arts*, Harmondsworth, 1972, pp. 226—7.
121. Ibid., p. 229.
122. Laurenson and Swingewood, *The Sociology of Literature*, op. cit., p. 214.
123. For Marx's theory of alienation, cf. Marx, *Economic and Philosophic Manuscripts of 1844*, pp. 67—83.
124. Laurenson and Swingewood, *The Sociology of Literature*, p. 244.
125. Cf. Lukács, *Solzhenitsyn*.

126. Lukács, *Studies in European Realism*, p. 86.
127. Ibid., p. 11.
128. Ibid., p. 89.
129. Ibid., p. 13.
130. Ibid., p. 86.
131. Ibid., p. 89.
132. Ibid., p. 135.
133. G. Lukács, *The Historical Novel*, Harmondsworth, 1969, p. 20.
134. Ibid., p. 31.
135. Lukács, *Studies in European Realism*, p. 77.
136. Lukács, *The Historical Novel*, pp. 219–20.
137. Sparks, 'George Lukács', p. 83.
138. G. Lukács, *Essays on Thomas Mann*, London, 1962, p. 12.
139. Ibid., pp. 13–14.
140. Ibid., p. 114.
141. Ibid., pp. 114–15.
142. A. Swingewood, 'Lukács' Theory of Literature' (unpublished paper).
143. Ibid.
144. R. Williams, 'Literature and Society: in memory of Lucien Goldmann', in *New Left Review*, no. 67, May/June 1971, pp. 7–8.
145. E. M. W. Tillyard, *The Miltonic Setting*, London, 1966, Ch. 8, pp. 141–68.
146. The English Marxism of the 1930s was particularly influential amongst two specific groups within the intelligentsia, the natural scientists, and the practitioners of both 'literature' itself and literary criticism. This latter group included figures such as C. Day Lewis, W. H. Auden, Stephen Spender, Christopher Caudwell, Maurice Cornforth, Edward Upward, and Alick West. Cf. C. Day Lewis (ed.), *The Mind in Chains*, London, 1937; A. West, *Crisis and Criticism*, London, 1937; Caudwell, op. cit. For a recent account of Caudwell's literary criticism cf. F. Mulhern, 'The Marxist Aesthetics of Christopher Caudwell', in *New Left Review*, no. 85, May/June 1974. For a more detailed account of Leavis cf. A. Milner, 'Leavis and English Literary Criticism', in *Praxis*, Berkeley, California, vol. 1, no. 2, Winter 1976.
147. F. R. Leavis, *Scrutiny: A Retrospect*, vol. xx, p. 4.
148. Leavis, *The Common Pursuit*, p. 213.
149. Williams, 'Literature and Society: in memory of Lucien Goldmann', p. 9.
150. S. Saunders, 'Towards a Social Theory of Literature', in *Telos*, no. 18, Winter 1973–74, p. 110.
151. Anderson, op. cit., p. 268.
152. F. R. Leavis, *Nor Shall My Sword*, London, 1972, p. 15.
153. F. R. Leavis, *The Great Tradition*, Harmondsworth, 1967, p. 10.
154. Ibid., p. 17.
155. F. R. Leavis, *New Bearings in English Poetry*, London, 1938, p. 25.
156. Leavis, *The Great Tradition*, p. 35.
157. Ibid., p. 36.
158. Leavis, *The Common Pursuit*, p. 184.
159. Ibid.
160. F. R. Leavis and D. Thompson, *Culture and Environment*, London, 1960, p. 91.
161. Ibid., p. 87.
162. F. R. Leavis, *Two Cultures?*, London, 1962, p. 24.

163. Leavis, *The Common Pursuit*, p. 190.
164. Leavis, *New Bearings in English Poetry*, p. 5.
165. Ibid., p. 6.
166. Ibid., pp. 213–14.
167. Leavis, *Nor Shall my Sword*, p. 94.
168. Leavis's theory of cultural decline is, of course, closely related to that developed by T. S. Eliot. Leavis's specific criticisms of Milton's poetry run parallel to those propounded by Eliot. And both writers are similarly concerned to emphasise the social determinants of this process of cultural decline (for Eliot, cf. *Milton: Two Studies*, p. 34). But at no point does Leavis specifically commit himself to the notion of a seventeenth-century 'dissociation of sensibility'. And as Eliot's theory came under fire, Leavis found himself able to switch ground, or, at least, to abandon an increasingly offensive terminology. For criticisms of the 'dissociation' thesis cf. F. W. Bateson, 'Contribution to a Dictionary of Critical Terms: II Dissociation of Sensibility' in *Essays in Criticism*, vol. 1, no. 3, 1951; Kermode, op. cit.; B. Dobree, "The Claims of Sensibility', in *Humanitas*, vol. 1, no. 2, Autumn 1946. But, even if both Eliot's and Leavis's *aesthetic* judgements can be faulted, their understanding that something of significance happened to English poetry in the seventeenth century, and that that something had extra-literary origins, is extremely valuable. One member of the Scrutiny school actually went so far as to relate the 'dissociation' thesis to the Tawney thesis; cf. H. Wendell Smith, 'The Dissociation of Sensibility' in *Scrutiny*, vol. XVIII, no. 3, Winter, 1951–52.
169. A. Shuttleworth, *Two Working Papers in Cultural Studies*, Birmingham, 1967.
170. Anderson, op. cit., p. 269.
171. Ibid., p. 277.
172. Ibid., p. 271.
173. F. R. Leavis, *Revaluation*, Harmondsworth, 1972, p. 54.
174. *Paradise Lost*, I, 25–6.
175. Tillyard, op. cit.
176. Leavis, *The Common Pursuit*, p. 36.
177. Leavis, *Revaluation*, p. 60.
178. Goldmann, 'The sociology of literature: status and problems of method', p. 498.
179. Tillyard, op. cit., pp. 168–204.
180. Goldmann, 'The sociology of literature: status and problems of method', p. 498.
181. J.-P. Sartre, *The Problem of Method*, London, 1963.
182. J. -P. Sartre, *L'Idiot de la famille*, Paris, 1971. Cf. R. Aronson, 'L'Idiot de la famille: The Ultimate Sartre?', in *Telos*, Summer 1974 pp. 90–107.
183. K. Marx and F. Engels, *The Communist Manifesto*, Harmondsworth, 1969, p. 79.
184. Goldmann, 'The sociology of literature: status and problems of method', p. 507.
185. Ibid.
186. J. Milton, 'The Doctrine and Discipline of Divorce', *Prose Works*, Bohn Edition, London, 1848, III, pp. 169–273; 'The Judgement of Martin Bucer Concerning Divorce', *Prose Works*, III, pp. 274–314; 'Tetrachordon', *Prose Works*, III, pp. 315–433; 'Colasterion', *Prose Works*, III, pp. 434–61.

187. *Paradise Lost*, IX, 82—6.
188. Sartre, *The Problem of Method*, p. 56.

CHAPTER TWO

1. L. Goldmann, *The Hidden God*, London, 1964, p. 23.
2. D. Hume, 'An Enquiry Concerning Human Understanding', Section VII, *Enquiries concerning Human Understanding and concerning the Principles of Morals*, Oxford, 1975, pp. 60—79.
3. L. Goldmann, *Immanuel Kant*, London, 1971, pp. 37—8.
4. P. Anderson, 'Components of the National Culture', in A. Cockburn and R. Blackburn, (ed.), *Student Power*, Harmondsworth, 1970, p. 226.
5. K. Marx and F. Engels, *Selected Works*, Moscow, 1970, pp. 375—93.
6. M. Weber, *The Protestant Ethic and the Spirit of Capitalism*, London, 1930.
7. Ibid., p. 154.
8. Notable exceptions include B. Willey, *The Seventeenth Century Background*, Harmondsworth, 1972 and, more especially, D. Saurat, *Milton: Man and Thinker*, London, 1924. But the latter work is marred somewhat by its tendency to blur the distinction between Milton's protestant rationalism and nineteenth-century French rationalism, and by its relative indifference to Milton's *poetry*.
9. J. Milton, 'Areopagatica', *Prose Works*, Bohn Edition, London, 1848, II, pp. 48—101.
10. For example, Lord Brooke's *A Discourse Opening the Nature of . . . Episcopacie*, Roger Williams's *The Bloody Tenent*, John Goodwin's *Anapologesiates Antapologias*, Richard Overton's *The Araignement of Mr. Persecution*.
11. 'The Ancient Bounds', in A. S. P. Woodhouse (ed.), *Puritanism and Liberty*, London, 1965, p. 247.
12. Cf. Woodhouse, ibid., Parts III and VIII, and Appendix: D.
13. On the significance of this issue cf. G. Yule, *The Independents in the English Civil War*, Cambridge, 1958, pp. 42—3.
14. Willey, op. cit., p. 72.
15. On the agrarian policy of the revolutionary governments cf. C. Hill, *Puritanism and Revolution*, London, 1968, ch. 5.
16. J. Lilburne, 'Legal Fundamental Liberties' in Woodhouse, op. cit., p. 348.
17. Ibid., p. 353.
18. J. Milton, 'A Defence of the English People', *Prose Works*, I, p. 143.
19. T. Collier, 'A Discovery of the New Creation' in Woodhouse, op. cit., p. 394.
20. *Cromwell's Letters*, ed. Carlyle, I, p. 265, quoted in H. A. Taine, *History of English Literature*, London, 1907, II, p. 212.
21. Whereas, in fact, he was a silk merchant.
22. 'The Tenure of Kings and Magistrates', *Prose Works*, II, p. 2.
    p. 2
23. Collier, op. cit., p. 395. (my emphasis).
24. A. Cole, 'The Quakers and the English Revolution', *Past and Present*, no. 10, November 1956, p. 42.

CHAPTER THREE

1. C. Hill, *Puritanism and Revolution*, London, 1968, p. 38.
2. H. R. Trevor-Roper, 'The General Crisis of the Seventeenth Century' in *Past and Present*, no. 16, November 1959, p. 36. This essay is reprinted in H. R. Trevor-Roper, *Religion, the Reformation and Social Change*, London, 1967, pp. 46–89.
3. E. J. Hobsbawm, 'Discussion', in *Past and Present*, no. 18, November 1960, p. 14.
4. For example, Weber's understanding of the triumph of Protestant asceticism as an essentially tragic process derives precisely from his recognition of its unintended consequences. Thus: 'Since asceticism undertook to remodel the world and to work out its ideals in the world, material goods have gained an increasing and finally an inexorable power over the lives of men as at no previous period in history.' (M. Weber, *The Protestant Ethic and the Spirit of Capitalism*, London, 1930, p. 181.)
5. H. K. Takahashi, 'The Transition from Feudalism to Capitalism: A contribution to the Sweezy–Dobb controversy', in *Science and Society*, vol. XVI, no. 4, Fall 1952, pp. 333–4.
6. M. Dobb, 'Reply', in *Science and Society*, vol. XIV, no. 2, Spring 1950, p. 157.
7. Paul Sweezy dissents from this view: cf. P. Sweezy, 'The Transition from Feudalism to Capitalism', in *Science and Society*, vol. XIV, no. 2, Spring 1950, and P. Sweezy, 'Comments', in *Science and Society*, vol. XVII, no. 2, Spring 1953. Sweezy's insistence on 'pre-capitalist commodity production' as a distinct transitional form between feudalism and capitalism seems unwarranted. It has the unfortunate consequence that he sees the development of capitalism out of feudalism as a product of exogenous, and hence essentially contingent, factors (those associated with trade), rather than of factors internal to feudalism itself. His unwillingness to recognise the absolutist state as a form of feudal class rule derives from the same source.
8. P. Anderson, *Lineages of the Absolutist State*, London, 1974, p. 403.
9. Ibid., p. 407.
10. Ibid., p. 19.
11. Ibid., p. 18.
12. Ibid., p. 17.
13. Characteristically, Weber interprets the difference between merchant and industrial capitalism in ideological terms as a difference between, respectively, the Jewish and Protestant ethics: cf. *The Protestant Ethic and the Spirit of Capitalism*, pp. 165–6.
14. R. Hilton, 'The Transition from Feudalism to Capitalism' in *Science and Society*, vol. XVII, no. 4, Fall 1953, p. 343.
15. Ibid., pp. 347–8.
16. Hill, *Puritanism and Revolution*, pp. 48–50.
17. L. Stone, *The Causes of the English Revolution*, London, 1972, p. 72.
18. L. Stone, *The Crisis of the Aristocracy 1558–1641*, Oxford, 1965; cf. also J. H. Hexter, 'The English Aristocracy, its Crises, and the English Revolution, 1558–1660', in *Journal of British Studies*, vol. VIII, no. 1, November 1968.
19. Anderson, op. cit., p. 142.

20. E. H. Kossmann, 'Discussion', in *Past and Present*. no. 18, November 1960, pp. 8—11.
21. H. R. Trevor-Roper, 'The Gentry, 1540—1640', in *Economic History Review Supplement*.
22. R. H. Tawney, 'The Rise of the Gentry', in *Economic History Review*, vol. XI, no. 1.
23. H. R. Trevor-Roper, 'The General Crisis of the Seventeenth Century', p. 61.
24. K. Marx, Art. II (1844), *Marx-Engels Gesamtausgabe* 1/3, p. 22, quoted in T. B. (ed.), and M. Rubel (ed.)., *Karl Marx, Selected Writings in Sociology and Social Philosophy*, Harmondsworth, 1963, p. 243.
25. Cf. Anderson, op. cit., pp. 15—18.
26. C. Hill, 'The Transition from Feudalism to Capitalism', in *Science and Society*, vol. XVII, no. 4, Fall 1953, p. 351.
27. Anderson, op. cit., p. 19.
28. C. Hill, *The Century of Revolution*, Edinburgh, 1961, p. 33.
29. Ibid., pp. 46—7.
30. Stone, *The Causes of the English Revolution*, pp. 117—35.
31. Cf. R. Blackburn, 'A Brief Guide to Bourgeois Ideology' in A. Cockburn and R. Blackburn (ed.), *Student Power*, Harmondsworth, 1970, pp. 182—8, and C. Johnson, *Revolution and the Social System*, Stanford, 1964.
32. Stone, *The Causes of the English Revolution*, p. 11.
33. Ibid., p. 118.
34. K. Marx, *Gesamtausgabe*, Abt. 1, Bd, VI, p. 320, quoted in C. Hill, 'The English Civil War Interpreted by Marx and Engels', in *Science and Society*, vol. XII, no. 1, Winter 1948, p. 142.
35. Hill, *The Century of Revolution*, pp. 200—41.
36. Stone, *The Causes of the English Revolution*, p. 72.
37. Hill, *Puritanism and Revolution*, pp. 192—3.
38. Cf. P. Anderson,· *Passages from Antiquity to Feudalism*, London, 1974, pp. 190—5.
39. F. Engels, 'Introduction', *Socialism: Utopian and Scientific*, in K. Marx and F. Engels, *Selected Works*, Moscow, 1970, p. 385.
40. Stone, *The Causes of the English Revolution*, p. 144.
41. Ibid.
42. Stone, *The Crisis of the Aristocracy, 1558—1641*, ch. III.
43. J. H. Hexter, 'The English Aristocracy, its Crises, and the English Revolution, 1558—1660', p. 29.
44. D. Brunton and D. H. Pennington, *Members of the Long Parliament*, London, 1954, pp. 19—20.
45. The only possible exception is Sir Arthur Ingram, but he died before the outbreak of war.
46. Brunton and Pennington, op. cit., pp. 53—64.
47. See p. 65.
48. B. Manning, 'The Nobles, The People, and the Constitution', in *Past and Present*, no. 9, April 1956, p. 49.
49. Takahashi, op. cit., p. 342.
50. G. Yule, 'Independents and Revolutionaries' in *Journal of British Studies*, vol. VII no. 2, May 1968, p. 16.
51. Brunton and Pennington, op. cit., p. 128.

52. G. Yule, *The Independents in the English Civil War*, Cambridge, 1958, pp. 81—2.
53. Hill, *Puritanism and Revolution*, p. 25.
54. Brunton and Pennington, op. cit., pp. 177—9.
55. Ibid., pp. 66—7.
56. J. H. Hexter, 'The Problem of the Presbyterian Independents', *Reappraisals in History*, London, 1961.
57. Yule, The *Independents in the English Civil War*, p. 38.
58. Yule, 'Independents and Revolutionaries', p. 16.
59. Ibid., p. 31.
60. D. Underdown, 'The Independents Again', in *Journal of British Studies*, vol..VIII, no. 1, November 1968, p. 88.
61. Yule, 'Independents and Revolutionaries', p. 19.
62. L. Trotsky, 'Two Traditions: The Great Rebellion and Chartism', *On Britain*, New York, 1973, p. 112.
63. See pp. 83—4.
64. Cf. Yule, *The Independents in the English Civil War*, p. 60.
65. Cf. C. B. Macpherson, *The Political Theory of Possessive Individualism*, Oxford, 1962, pp. 154—5.
66. Trevor-Roper, *Religion, the Reformation and Social Change*, pp. 346—7.
67. Other members included Samuel Moyer, Rowland Wilson, John Foulkes, and William Gibbs. Cf. Yule, *The Independents in the English Civil War*, p. 52.
68. Brunton and Pennington, op. cit., p. 44.
69. Ibid.
70. H. N. Brailsford, *The Levellers and the English Revolution*, London, 1961, p. 9.
71. F. Engels, *Anti-Dühring*, Moscow, 1954, pp. 29—30.
72. The term 'petty bourgeois' is here used in a purely analytical sense, rather than in the pejorative sense of vulgar usage.
73. Cf. Brailsford, op. cit., ch. XIII, pp. 267—304.
74. 'The Putney Debates' in A. S. P. Woodhouse (ed.), *Puritanism and Liberty*, London, 1965, p. 53.
75. Brailsford, op. cit., p. 274.
76. That is, *wage* servants.
77. Which would include all *unemployed* wage servants.
78. 'The Putney Debates' in Woodhouse, op. cit., p. 83.
79. Macpherson, op. cit., p. 129.
80. 'In my opinion and judgement this conceit of levelling propriety and magistracy is so ridiculous and foolish an opinion as no man of brains, reason or ingenuity can be imagined such a sot as to maintain such a principle, because it would, if practised, destroy not only any industry in the world, but raze the very foundation of generation and of subsistence.'—*Lt. Colonel John Lilburne his Apologetical Narration*, quoted in Brailsford, op. cit., p. 525.
81. Cf. Macpherson, op. cit., pp. 107—59.
82. Cf. Brailsford, op. cit., ch. XXI, pp. 417—52.
83. For a detailed account of the Leveller programme cf. Brailsford, op. cit., ch. XXVII, pp. 523—39, and Woodhouse, op. cit., Part III, ch. VIII, pp. 317—78.
84. 'The Putney Debates' in Woodhouse, op. cit., p. 67.
85. Engels, *Socialism: Utopian and Scientific*, pp. 384—5.

86. *The English Soldier's Standard*, quoted in Brailsford, op. cit., p. 499.
87. 'Introduction', Woodhouse, op. cit., pp. (15)–(16).
88. Hill, *Puritanism and Revolution*, p. 158.
89. H. R. Trevor-Roper, *Historical Essays*, London, 1975, p. 204.
90. 'The Heads of Proposals' in Woodhouse, op. cit., p. 204.
91. F. Engels, 'Introduction' to K. Marx, *The Class Struggles in France, 1848 to 1850, Selected Works*, p. 645. In a commentary on this passage, Christopher Hill suggests that the equivalent in the English Revolution of Engels's radicals were the Levellers: cf. 'The English Civil War Interpreted by Marx and Engels', p. 147. But it is clear from the context of the passage that the radicals are normally a section of the 'victorious minority' rather than of the 'ruled majority'. It would seem, then, that Engels's analysis can only be applicable, not to the Levellers, but to the Independents. We should note that the defeated English radicals did not confine themselves merely to shrieks of treachery and explanations in terms of accident. Milton, in fact, proceeded to an explanation which, in the form in which it appears in the last great epic poems, is profoundly historical.
92. W. Prynne, 'Anti-Arminianism', in Woodhouse, op. cit., p. 232.
93. Yule, *The Independents in the English Civil War*, p. 11.
94. Ibid., p. 79.
95. Brailsford, op. cit., p. 398.
96. 'The Heads of Proposals', in Woodhouse, op. cit., p. 424 (my emphasis).
97. 'A Representation of the Army', quoted in Brailsford, op. cit., p. 390—this part of Article IX is ommitted from Woodhouse's selection and the document thus appears as more genuinely tolerationist than it actually is.
98. Cf. Brailsford, op. cit., ch. XIX, pp. 379–99.
99. Milton, 'A Treatise of Civil Power in Ecclesiastical Causes', *Prose Works*, Bohn Edition, London, 1848, II, p. 533.
100. J. Illo, 'The Misreading of Milton', in L. Baxandall (ed.), *Radical Perspectives in the Arts*, Harmondsworth, 1972, p. 189. The flawed nature of Illo's commentary derives from its evident relish at revolutionary intolerance. He interprets that intolerance as a matter of political principle, rather than of political necessity—a dangerous conclusion, one would have thought, in the contemporary Cuban context. St. Paul's status as a 'humanist revolutionary' is also rather less self-evident than Illo, a Catholic Marxist, would have us believe.
101. Cf. C. H. George, 'A Social Interpretation of English Puritanism', in the *Journal of Modern History*, vol. xxv, no. 4, December 1953.
102. Cf. Woodhouse, op. cit., pp. 126–7, 156–9, 168–9.
103. Cf. the extract in Woodhouse, op. cit., p. 186, on toleration.
104. In Woodhouse, op. cit., pp. 212–20.
105. Yule, *The Independents in the English Civil War*, p. 13.
106. Ibid., p. 112.
107. Ibid., pp. 84–127.
108. 'Of True Religion, Heresy, Schism, Toleration', *Prose Works*, II, p. 511, Cf. also 'A Treatise of Christian Doctrine', Bk. 1, ch. IV, *Prose Works*, IV, pp. 43–77.
109. Trevor-Roper, *Religion, the Reformation and Social Change*, p. 207.
110. Weber, op. cit., p. 115.
111. Engels, *Socialism: Utopian and Scientific*, p. 384.
112. Cf. Weber. op. cit., pp. 79–87, and Engels, op. cit., p. 384.
113. Trevor-Roper, *Religion, the Reformation and Social Change*, pp. 6–7.

114. Ibid., p. 214.
115. Weber, op. cit., pp. 110–12.
116. 'A Treatise of Christian Doctrine', *Prose Works*, IV, p. 399.
117. L. Goldmann, *The Human Sciences and Philosophy*, London, 1970, p. 130.

CHAPTER FOUR

1. Sir Herbert J. C. Grierson, *Milton and Wordsworth*, Cambridge, 1937, pp. 65–131, 147–82.
2. J. Milton, *Prose Works*, Bohn Edition, London, 1848, II, 108–38.
3. Cf. J. Milton, *Poetical Works*, Oxford, 1966, p. 78.
4. *Sonnet VII*, 1–4.
5. 'Areopagatica', *Prose Works*, II, p. 66.
6. Ibid., p. 74.
7. W. Prynne, 'Anti-Arminianism' in A. S. P. Woodhouse (ed.), *Puritanism and Liberty*, London, 1965, p. 232.
8. 'A Treatise on Christian Doctrine', *Prose Works*, IV, p. 33.
9. Ibid., p. 36.
10. Ibid., p. 40.
11. Ibid., p. 51.
12. Ibid., p. 57–8.
13. Ibid., p. 63.
14. *At A Solemn Music*, 25–8.
15. 'Of Reformation in England', *Prose Works*, II, p. 373.
16. 'An Apology for Smectymnuus', *Prose Works*, III, p. 138.
17. 'Of Prelatical Episcopacy', *Prose Works*, II, p. 422.
18. 'An Apology for Smectymnuus', *Prose Works*, III, p. 139.
19. 'The Doctrine and Discipline of Divorce', *Prose Works*, III, p. 215.
20. Ibid., p. 217.
21. Ibid.
22. 'A Treatise on Christian Doctrine', *Prose Works*, IV, p. 447.
23. Ibid., p. 450.
24. 'Of Reformation in England', *Prose Works*, II, p. 387.
25. 'An Apology for Smectymnuus', *Prose Works*, III, p. 154.
26. Ibid., pp. 155–6. Milton expresses similar sentiments in 'Animadversions Upon the Remonstrant's Defence Against Smectymnuus': 'Our great clerks think that these men, because they have a trade . . . cannot therefore attain to some good measure of knowledge, and to a reason of their actions, as well as they that spend their youth in loitering, bezzling, and harlotting, their studies in unprofitable questions and barbarous sophistry, their middle age in ambition and idleness, their old age in avarice, dotage, and diseases.' *Prose Works*, III, p. 51.
27. 'The Second Defence of the People of England', *Prose Works*, I, pp. 298–9.
28. Ibid., p. 298.
29. 'The Reason of Church Government', *Prose Works*, II, p. 490.
30. 'Areopagatica', *Prose Works*, II, p. 97.
31. *On the New Forces of Conscience Under the Long Parliament*, 20.
32. *Sonnet XV*.

33. *Sonnet XVI.*
34. *Sonnet XVII.*
35. Ibid., 9—11.
36. *Lycidas*, 114—18.
37. 'A Treatise on Christian Doctrine', *Prose Works*, IV, p. 463.
38. Ibid., p. 454.
39. *Prose Works*, II, pp. 520—48.
40. 'A Treatise of Civil Power in Ecclesiastical Causes', *Prose Works*, II, p. 523.
41. Ibid., p. 532.
42. 'A Defence of the People of England', *Prose Works*, I, p. 33.
43. Ibid., p. 63.
44. 'The Tenure of Kings and Magistrates', *Prose Works*, II, pp. 8—9.
45. Ibid., p. 9.
46. Ibid., pp. 9—10.
47. Ibid., p. 11.
48. Ibid., p. 14.
49. The problem was, in fact, extremely urgent. *The Tenure of Kings and Magistrates* was published on 13 February 1649, just over two months after the purging of the Presbyterian members from Parliament, only a fortnight after the execution of the king, and almost exactly three months before the final defeat of the Levellers at Burford.
50. 'The Tenure of Kings and Magistrates', *Prose Works*, II, p. 10.
51. 'A Defence of the People of England', *Prose Works*, I, pp. 168—9.
52. 'The Second Defence of the People of England', *Prose Works*, I, p. 265.
53. Ibid., p. 258.
54. Cf. 'On Education', *Prose Works*, III, pp. 462—78.
55. Cf. 'Areopagatica', *Prose Works*, II, pp. 48—101.
56. 'Tetrachordon', *Prose Works*, III, p. 335.
57. 'The Doctrine and Discipline of Divorce', *Prose Works*, III, p. 176.
58. Milton makes it quite clear that both men *and* women should be able to sue for divorce. Cf. 'Tetrachordon', *Prose Works*, III, pp. 345—6 and p. 356.
59. 'The Doctrine and Discipline of Divorce', *Prose Works*, III, p. 205.
60. Ibid., p. 210.
61. Ibid., pp. 263—4. Marriage 'being of itself a civil ordinance, a household contract, a thing indifferent and free to the whole of mankind, not as religious, but as men . . . not therefore invalid or unholy without a minister and his pretended necessary hallowing, more than any other act, enterprise, or contract of civil life'. ('Considerations Touching the Likeliest Means to Remove Hirelings Out of the Church', *Prose Works*, III, p. 22.)
62. 'The Doctrine and Discipline of Divorce', *Prose Works*, III, p. 268.
63. 'Tetrachordon', *Prose Works*, III, p. 354.
64. V. I. Lenin, *The State and Revolution*, Peking, 1965, p. 10.
65. 'A Treatise on Christian Doctrine', *Prose Works*, IV, p. 49.
66. Ibid., p. 59.
67. Ibid., pp. 398—9 (my emphasis).
68. 'A Defence of the People of England', *Prose Works*, I, p. 111.
69. Ibid., p. 155.
70. D. Saurat, *Milton: Man and Thinker*, London, 1924, pp. 149—71.
71. H. Agar, *Milton and Plato*, Princeton, 1928, pp. 6—9.

72. F. M. Cornford (trans.), *The Republic of Plato*, Oxford, 1945, pp. 129–38.
73. E. Gellner, *Thought and Change*, London, 1964, pp. 86–99.
74. 'Tetrachordon', *Prose Works*, III, p. 432.
75. 'A Treatise on Christian Doctrine', *Prose Works*, V, p. 79.
76. 'Aeropagatica', *Prose Works*, II, p. 68.
77. 'The Doctrine and Discipline of Divorce', *Prose Works*, III, p. 210.
78. Ibid., p. 187.
79. Ibid., p. 205.
80. Ibid.
81. Ibid.
82. Cf. 'Tetrachordon', *Prose Works*, III, p. 333.
83. Ibid., p. 332.
84. 'Of Reformation in England, *Prose Works*, II, p. 391.
85. 'The Ready and Easy Way to Establish a Free Commonwealth', *Prose Works*, II, p. 118.
86. 'Law in a free nation hath ever been public reason, the enacted reason of a parliament.' ('Eikonoklastes', *Prose Works*, I, p. 324.)
87. 'Nothing in the world is more pleasing to God, more agreeable to reason, more politically just, or more generally useful, than that the supreme power should be vested in the best and wisest of men.' ('The Second Defence of the People of England', *Prose Works*, I, p. 288.)
88. Cf. 'The Ready and Easy Way to Establish a Free Commonwealth', *Prose Works*, II, pp. 122–33.
89. 'The Tenure of Kings and Magistrates', *Prose Works*, II, p. 13.
90. Ibid., p. 17.
91. 'The Second Defence of the People of England', *Prose Works*, I, p. 297.
92. *Sonnet XII*, 11–14.
93. 'Eikonoklastes', *Prose Works*, I, p. 399.
94. 'The Second Defence of the People of England', *Prose Works*, I, p. 286.
95. Ibid., p. 295.
96. This is intended just as much to protect the state from the church as *vice versa*. For example, Milton warned the Belfast Presbyterians that 'affairs of state are not for their meddling', and that in civil matters they should 'assume nothing above other private persons', and should refrain from speaking separately and collectively 'as if they were a tribe and party by themselves'. ('Observations on the Articles of Peace', *Prose Works*, II, 189–90.)
97. And also of *burial*; cf. 'Considerations Touching the Likeliest Means to Remove Hirelings Out of the Church', *Prose Works*, III, p. 21.
98. 'The Tenure of Kings and Magistrates', *Prose Works*, II, p. 34.
99. Ibid., p. 17.
100. 'The Doctrine and Discipline of Divorce', *Prose Works*, III, p. 258.
101. 'A Treatise on Christian Doctrine', *Prose Works*, IV, p. 86. In Milton's view strict logic forbids the notion that God the Father and God the Son constitute a unity: 'if two subsistences or two persons be assigned to one essence, it involves a contradiction of terms, by representing the essence as at once simple and compound'. ('A Treatise on Christian Doctrine', *Prose Works*, IV, p. 86.)
102. Ibid., p. 415.
103. 'Tetrachordon', *Prose Works*, III, p. 365.
104. 'A Defence of the People of England', *Prose Works*, I, p. 96.

105. 'A Treatise on Christian Doctrine', *Prose Works*, IV, p. 14.
106. Ibid., p. 15.
107. Ibid.
108. Milton has regular resort to such arguments. For example, his proof of the afterlife, which clearly anticipates Kant, is based on the notion that 'were there no resurrection, the righteous would be of all men the most miserable, and the wicked, who have a better portion in this life, most happy'. ('A Treatise on Christian Doctrine', *Prose Works*, IV, p. 481.)
109. Ibid., p. 29.
110. Ibid., pp. 177–8.
111. Ibid., pp. 150–69.
112. Ibid., p. 342.
113. L. Trotsky, 'Two Traditions: The Great Rebellion and Chartism', *On Britain*, New York, 1973, p. 117.
114. B. Willey, *The Seventeenth Century Background*, Harmondsworth, 1972, p. 19.
115. 'Considerations Touching the Likeliest Means to Remove Hirelings Out of the Church', *Prose Works*, III, p. 37.
116. 'Tetrachordon', *Prose Works*, III, p. 414.
117. 'The Second Defence of the People of England', *Prose Works*, I, p. 248.
118. My usage here is intended as more than a simple pun. The political implications of scholasticism are, in the conventional sense of the term, authoritarian.
119. 'Animadversions Upon the Remonstrant's Defence Against Smectymnuus', *Prose Works*, III, pp. 56–7.
120. C. Hill, *Intellectual Origins of the English Revolutions*, London, 1972, p. 294.
121. London, 1975.
122. J. H. Hexter, 'The Burden of proof', *Times Literary Supplement*, 24 October, 1975, p. 1250.
123. Locke distinguishes between *thinking*, on the one hand, which is active, and which consists in the Mind reflecting on its own ideas, and perception, on the other, which is passive: 'in bare naked Perception, the Mind is for the most part, only passive; and what it perceives, it cannot avoid perceiving'. (J. Locke, *An Essay concerning Human Understanding*, Oxford, 1975, p. 143.)
124. 'Of Reformation in England', *Prose Works*, II, p. 364.
125. 'The Second Defence of the People of England', *Prose Works*, I, p. 239.
126. *Sonnet XXII*, 9–14.
127. 'A Defence of the People of England', *Prose Works*, I, pp. 140–1.
128. 'Tetrachordon', *Prose Works*, III, p. 341.
129. 'The Tenure of Kings and Magistrates', *Prose Works*, II, p. 29.
130. Ibid., p. 31.
131. A. J. A. Waldock, *Paradise Lost and Its Critics*, Cambridge, 1966, p. 59
132. *The Shorter Oxford Dictionary*, Oxford, 1973, p. 1758.
133. Willey, op. cit., p. 185.
134. As Willey observes, an empiricist poetics was logically possible, and was indeed ultimately developed by Wordsworth—cf. pp. 266–77.
135. *At a Vacation Exercise in the College*, 29–32.
136. 'An Apology for Smectymnuus', *Prose Works*, III, p. 117.
137. 'The Reason of Church Government', *Prose Works*, II, p. 479.
138. Ibid., p. 480.
139. 'An Apology for Smectymnuus', *Prose Works*, III, p. 141.

140. E. M. W. Tillyard, *Milton*, Harmondsworth, 1968, p. 304.

141. R. W. Condee, *Structure in Milton's Poetry*, Pennsylvania, 1974, p. 1.

142. 'True eloquence I find to be none, but the serious and hearty love of truth' ('An Apology for Smectymnuus', *Prose Works*, III, p. 165.)

143. Indeed, Walter J. Ong has been prompted to observe that 'paradoxically, in Milton's poetry logic appears perhaps more assertive than in his prose'. ('Logic and Epic Muse: Reflections on Poetic Structure in Milton's Milieu'), in M. Lieb and J. T. Shawcross (ed.), *Achievements of the Left Hand*, Amherst, 1974, p. 239.

144. 'On Education', *Prose Works*, III, p. 473.

145. F. Kermode, 'Dissociation of Sensibility', in *The Kenyon Review*, vol. XIX, no. 2 Spring 1957, p. 191.

146. One would have thought that the least the sociologist had the right to expect from the literary critic was textual accuracy. Sadly, such expectations are often unwarranted.

147. T. S. Eliot, *Milton: Two Studies*, London, 1968, pp. 18–19.

148. Or, at least, as he appeared to believe in 1936. By 1947 his assessment of Milton's poetic worth had undergone some considerable transformation. Cf. Eliot, op. cit., pp. 22–48.

149. F. W. Bradbrook, 'Ben Jonson's Poetry', in B. Ford (ed.), *From Donne to Marvell*, Harmondsworth, 1968, p. 137.

150. *Comus*, 5–10.

151. Ibid., 1018–19.

152. Ibid., 591–2.

153. Ibid., 806.

154. Ibid., 813.

155. Ibid., 211–12.

156. Ibid., 1022–3.

157. Ibid., 909.

158. Ibid., 8–9.

159. Ibid., 662–5.

160. Ibid., 102–10.

161. Ibid., 710–14.

162. Ibid., 721–7.

163. Ibid., 764–7.

164. Ibid., 768–74.

165. Cf. especially lines 710–36. It is, of course, extremely significant that Leavis, the grand empiricist whose own literary criticism persistently refuses to forsake the concrete for the realms of abstraction, should select this particular passage from *Comus* as one of the few of Milton's 'better' passages. (F. R. Leavis *Revaluation*, Harmondsworth, 1972, pp. 50–2.) Leavis's view, in fact, pays a back-handed compliment to Milton's considerable ability to represent in poetic form a view of the world, and indeed a view of poetry, with which he actually had very little sympathy.

166. *Comus*, 666–89.

167. Ibid., 706–36.

168. Ibid., 737–55.

169. Ibid., 800–5.

170. Ibid., 805–13.

171. Ibid., 205.

172. Ibid., 210–11. There is an obvious point of comparison here between *Comus* and the views later expressed in the *Areopagatica*: 'the knowledge cannot defile, nor consequently the books, if the will and conscience be not defiled'. (*Prose Works*, II, p. 65.)
173. *Comus*, 359–63.
174. Ibid., 966–75.
175. Ibid., 381–5.
176. Ibid., 460–3.
177. Ibid., 463–9.
178. Ibid., 321–6.
179. Ibid., 122–3.
180. W. Cartwright, "Drinking Song" from *The Royal Slave*, 1636, in W. Lamont and S. Oldfield, *Politics, Religion and Literature in the Seventeenth Century*, London, 1975, p. 36.
181. These lines, for example, express Suckling's view of the world better than anything that Suckling himself wrote:

> 'List, lady, be not coy, and be not cozened
> With that same vaunted name Virginity;
> Beauty is Nature's coin, must not be hoarded,
> But must be current, and the good thereof
> Consists in mutual and partaken bliss,
> Unsavory in th'enjoyment of itself.
> If you let slip time, like a neglected rose
> It withers on the stalk with languished head.'

(*Comus*, 737–44)

182. *Comus*, 608.
183. Ibid., 125.
184. Ibid., 807–8.
185. As Comus is the priest, so too, perhaps, his glass is the chalice, and his wand, or 'rod', the bishop's staff?

CHAPTER FIVE

1. The early poems, for example, *Lycidas*, do, of course, deal with 'pessimistic' themes. But the problems there posed are solved in a distinctly 'ready and easy' manner.
2. General George Monck played a decisive role in placing the Army at the disposal of the Restoration, and received in return the title of Duke of Albemarle from Charles II; 'some men will betray three kingdoms for filthy lucre's sake', a minister said to his face (quoted in C. Hill, *The Century of Revolution*, Edinburgh, 1961, p. 189).
3. *Paradise Lost*, I, 22–6.
4. *Samson Agonistes*, 1745–8.
5. Cf. above, p. 117.
6. 'Eikonoklastes', *Prose Works*, I, p. 494.

7. T. S. Eliot, *Milton: Two Studies*, London, 1968, p. 38.

8. Ibid., p. 12.

9. F. R. Leavis, *Revaluation*, Harmondsworth, 1972, p. 53.

10. Ibid., pp. 46–63; F. R. Leavis, *The Common Pursuit*, London, 1952, 9–32.

11. Eliot: 'A theology that I find in large part repellent, expressed through a mythology which would have been better left in the book of *Genesis*' (op. cit., p. 19); Leavis: 'He has "character", moral grandeur, moral force; but he is, for the purpose of his undertaking, disastrously single-minded and simple-minded. He reveals everywhere a dominating sense of righteousness and a complete incapacity to question or explore its significance and conditions. . . . He offers as ultimate for our worship mere brute assertive will.' (*Revaluation*, p. 60.)

12. D. Bush, *Paradise Lost in Our Time*, Gloucester, Mass., 1957, pp. 88–117; C. S. Lewis, *A Preface to Paradise Lost*, Oxford, 1942, pp. 51–60.

13. Lewis, op. cit., p. 130.

14. Significantly the three share similar intellectual origins i.e. Leavis/Collingwood; Eliot/Bradley; Lukács/Hegel.

15. B. Bergonzi, 'Criticism and the Milton Controversy', in F. Kermode (ed.), *The Living Milton*, London, 1960, p. 176.

16. Eliot, op. cit., p. 42.

17. T. S. Eliot, *Selected Essays*, London, 1963, pp. 281–91.

18. T. S. Eliot, 'Donne In Our Time', in T. Spencer (ed.), *A Garland for John Donne*, Cambridge, Mass., 1931, pp. 1–19.

19. E. M. W. Tillyard, *The Miltonic Setting*, London, 1938, pp. 141–68.

20. Bush, op. cit., p.91.

21. Leavis, *Revaluation*, p. 58.

22. G. Lukács, *The Theory of the Novel*, London, 1971, p. 46.

23. Ibid., pp. 68–9.

24. Ibid., p. 68.

25. For example, I. Samuel, *Dante and Milton*, New York, 1966,

26. op. cit., pp. 48–9.

27. Lewis op. cit., pp. 12–50.

28. B. Willey, *The Seventeenth Century Background*, Harmondsworth, 1972, p. 212.

29. *Paradise Lost*, I, 13–16.

30. Lukács, op. cit., pp. 34–6.

31. J. Milton, *Poetical Works*, Oxford, 1966, p. 518.

32. Cf. G. Lukács, *The Historical Novel*, Harmondsworth, 1969, pp. 106–107.

33. Ibid., pp. 123–44.

34. Ibid., pp. 143–4.

35. Ibid., pp. 150–2.

36. Tillyard, op. cit., pp. 88–9.

37. *Samson Agonistes*, 1708–11.

38. Eliot, *Milton: Two Studies*, p. 26.

39. Lewis, op. cit., p. 64.

40. Bush, op. cit., pp. 55–7.

41. A. J. A. Waldock, *Paradise Lost and Its Critics*, Cambridge, 1961, p. 96.

42. E. M. W. Tillyard, *Milton*, Harmondsworth, 1968, p. 312.

43. Cf. J. H. Hanford, 'Milton and the Return to Humanism', *Studies in Philology*,

vol. XVI, April 1919, pp. 126–47.
44. Cf. D. Saurat, *Milton: Man and Thinker*, London, 1924.
45. The terms are significant. Engels: 'The grand period of English history, known to respectability under the name of "the Great Rebellion", and the struggles succeeding it, were brought to a close by the comparatively puny event entitled by liberal historians "the Glorious Revolution".' *Socialism: Utopian and Scientific*, in K. Marx and F. Engels, *Selected Works*, Moscow, 1970, p. 385.
46. *Paradise Lost*, V, 490.
47. Lukács, *The Theory of the Novel*, p. 66.
48. 'The "character", in short, disintegrates into what is really a succession of unrelated moods': Waldock, op. cit., p. 87.
49. J. Peter, *A Critique of Paradise Lost*, London, 1960, pp. 61–2.
50. *Paradise Lost*, IX, 99–178.
51. Ibid., II, 498.
52. Ibid., III, 98–102.
53. Ibid., III, 108.
54. Ibid., III, 96–7.
55. Ibid., III, 116–19.
56. Ibid., VIII, 635–7.
57. Ibid., III, 309–11.
58. Ibid., V, 809–48.
59. Ibid., II, 5–6.
60. Ibid., V, 493–503. God himself outlines a similarly meritocratic theory of the cosmos, when he determines, at the beginning of Book VII, to create a new world and a new race of men,

'. . . there to dwell,
Not here, till by degrees of merit raised
They open to themselves at length the way
Up hither, . . .'

(*Paradise Lost*, VII, 156–9)

61. Lewis, op. cit., pp. 72–80.
62. *Paradise Lost*, VIII, 398–451.
63. Ibid., VIII, 329–30.
64. Peter, op. cit., p. 11. Similar points are made by Waldock, op. cit., p. 103, and even by Lewis, op. cit., pp. 126–7.
65. Waldock, op. cit., p. 21.
66. Willey, op. cit., p. 231.
67. *Paradise Lost*, IV, 524–6, and IX, 692–9.
68. Ibid., IV, 526–7.
69. Ibid., IX, 1071–3.
70. Ibid., III, 94–5.
71. Ibid., IV, 428–30.
72. Saurat, op. cit., pp. 150–2.
73. *Paradise Lost*, VIII, 635–7.
74. Ibid., VI, 174–81.
75. Ibid., IV, 957–61.
76. Peter, op. cit., pp. 66–71.

77. Ibid., pp. 72–3.
78. The war in Heaven which follows the act of rebellion itself is, of course, much less successful. There can be little doubt that Milton's treatment of this particular episode would have been greatly improved by a firm decision to avoid all speculation about the properties of angelic bodies. There can inevitably be little interest in the process itself, as opposed to the outcome, of a battle between immortal creatures in possession of self-healing bodies.
79. Saurat, op. cit., pp. 152–5.
80. Indeed, from Milton's own point of view, the Genesis story is extremely unfortunate. For it does, in fact, specifically state that the tree did confer knowledge: 'when the woman saw that the tree was good for food, and that it was pleasant to the eyes, and *a tree to be desired to make one wise*, she took of the fruit thereof, and did eat'—Genesis 3, 6 (my emphasis).
81. *Paradise Lost*, IX, 791–3.
82. Ibid., IX, 999.
83.   'But that false fruit
            Far other operation first displayed,
            Carnal desire inflaming: he on Eve
            Began to cast lascivious eyes, she him
            As wantonly repaid; in lust they burn,'

                                                (Ibid., IX, 1011–15.)

84.   'but high winds worse within
            Began to rise, high passions, anger, hate,
            Mistrust, suspicion, discord, and shook sore
            Their inward state of mind, calm region once'

                                                (Ibid., IX, 1122–5.)

85. Tillyard, *Milton*, pp. 218–33.
86. Lewis, op. cit., pp. 121–4.
87. Waldock, op. cit., p. 41 and pp. 51–2.
88. Peter, op. cit., p. 137.
89. Waldock, op. cit., pp. 51–7.
90. Eliot, *Milton: Two Studies*, p. 38.
91. *Paradise Lost*, XII, 82–101.
92. Ibid., III, 128–32.
93. This point is made by F. T. Prince, 'On the Last Two Books of *Paradise Lost*', in *Essays and Studies*, 1958, vol. XI Series 2). But Prince's reading of Books XI and XII seems to me to be mistaken.
94. R. W. Condee, *Structure in Milton's Poetry*, Pennsylvania, 1974, pp. 1–4 and pp. 175–9.
95. F. Kermode, 'Adam Unparadised', in Kermode (ed.), op. cit., pp. 85–123.
96. *Paradise Lost*, XII, 463–5.
97. Ibid., XII, 487–91.
98. Ibid., XII, 585–7.
99. Ibid., XII, 646–9.
100. Ibid., IX, 13–47.
101. Saurat, op. cit., p. 235.
102. Indeed, those few critics who have looked favourably on *Paradise Regained* have emphasised precisely this exceptional control over the poetic materials at hand.

Cf. F. W. Bateson, '*Paradise Regained*: A Dissentient Appendix', in Kermode (ed.), op. cit., pp. 138–40.

103. *Paradise Regained*, I, 4–5.
104. Ibid., IV, 534–5.
105. Ibid., I, 196–267.
106. Ibid., I, 215–23.
107. Ibid., III, 357–70.
108. Ibid., IV, 90–102.
109. Ibid., I, 163–7.
110. This is evidently the case since the sequence in which the separate temptations arise in *Paradise Regained* is the same as that outlined in *St. Luke*. In *St. Matthew*, the order of the second and third temptations is reversed (ch. 4, 5–10), in *St. Mark* the details are omitted (ch. 1, 12–13), and in *St. John* there is no mention of the entire incident.
111. *St. Luke*, ch. 4, 3–4.
112. Ibid., ch. 4, 5–8.
113. Ibid., ch. 4, 9–12.
114. *Paradise Regained*, I, 314–56. Satan's first encounter with Christ, though not the incident of the temptation itself, is actually prolonged until the end of Book I.
115. Ibid., II, 241–403.
116. Ibid., II, 404–86.
117. 443 lines.
118. Ibid., IV, 1–393.
119. Ibid., IV, 499–639.
120. Ibid., I, 355–6.
121. Ibid., I, 349–50.
122. Ibid., II, 153.
123. Ibid., II, 340–4.
124. Ibid., II, 338–65.
125. Ibid., IJ, 412.
126. Ibid., III, 175–6.
127. Ibid., III, 368–85.
128. Ibid., IV, 100–2.
129. Ibid., I, 215–20.
130. Ibid., II, 42–8.
131. Ibid., II, 432–56.
132. Ibid., II, 466–76.
133. Ibid., III, 1–144.
134. Ibid., III, 188–95.
135. 'Eikonoklastes', *Prose Works*, I, p. 423.
136. *Paradise Regained*, III, 374–80 and IV, 90–102.
137. Ibid., III, 427–31.
138. Ibid., IV, 143–5.
139. Ibid., II, 321–2.
140. Ibid., IV, 154–94.
141. Ibid., IV, 286–364.
142. Ibid., IV, 322–4, 326–7.
143. Ibid., IV, 351–2.

144. Ibid., I, 290—4; II, 245—59; III, 182—94.
145. Ibid., IV, 538—40.
146. Ibid., IV, 518—20.
147. Ibid., IV, 560—2.
148. Condee, op. cit., pp. 153—73.
149. Hamburger's fascinating comparison between Milton's *Samson Agonistes* and Hölderlin's *Empedocles* serves only to emphasise the uniqueness of Milton's achievement. For, whilst Hölderlin embarked upon the self-same project as Milton, his *Empedocles* remained, nonetheless, ultimately unrealisable. Cf. M. Hamburger, 'The Sublime Art: Notes on Milton and Hölderlin', in Kermode (ed.), op. cit., pp. 141—61.
150. Saurat, op. cit., pp. 237—9.
151. Condee, op. cit., pp. 123—52.
152. A. S. P. Woodhouse, 'The Historical Criticism of Milton' in *Publications of the Modern Language Association of America*, vol. LXVI, no. 6, December 1951, p. 1036.
153. Cf. Hill, op. cit., pp. 222—41.
154. Our analysis of the problem of dating *Samson Agonistes* reveals, incidentally, the methodological limitations of formalistic, as opposed to genetic, structuralisms. Much of Condee's account of the structural organising principles of Milton's poetry is extremely valuable. It stands in marked contrast to the moralising tone of the literary criticism of writers, such as Douglas Bush, who are more concerned to take Milton's work as the text for a sermon on the iniquities of modern life, than to analyse it in terms of its specifically literary qualities. But in refusing to contemplate an explicitly sociological analysis of the wider context within which Milton's thought is formed, Condee finds himself obliged to posit an implicit and unspoken and, therefore, an assumed rather than a proven, account of the course of the poet's intellectual development, as the basis for his account of the poetry. Trotsky's observation that 'the artist who creates form, and the spectator who is enjoying it are not mere empty machines . . . They are living people' appears extremely apposite. (L. Trotsky, *Literature and Revolution*, Michigan, 1971, p. 171.)
155. *Samson Agonistes*, 170—5.
156. *Poetical Works*, op. cit., p. 517.
157. *Samson Agonistes*, 1758.
158. Ibid., 46—54.
159. Ibid., 356—80.
160. Ibid., 294—9.
161. Ibid., 667—70.
162. Ibid., 674.
163. Ibid., 680—1.
164.   Nor only dost degrade them, or remit
         To life obscured, which were a fair dismission,
         But throw'st them lower than thou didst exalt them high,
         Unseemly falls in human eye,
         Too grievous for the trespass or omission;
         Oft leav'st them to the hostile sword
         Of heathen and profane, their carcasses
         To dogs and fowls a prey, or else captived,

Or to the unjust tribunals, under change of times,
And condemnation of the ingrateful multitude.
(*Samson Agonistes*, 687—96.)

165. Quoted in W. Lamont and S. Oldfield, *Politics, Religion and Literature in the Seventeenth Century*, London, 1975, p. 235.
166. *Samson Agonistes*, 647—8.
167. Ibid., 654.
168. Ibid., 632.
169. Condee, op. cit., p. 132.
170. *Samson Agonistes*, 914—17.
171. Ibid., 932—5.
172. Of the poem's leading characters, Harapha alone is Milton's own creation. Cf. *Judges* 13, 14, 15 and 16, especially 16, 18—31.
173. *Samson Agonistes*, 1180.
174. Ibid., 1211—17.
175. Ibid., 1265—7.
176. Ibid., 1268—73.
177. Ibid., 1287—91.
178. Ibid., 1294—6.
179. Ibid., 1404—7.
180. Ibid., 1369—74.
181. Ibid., 1381—9.
182. Ibid., 1679.
183. Ibid., 1689.
184. Ibid., 1714—16.
185. Ibid., 1733—40.
186. Tillyard, *The Miltonic Setting*, pp. 88—9.
187. *Samson Agonistes*, 1721—4.
188. *Paradise Regained*, IV, 636—9.
189. *Samson Agonistes*, 1755—8.
190. A. S. P. Woodhouse, 'Tragic Effect in *Samson Agonistes*', in A. E. Barker (ed.), *Milton: Modern Essays in Criticism*, New York, 1965, pp. 447—66.
191. *Poetical Works*, op. cit., p. 517.
192. *Samson Agonistes*, 1387—9.

CHAPTER SIX

1. C. Hill, *Milton and the English Revolution*, London, 1977.
2. Ibid., pp. 17—21.
3. Ibid., pp. 69—79.
4. Ibid., p. 93.
5. Ibid., pp. 114—15.
6. Ibid., p. 250.
7. Ibid., p. 337.
8. Ibid., p. 345.
9. Ibid., p. 360.

10. Ibid., p. 472.
11. Ibid., p. 267.
12. See, for example, C. Hill, 'The English Civil War Interpreted by Marx and Engels', *Science and Society*, vol. XII, no. 1, Winter 1948.
13. Hill, *Milton and the English Revolution*, p. 13.
14. See, for example, C. Hill, *The Century of Revolution*, Edinburgh, 1961, ch. 8.
15. Hill, *Milton and the English Revolution*, p. 99.
16. Ibid., pp. 71—74, 100—7.
17. Ibid., p. 22.
18. Ibid., pp. 22—3.
19. 'We see Milton as a strict business-man, . . . Milton had a range of vision which included both God and the main chance.' (J. M. French, 'The Powell—Milton Bond', *Harvard Studies and Notes*, vol. XX, 1938, p. 73.)
20. Milton's most precise constitutional proposals are contained in 'The Ready and Easy Way to Establish A Free Commonwealth', J. Milton, *Prose Works*, Bohn Edition, London, II, pp. 108—38. There he specifically argues against popular elections: 'not committing all to the noise and shouting of a rude multitude, but permitting only those of them who are rightly qualified' (p. 126).
21. Cf. 'Observations on the Articles of Peace', *Prose Works*, II, pp. 139—99; 'The Second Defence of the People of England', *Prose Works*, I, p. 287.
22. Cf. 'A Manifesto of the Lord Protector', *Prose Works*, II, pp. 333—53.
23. See, for example, *Sonnet XV*, on Fairfax, and *Sonnet XVI*, on Cromwell.
24. 'A Second Defence of the People of England', *Prose Works*, I, pp. 286—288.
25. Hill, *Milton and the English Revolution*, p. 165.
26. Ibid., p. 115.
27. Ibid., pp. 451—8.
28. Ibid., p. 6.
29. Ibid.
30. Ibid., p. 472.
31. Ibid., pp. 242—52.
32. Ibid., p. 249.
33. Ibid., p. 170.
34. Ibid., p. 140.
35. Ibid., p. 466.
36. Ibid., pp. 371—2.
37. Ibid., p. 372.
38. Ibid., pp. 259—62.
39. Ibid., pp. 356—60.
40. Ibid., p. 352.
41. Ibid., p. 434.
42. J. H. Hexter, 'The burden of proof', *Times Literary Supplement*, 24 October 1975, p. 1252.
43. D. Widgery, 'The Two New Lefts', in D. Widgery (ed.), *The Left in Britain 1956—68*, Harmondsworth, 1976, pp. 131—53.
44. Widgery's essay, written in 1964, fails to anticipate this development.
45. Hill, *Milton and the English Revolution*, p. 459.

Bibliography

BOOKS

The Bible, Authorized Version, Oxford, 1960.
Milton, J., *Prose Works* (5 volumes), Bohn Edition, London, 1848.
Milton, J., *Poetical Works*, Oxford, 1966.
The Oxford Book of Seventeenth Century Verse, Oxford, 1968.
The Shorter Oxford Dictionary, Oxford, 1973.

Agar, H., *Milton and Plato*, Princeton, 1928.
Anderson, P., *Passages from Antiquity to Feudalism*, London, 1974.
Anderson, P., *Lineages of the Absolutist State*, London, 1974.
Anderson, P., *Considerations on Western Marxism*, London, 1976.
Ayer, A. J., *Language, Truth and Logic*, London, 1967.
Barker, A. E. (ed.), *Milton: Modern Essays in Criticism*, New York, 1965.
Barker, Sir Ernest (ed.), *Social Contract: Essays by Locke, Hume and Rousseau*, London, 1960.
Barthes, R., *Mythologies*, London, 1973.
Baxandall, L. (ed.), *Radical Perspectives in the Arts*, Harmondsworth, 1972.
Benjamin, W., *Understanding Brecht*, London, 1973.
Berger, P. L. and Luckmann, T., *The Social Construction of Reality*, Harmondsworth, 1971.
Blackburn, R. (ed.), *Ideology in Social Science*, London, 1972.
Bottomore, T. B. and Rubel, M. (ed.), *Karl Marx: Selected Writings in Sociology and Social Philosophy*, Harmondsworth, 1973.
Brailsford, H. N., *The Levellers and the English Revolution*, London, 1961.
Brunton, D. and Pennington, D. H., *Members of the Long Parliament*, London, 1954.
Bunyan, J., *Pilgrim's Progress*, London, 1903.
Burns, E. and Burns, T. (ed.), *Sociology of Literature and Drama*, Harmondsworth, 1973.

Bush, D., *Paradise Lost in Our Time*, Gloucester, Mass., 1957.
Caudwell, C., *Illusion and Reality*, London, 1946.
Clark, Sir George, *The Seventeenth Century*, Oxford, 1972.
Cockburn, A. and Blackburn, R. (ed.), *Student Power*, Harmondsworth, 1970.
Collingwood, R. G., *The Idea of History*, Oxford, 1946.
Condee, R. W., *Structure in Milton's Poetry*, Pennsylvania, 1974.
Cooper, D. (ed.), *The Dialectics of Liberation*, Harmondsworth, 1971.
Cornford, F. M. (trans.), *The Republic of Plato*, Oxford, 1945.
Day Lewis, C. (ed.), *The Mind in Chains*, London, 1937.
de George, R. T. and de George, F. M., *The Structuralists: From Marx to Levi-Strauss*, New York, 1972.
Durkheim, E., *The Rules of Sociological Method*, Chicago, 1962.
Eliot, T. S., *Selected Essays*, London, 1963.
Eliot, T. S., *Milton: Two Studies*, London, 1968.
Engels, F., *Anti-Dühring*, Moscow, 1954.
Fischer, E., *The Necessity of Art*, Harmondsworth, 1971.
Ford, B. (ed.), *The Age of Shakespeare*, Harmondsworth, 1966.
Ford, B. (ed.), *From Donne to Marvell*, Harmondsworth, 1968.
Gellner, E., *Thought and Change*, London, 1964.
Goldmann, L., *The Hidden God*, London, 1964.
Goldmann, L., *The Human Sciences and Philosophy*, London, 1970.
Goldmann, L., *Immanuel Kant*, London, 1971.
Goldmann, L., *Power and Humanism*, Nottingham, 1971.
Goldmann, L., *The Philosophy of the Enlightenment*, London, 1973.
Goldmann, L., *Towards a Sociology of the Novel*, London, 1977.
Gouldner, A. W., *The Coming Crisis of Western Sociology*, London, 1971.
Grierson, Sir Herbert J. C., *Milton and Wordsworth*, Cambridge, 1937.
Hexter, J. H., *Reappraisals in History*, London, 1961.
Hill, C., *The Century of Revolution*, Edinburgh, 1961.
Hill, C., *Puritanism and Revolution*, London, 1968.
Hill, C., *Intellectual Origins of the English Revolution*, London, 1972.
Hill, C., *Milton and the English Revolution*, London, 1977.
Hobbes, T., *Leviathan*, Harmondsworth, 1968.
Homer, *Iliad*, Harmondsworth, 1969.
Homer, *Odyssey*, Harmondsworth, 1970.
Hume, D., *Enquiries concerning Human Understanding and concerning the Principles of Morals*, Oxford, 1975.
Johnson, C., *Revolution and the Social System*, Stanford, 1964.

Kermode, F. (ed.), *The Living Milton*, London, 1960.

Knights, L. C., *Explorations*, London, 1958.

Lamont, W. and Oldfield, S., *Politics, Religion and Literature in the Seventeenth Century*, London, 1975.

Laurenson, D. T. and Swingewood, A., *The Sociology of Literature*, London, 1972.

Leavis, F. R., *New Bearings in English Poetry*, London, 1938.

Leavis, F. R., *The Common Pursuit*, London, 1952.

Leavis, F. R., *Two Cultures?*, London, 1962.

Leavis, F. R., *The Great Tradition*, Harmondsworth, 1967.

Leavis, F. R., *Nor Shall My Sword*, London, 1972.

Leavis, F. R., *Revaluation*, Harmondsworth, 1972.

Leavis, F. R. and Thompson, D., *Culture and Environment*, London, 1960.

Lenin, V. I., *The State the Revolution*, Peking, 1965.

Lewis, C. S., *A Preface to Paradise Lost*, Oxford, 1942.

Lichtheim, G., *Lukács*, London, 1970.

Lieb, M. and Shawcross, J. T. (ed.), *Achievements of the Left Hand*, Amherst, 1974.

Lifshitz, M., *The Philosophy of Art of Karl Marx*, London, 1973.

Locke, J., *An Essay Concerning Human Understanding*, Oxford, 1975.

Lukács, G., *Essays on Thomas Mann*, London, 1964.

Lukács, G., *The Historical Novel*, Harmondsworth, 1969.

Lukács, G., *Solzhenitsyn*, London, 1970.

Lukács, G., *Writer and Critic*, London, 1970.

Lukács, G., *History and Class Consciousness*, London, 1971.

Lukács, G., *The Theory of the Novel*, London, 1971.

Lukács, G., *Studies in European Realism*, London, 1972.

Lukács, G., *The Meaning of Contemporary Realism*, London, 1972.

MacIntyre, A. C., *A Short History of Ethics*, London, 1967.

McLennan, D., *Marx's Grundrisse*, London, 1973.

Macksey, R. and Donato, E. (ed.), *The Languages of Criticism and the Sciences of Man*, Baltimore, 1970.

Macpherson, C. B., *The Political Theory of Possessive Individualism*, Oxford, 1962.

Marx, K., *On Britain*, Moscow, 1953.

Marx, K., *Economic and Philosophic Manuscripts of 1844*, London, 1959.

Marx, K., *The Civil War in France*, Peking, 1966.

Marx, K., *Capital* (3 volumes), London, 1970.

Marx, K., *A Contribution to the Critique of Political Economy*, London, 1971.

Marx, K., *Grundrisse*, London, 1973.

Marx, K. and Engels, F., *Literature and Art*, New York, 1947.

Marx, K. and Engels, F., *The Holy Family or Critique of Critical Critique*, Moscow, 1956.

Marx, K. and Engels, F., *The Communist Manifesto*, Harmondsworth, 1969.

Marx, K. and Engels, F., *Selected Works*, Moscow, 1970.

Marx, K. and Engels, F., *The German Ideology*, Part One, London, 1970.

Murray, P., *Milton: The Modern Phase*, London, 1967.

Parker, W. R., *Milton*, Oxford, 1968.

Patrides, C. A., *Milton and the Christian Tradition*, Oxford, 1966.

Peter, J., *A Critique of Paradise Lost*, London, 1960.

Robey, D. (ed.), *Structuralism: An Introduction*, Oxford, 1973.

Runciman, W. G., *Social Science and Political Theory*, Cambridge, 1969.

Samuel, I., *Dante and Milton*, New York, 1966.

Sartre, J.-P., *The Problem of Method*, London, 1963.

Sartre, J.-P., *What is Literature?* London, 1967.

Sartre, J.-P., *Politics and Literature*, London, 1973.

Saurat, D., *Milton: Man and Thinker*, London, 1924.

Sewell, A., *A Study in Milton's Christian Doctrine*, Oxford, 1939.

Shakespeare, W., *Complete Works*, London, 1966.

Shaw, M., *Marxism and Social Science*, London, 1975.

Shklovsky, V., *Mayakovsky and His Circle*, London, 1974.

Sophocles, *Theban Plays*, Harmondsworth, 1969.

Spencer, T. (ed.), *A Garland for John Donne*, Cambridge, Mass., 1931.

Stone, L., *The Crisis of the Aristocracy, 1558–1641*, Oxford, 1965.

Stone, L., *The Causes of the English Revolution*, London, 1972.

Swingewood, A., *The Novel and Revolution*, London, 1975.

Taine, H. A., *History of English Literature* (4 volumes), London, 1907.

Tawney, R. H., *Religion and the Rise of Capitalism*, Harmondsworth, 1972.

Tillyard, E. M. W., *The Miltonic Setting*, London, 1938.

Tillyard, E. M. W., *Milton*, Harmondsworth, 1968.

Trevor-Roper, H. R., *Religion, the Reformation and Social Change*, London, 1967.

Trevor-Roper, H. R., *Historical Essays*, London, 1975.

Trotsky, L., *The Revolution Betrayed*, London, 1937.

Trotsky, L., *On Literature and Art*, New York, 1970.

Trotsky, L., *Literature and Revolution*, Michigan, 1971.

Trotsky, L., *On Britain*, New York, 1973.
Virgil, *Aeneid*, Harmondsworth, 1969.
Waldock, A. J. A., *Paradise Lost and Its Critics*, Cambridge, 1961.
Walton, P. and Hall, S., *Situating Marx*, London, 1972.
Watt, I., *The Rise of the Novel*, Harmondsworth, 1966.
Weber, M., *The Protestant Ethic and the Spirit of Capitalism*, London, 1930.
Weber, M., *The Methodology of the Social Sciences*, New York, 1949.
West, A., *Crisis and Criticism*, London, 1937.
Widgery, D. (ed.), *The Left in Britain 1956–68*, Harmondsworth, 1976.
Willey, B., *The Seventeenth Century Background*, Harmondsworth, 1972.
Williams, R., *Culture and Society 1780–1950*, Harmondsworth, 1971.
Williams, R., *The English Novel*, London, 1974.
Wolfe, D. M., *Milton in the Puritan Revolution*, New York, 1941.
Woodhouse, A. S. P. (ed.), *Puritanism and Liberty*, London, 1965.
Yule, G., *The Independents in the English Civil War*, Cambridge, 1958.

ARTICLES

Anderson, P., 'Origins of the Present Crisis', *New Left Review*, no. 23, January/February 1964.
Aronson, R., 'L'Idiot de la famille: The Ultimate Sartre', *Telos*, Summer 1974.
Bateson, F. W., 'Contribution to a Dictionary of Critical Terms: II Dissociation of Sensibility', *Essays in Criticism*, vol. 1, no. 3, 1951.
Birchall, I., 'Sartre and the Myth of Practice', Part 1, *International Socialism*, no. 45, November/December 1970; Part 2, *International Socialism*, no. 46, February/March 1971.
Brecht, B., 'Against Georg Lukács', *New Left Review*, no. 84, March/April 1974.
Cole, A., 'The Quakers and the English Revolution', *Past and Present*, no. 10, November 1956.
Dahmer, H., 'Brecht and Stalinism', *Telos*, no. 22, Winter 1974–75.
Dobb, M., 'Reply', *Science and Society*, vol. xiv, no. 2, Spring 1950.
Dobree, E., 'The Claims of Sensibility', *Humanitas*, vol. 1, no. 2, Autumn 1946.
Eagleton, T., 'Ideology and Literary Form', *New Left Review*, no. 90, March/April 1975.

Eagleton, T., 'Criticism and Politics: the work of Raymond Williams', *New Left Review*, no. 95, January/February 1976.

Fekete, J., 'The New Criticism: Ideological Evolution of the Right Opposition', *Telos*, no. 20, Summer 1974.

French, J. M., 'The Powell-Milton Bond', *Harvard Studies and Notes*, vol. xx, 1938.

Gallas, H., 'The Part Played by Georg Lukács in Working Out a Marxist Theory of Literature in the League of Proletarian Writers', *Working Papers in Cultural Studies*, no. 4.

George, C. H., 'A Social Interpretation of English Puritanism', *Journal of Modern History*, vol. xxv, no. 4, December 1953.

Goldmann, L., 'The sociology of literature: status and problems of method', *International Social Science Journal*, vol. xix, no. 4, 1967.

Goldmann, L., 'Is There a Marxist Sociology?', *International Socialism*, no. 34, Autumn 1968.

Goldmann, L., 'The Aesthetics of the Young Lukács', *New Hungarian Quarterly*, vol. xiii, no. 47, Autumn 1972.

Goldmann, L., 'Dialectical Materialism and Literary History', *New Left Review*, no. 92, July/August 1975.

Hanford, J. H., 'Milton and the Return to Humanism', *Studies in Philology*, vol. xvi, no. 2, April 1919.

Hexter, J. H., 'The English Aristocracy, its Crises, and the English Revolution, 1558–1660', *Journal of British Studies*, vol. viii, no. 1, November 1968.

Hexter, J. H., 'The burden of proof', *Times Literary Supplement*, 24 October 1975.

Hill, C., 'The English Civil War Interpreted by Marx and Engels', *Science and Society*, vol. xii, no. 1, Winter 1948.

Hill, C., 'The Transition from Feudalism to Capitalism', *Science and Society*, vol. xvii, no. 4, Fall 1953.

Hobsbawm, E. J., 'The General Crisis of the European Economy in the Seventeenth Century', Part 1, *Past and Present*, no. 5, May 1954; Part 2, *Past and Present*, no. 6, November 1954.

Hobsbawm, E. J., 'Discussion', *Past and Present*, no. 18, November 1960.

Kermode, F., 'Dissociation of Sensibility', *The Kenyon Review*, vol. xix, no. 2, Spring 1957.

Kiernan, V. G., 'Art and the Necessity of History', *The Socialist Register*, 1965.

Kossmann, E. H., 'Discussion', *Past and Present*, no. 18, November 1960.

Leavis, F. R., 'Scrutiny: A Retrospect', *Scrutiny*, vol. xx, Cambridge, 1963.

Löwy, M., 'Lukács and Stalinism', *New Left Review*, no. 91, March/June 1975.

Lukács, G., 'On his Life and Work', *New Left Review*, no. 68, July/August 1971.

Manning, B., 'The Nobles, the People, and the Constitution', *Past and Present*, no. 9, April 1956.

Milner, A., 'Leavis and English Literary Criticism', *Praxis*, vol. 1, no. 2, Winter 1976.

Mulhern, F., 'The Marxist Aesthetics of Christopher Caudwell', *New Left Review*, no. 92, July/August 1975.

Noble, T., 'Sociology and literature', *British Journal of Sociology*, vol. XXVII, no. 2, June 1976.

Prince, F. T., 'On the Last Two Books of Paradise Lost', *Essays and Studies*, vol. XI, 1958, (New Series).

Saunders, S., 'Towards a Social Theory of Literature', *Telos*, no. 18, Winter 1973−4.

Shuttleworth, A., 'Two Working papers in Cultural Studies', Birmingham, 1967 (cyclostyled).

Sparks, C., 'George Lukács', *Working Papers in Cultural Studies*, no. 4.

Sparks, C., 'Shakespeare and Society' (unpublished paper).

Stedman-Jones, G., 'The Marxism of the Early Lukács', *New Left Review*, no. 70, November/December 1971.

Sweezy, P., 'The Transition from Feudalism to Capitalism', *Science and Society*, vol. XIV, no. 2, Spring 1950.

Swingewood, A., 'Lukács's Theory of Literature' (unpublished paper).

Takahashi, H. K., 'The Transition from Feudalism to Capitalism: A Contribution to the Sweezy−Dobb Controversy', *Science and Society*, vol. XVI, no. 4, Fall 1952.

Tawney, R. H., 'The Rise of the Gentry', *Economic History Review*, vol. XI, no. 1, 1941.

Thompson, E. P., 'The Peculiarities of the English', *The Socialist Register*, 1965.

Trevor-Roper, H. R., 'The General Crisis of the Seventeenth Century', *Past and Present*, no. 16, November 1959.

Trevor-Roper, H. R., 'The Gentry, 1540−1640', *Economic History Review Supplements*, I, London, 1953.

Underdown, D., 'The Independents Reconsidered', *Journal of British Studies*, vol. III, no. 2, May 1964.

Underdown, D., 'The Independents Again', *Journal of British Studies*, vol. VIII, no. 1, November, 1968.

Wellek, R., 'Literary Criticism and Philosophy', *Scrutiny*, vol. V, no. 4, March 1937.

Wendell Smith, H., 'The Dissociation of Sensibility', *Scrutiny*, vol. XVIII, no. 3, Winter 1951–52.

Williams, P., 'The Tudor State', *Past and Present*, no. 25, July 1963.

Williams, R., 'Literature and Society: in memory of Lucien Goldmann', *New Left Review*, no. 67, May/June 1971.

Williams, R., 'Base and Superstructure in Marxist Cultural Theory,' *New Left Review*, no. 82, November/December 1973.

Woodhouse, A. S. P., 'The Historical Criticism of Milton', *Publications of the Modern Language Association of America*, vol. LXVI, no. 6, December 1951.

Yule, G., 'Independents and Revolutionaries', *Journal of British Studies*, vol. VII, no. 2, May 1968.

'Special Lukács Issue' Part 1, *Telos*, no. 10, Winter 1971; Part 2, *Telos*, no. 11, Spring 1972.

'Georg Lukács: a Memorial Symposium', *Cambridge Review*, vol. 93, no. 2206, 28 January 1972.

'Literature/Society: Mapping the Field', *Working Papers in Cultural Studies*, no. 4.

'F. R. Leavis: b. 1895: "Stability and growth"', *The New Universities Quarterly*, vol. 30, no. 1, Winter 1975.

Index

243